TEACHING POSITIONS

DIFFERENCE, PEDAGOGY, and THE POWER OF ADDRESS

TEACHING POSITIONS

DIFFERENCE, PEDAGOGY, and THE POWER OF ADDRESS

Elizabeth Ellsworth

Teachers College, Columbia University
New York and London

Published by Teachers College Press, 1234 Amsterdam Avenue, New York, NY 10027

Cover photo by David M. Spradling.

Library of Congress Cataloging-in-Publication Data

Ellsworth, Elizabeth Ann.
　　Teaching positions : difference, pedagogy, and the power of
　address / Elizabeth Ellsworth.
　　　　p.　　cm.
　　Includes bibliographical references (p.　) and index.
　　ISBN 0-8077-3668-6 (cloth : alk. paper). — ISBN 0-8077-3667-8
　(pbk. : alk. paper)
　　　1. Communication in education — Social aspects.　2. Teaching.
　3. Teacher-student relationships.　4. Forms of address.　I. Title.
　LB1033.5.E53　　　1997
　371.102′2 — dc21　　　　　　　　　　　　　　　　　97-27095

ISBN 0-8077-3667-8 (paper)
ISBN 0-8077-3668-6 (cloth)

Printed on acid-free paper

Manufactured in the United States of America

04　03　02　01　00　99　98　97　　8　7　6　5　4　3　2　1

For my mother and father, Emily and Ray Ellsworth, who, when faced as my parents with the impossibilities of teaching, loved me

Contents

Acknowledgments

I THANK Mimi Orner, Karen Evans, and Janet L. Miller for reading various drafts of this book. Their patience, enthusiasm, and generosity—not to mention their comprehension—were taxed by the fact that it took me a long time and many revisions to complete this project. I'm extremely grateful for their support, their keen and incisive criticisms, and for the opportunity to spin ideas together with them as colleagues and friends. I thank Brian Ellerbeck for his thoughtful and intelligent editing of the manuscript, especially for his precise identification of points that needed clarification, elaboration, and stronger support. I met Carole Saltz for the first time at a crucial point in the writing of this book, and her expressions of encouragement and interest renewed my confidence in its worth. I thank as well the students of C&I 800 and C&I 607 who, over the past several years, have been not only the audience for the beginnings of the ideas offered here, but the inspiration for them as well.

I received much-appreciated institutional support toward writing this book from the University of Wisconsin-Madison in the form of a sabbatical leave and, in part, in the form of the Vilas Fellow Award for research on the relation between interaction design and pedagogy. Just as I began the final revision of this manuscript, I was invited to present work-in-progress before students and faculty at the Ontario Institute for Studies in Education in Toronto, and also at the Departments of Education and Women's Studies, Umea Universitet, Umea, Sweden. The opportunity to offer some of these ideas before live audiences of very committed students and faculty was invaluable. The thoughtful questions and challenges raised by gracious hosts in Toronto and Umea informed much of the revision of the manuscript.

Living with a writing project like this means, for me, coming up against stuck place after stuck place, day after day, and then trying to find the words, ideas, connections, rhetorical moves, and learnings capable of getting me moving again. For 2 years, I took my daily stuck places to the breakfast, lunch, or dinner table, where Janet Miller read them, listened to them, and then offered thoughts, reminders, phrases, stories, arguments, analyses, theoretical framings, and countless urgings to just "go back up-stairs and write what you just said!" Anyone who has been fortunate enough to work with her as a colleague can guess how this book has been strengthened by her powerful mix of intellect, gentle teaching, and literary sensibility.

Finally, I thank my mother and father for my passion for learning, and for showing me what 70-plus years of life can look like if one never stops learning.

Introduction

IN THESE ESSAYS I take up the question of pedagogy and pursue it into some rather unlikely places. I take it to film studies, where I did my graduate work. There, I revisit the concept of mode of address — a key concept in film criticism — to see what it might mean for teachers.

I take the question of pedagogy into psychoanalytic literary criticism. By daring to explore the meanings of the unconscious for the student-teacher relationship, educators such as James Donald (1992) and Shoshana Felman (1987, Felman & Laub, 1992) are making trouble for some of the reigning assumptions about teaching and the student-teacher relationship.

I take it along the path prescribed for teachers who would use dialogue as a pedagogical practice — only to find myself on a circular track that returns sameness in the name of bridging difference.

I take it into readings of several educational documentary films and web sites. There, I try to show how some pedagogical modes of address invite learning in the form of what Felman (1987) calls a surprising "return of a difference" (p. 82). But other pedagogies address me "perversely," as if they already know what is good for me.

And I take the question of pedagogy into the not quite imaginary world of magical realism — where I try to imagine a magical realist mode of address in academic writing. What might magical realism do for the field of education and the problem of teaching about and across social and cultural difference?

As you could expect, each of these essays takes me into very different landscapes of vocabulary, practice, and intention. But what they all share is a concern with "mode of address" and what it means for teaching.

Mode of address is an analytical concept that's been around for years in film and media studies. Film scholars use it to pose this question: Who does this film think you are? It's a question about how dynamics of social positioning get played out in film viewing — who does this film address you to be within networks of power relations associated with race, sexuality, gender, class, and so on? And what difference does address make to how you read and use a film? What difference does it make, even, to historical dynamics of social "control" and "change"?

But mode of address hasn't been taken up in education. I think it should be. I think it's a provocative and productive tool for those of us who are interested in pedagogy. We can use it to shake up solidified and limiting ways of thinking about and practicing teaching. We can use it to make visible and problematic the ways that all curricula and pedagogies invite their users to take up particular positions within relations of knowledge, power, and desire.

My reasons for building this book about teaching around the notion of mode of address are both theoretical and autobiographical. Let me explain.

TRACING THE POWER OF ADDRESS

It's taken me a long time to begin to find a way to explain to myself and to others what I mean when I say that my memories of school are "bad" ones. I had no vocabulary for speaking about and back to the slippery, indirect, and intricate workings of power in the student-teacher relations that I experienced.

My grade and high school days weren't dramatically abusive or oppressive. I didn't have particularly mean-spirited teachers, and the schools that I went to were relatively clean, safe, orderly, and integrated into their surrounding community. Social and economic status, gender, and physical "attractiveness" were the operative markers of difference. They made the difference in who was "in," who was "out," who was expected to be "bright," and who was expected to be "slow" in this small, overwhelmingly white, working-class-to-lower-middle-class, Euro-American ethnic city on Milwaukee's near south side.

But these were subtle markers. The ways in which they were taken up by teachers and students as bases for sorting and grading, rewarding and ignoring, celebrating and marginalizing, disciplining and stylizing were not all that blatant or nameable. The workings of power in my school were elusive, traditional, taken for granted, well intentioned, commonsensical, even unconscious. They include the power to suggest, subtly yet clearly, that some knowledges and aspirations are for boys while others are for girls. They include the power not to have to learn about the meanings and operations of race in the United States. They also include the power to invite passions for learning out to play or to squash budding curiosity and ideas; to delicately discipline and stylize who I was as a "good" or "bad" student; to address me as a teenager as if everyone in the room and in the world is and should be heterosexual; to provoke interest and excitement in

Workings of Power [handwritten marginal note]

some promised moment of opportunity or learning, only to miss the mark when it came to delivering on that promise (despite all of the best intentions, and often through no "fault" of teacher or student).

For example, one day in eighth grade, during the heat of the cold war, large cardboard boxes arrived at our very cramped classroom. Inside were dozens and dozens of test tubes, flasks, beakers, pipettes. Chemistry glassware.

Our teacher—a kind, very tall, balding man who reminded us all of the Addams family's Lurch—rearranged our desks, set up very large folding tables along one entire side of the room, and set out all of the glass.

But that was it. Just glass. No chemicals. No Bunsen burners. No chemistry experiment handbooks. Just rows and rows of glass. It was stunning. We were in awe of that side of the room. I have a vague memory of asking our teacher where it came from. His vague answer referred to the government. Sending us all that glass—trying to get our teacher to teach us chemistry—was part of a misfired attempt to teach us something we'd need to know in order to fight the cold war.

My teacher pulled me aside and said this glassware was for learning science, and if I could think of something I wanted to do with it to learn something, I could use it. I looked at the fragile collection and felt both performance anxiety and excitement.

I went home to consult with the real teacher in my life—a genuine mad scientist who spent all his spare time in the basement of our house despite the protests of my mother—the guy who knew more about science than my teacher ever would—my dad. We sat at his drafting table among torn-up televisions, poached radio sets, a complete library of *Scientific American*s, and we contemplated this challenge. Dad was quite excited because there was a citywide science fair coming up, and maybe we—I mean I—could enter some experiment in it.

We poured over back-issues of *Scientific American* and found an experiment that required lots of glassware. It's hard to remember now, but it involved steadily dripping drops of water past a magnet or something and creating an electrical charge that could be measured. I never fully understood what was happening, and that made me feel a little uneasy. But that was always the way it was with Dad. His explanations were always just a little over my head, so my brain had to stand on tiptoe most of the time. But I knew he got it. And with some things, months or years later I did too.

My eighth-grade teacher was happy. I took some of the glassware home and Dad and I built the exhibit.

I have three more memories of this whole affair that will become important to the moral of this story. One is that when we took it to the science fair, I really thought our exhibit had a chance to win a prize. But once there, I realized that our thing really wasn't an experiment, it didn't try to prove anything or generate new knowledge. It was more like a demonstration of principles already known. It lacked a "so what?" To this day I ask students if there's a so what to their research projects.

The second memory is that I was practically the only girl with an exhibit at the science fair. This made me feel a little freakish and kind of sorry for my dad, who had to be there with a daughter instead of a son.

The last memory is that soon after the science fair, I bumped into the glassware table in our classroom and broke a bunch of the stuff. My teacher packed the whole lot of it back up and we never saw it again.

The thing is, I loved learning and I adored science. The first thing I ever saved up for, by collecting newspapers from neighbors, was a $13 telescope from the Smith Merchandise catalogue. I saw the rings around Saturn and I was hooked. You couldn't stop me from learning. I spent Saturdays taking the bus to Milwaukee's big downtown public library and reading every nonfiction book I had time to read.

But nothing, not a thing that I remember in my public school experience, ever addressed the part of me that was passionate about learning. And if it tried, it missed.

It missed like the chemistry glassware missed. Those beakers and flasks could have brought alive the Junior Scholastic book I bought and read on my own about Leeuwenhoek discovering germs and saving people from plagues. But they didn't. Who the National Science Foundation thought we were when it sent that glass to my classroom was not who we were. My teacher's invitation to do something with our windfall was a very kind gesture and it boosted my battered adolescent ego, but it was an empty invitation without any follow-up.

And while the best education I got about anything to do with science came from wandering the aisles of the public libraries and watching Dad in his basement shop, it was far from systematic and didn't really give me what I needed to become a real scientist when I hit chemistry classes in high school or college.

Not to mention that I was a girl. As each year passed it got less and less OK to be a tomboy and excel at math and science. Dad's pedagogical address to me as he tried to answer a question I had about my Gilbert chemistry set was a gender-neutral address. That was great in some ways. But in another way, I had no preparation from Dad or from teachers for dealing with the gendered nature of all the science books in the library, all the science education films we saw on TV and in school, all the great sci-fi films and television programs from the fifties and sixties, and the boxes and handbooks that came with my telescope, chemistry set, microscope, crystal radio kit, and model rockets. I became a teacher because girls didn't become astronomers.

My memories of school are that it was all like the chemistry glassware. Exciting, promising invitations to learn—new school supplies in September; eager anticipation of discoveries, adventures, challenges—and then disappointment, boredom, patronizing lessons, interruption, rote memorization, no context, no passion . . .

For example, I came away from the Now You Are A Woman movie they showed to all us sixth-grade girls with some pretty huge unaddressed questions that I didn't even know how to ask. The tiny library in my seventh-grade classroom had a couple of dozen books. It also received monthly issues of the Boy Scout magazine Boy's Life. I read Boy's Life eagerly and surreptitiously. It had exciting articles about mountains, rafting, camping, flying model airplanes, and other adventures. It was in second grade, while reading that magazine, that it really dawned on me that being a girl meant not doing any of this—it was a boy's life.

That tiny library gave me another truncated lesson about social positioning. The only time I ever "learned" anything in grade school about African Americans was when I stumbled upon *Black Like Me* (Griffin, 1961), the "true" story of a white man "passing" as a black man in the South. I tried to read it. It was frightening, confusing, fascinating, and very powerful. I still can't imagine how that book got into that classroom. But there was nobody to talk to about it. I had no idea what to do with it.

The next time race came up in school, I was a freshman in my all-white high school (except for one Japanese American family). Martin Luther King Jr. had just been killed. They wheeled a television set into our classroom and we inexplicably watched the funeral. No context. No discussion. No acknowledgment that Milwaukee was under a curfew. No history. No social studies. Who was this man?

After drafting this book, I found Jane Tompkins's *A Life in School: What the Teacher Learned* (1996). In it, she worries that her experiences of school weren't "bad" enough to warrant the critique she's about to launch. She tells us that as she writes, a voice inside gets in the way, saying, "Whatever you felt wasn't that bad . . . most people experience the same things, or worse" (p. 8). But the fact that her experiences weren't all that bad only makes it worse, she says: "If I had anything real to complain about, beatings, mistreatment, neglect, it would be easier. The way it is, all the unhappiness seems to be my responsibility, my fault" (p. 11).

Tompkins persists in her efforts to uncover what was systematic, institutional, and socially sanctioned about the stomach-clenching fear and mind-numbing boredom that she experienced in school. She persists in showing how her personal "unhappiness" had a social and institutional reason to it:

> What I expected from school and what I got were different beyond belief. Though I never completely gave up hoping the two would coincide, something happened to my sense of possiblity there that cramped it permanently. I didn't know it was happening: it didn't happen all at once; and I couldn't have told you what it was exactly that was going on. But as what I experienced clashed absolutely with my inward expectations and desires, the shape of my future-desire or expectations I might have was forever blunted. (1996, p. 15)

Tompkins's memoir gives desperately needed voice to the intricate ways that one's experience of being taught shapes one's life. She focuses on the routines and repetitions that forced her obedience, subjected her "day to day to a boredom so complete it was a form of torture" (1996, p. 32), and deadened her passion for learning. She gives new meaning to the notion of a bad education, defining it as one not measured by low test scores, but by the extent to which we are left "alone to wander the world armed with plenty of knowledge but lacking the skills to handle things that are coming up in our lives" (p. xvi).

Some workings of power in pedagogy—like those Tompkins writes about, or like my experiences with the chemistry glassware from nowhere—may appear mild and quite ordinary. But they are powerful nonetheless because they are intimate.

Mode of address, the focus of this book, is one of those intimate relations of social and cultural power that shapes and misshapes who teachers think students are, and who students come to think themselves to be.

ADDRESS: WHERE THE "SOCIAL" MEETS (AND MISSES) THE "PERSONAL"

Pedagogy as a social relationship is very close in. It gets right in there—in your brain, your body, your heart, in your sense of self, of the world, of others, and of possibilities and impossibilities in all those realms. A pedagogical mode of address is where the social construction of knowledge and learning gets deeply personal. It's a relationship whose subtleties can shape and misshape lives, passions for learning, and broader social dynamics.

The workings of power and social positioning in the pedagogical relation—especially a pedagogical relation with all good intentions—can be delicate and seemingly intangible. Power and social positioning aren't always like those networks of power where force fields move in nearly straight, highly visible lines like thick high-tension wires. Often, the networks of power and social positioning in pedagogical relations can be made up of thin, stringy traces. They can be like the twisty and entwined chocolate bands running through a marbleized cake. Try to follow one of those bands. Better yet, try to extract one for a good look. It takes surgical skill.

The workings of power in a text's mode of address—such as those in the text of a curriculum or a pedagogical practice—are more often like marbleized traces than like high tension wires. As I explain in detail in the first chapter, you can't see a mode of address in a film, for example. Unlike a film's lighting, style of editing, or camerawork, its mode of address is invisible. You have to do an intricate analysis of a film's text to extract its address. But the repercussions of address for how we read a film, enjoy it, respond to it, resist it, and get offered particular places at the table of our popular culture are not subtle at all.

The mode of address in a particular pedagogical relation between teacher and student, curriculum and student, school and student is also invisible. It can be easily overlooked when "progressive" educators pose questions about power in education. But unlike many other vectors of power in schooling, the *terms of an address* are aimed precisely at shaping, anticipating, meeting, or changing who a student thinks she is. And this is done in relation to gender, race, sexuality, social status, ability, religion, ethnicity, and all those other differences that, at this historical moment, are used to make a difference in opportunity, health care, safety, sense of self, employment, quality of life.

As I was writing this introduction, an article appeared in the *New York Times Magazine,* titled "Flirting With Suicide" (Green, 1996). It begins: "Public health campaigns shout 'Just Say No,' but people don't listen. If they did, why would someone like Mark Ebenhoch still be having unsafe sex?" (1996, p. 39). This article is about emerging theories of how and why modes of address of current AIDS education campaigns "miss" their audiences. It's not because the gay men targeted by such campaigns are confused by or unable to read the texts being offered. It's much messier than that. It's about health campaigns (not only about AIDS, but also about teen pregnancy; alcohol, drug and tobacco use; driving motorcycles and bicycles without helmets) that tell people to stop doing things that they feel are part of their deepest core of identity. It's about telling them to give up something they profoundly enjoy and don't *want* to give up (p. 41). It's about how the history of AIDS in the gay men's community has left many young HIV-negative men with the "ghoulish" belief that they'll get AIDS no matter what they do, so why try to be safe (p. 43)? It's about the question that Walt Odets, a Berkeley psychologist, asks, of "whether one *ever* eliminates risk for things that are valuable" (p. 45). It's about what HIV-negative men think of themselves—in not necessarily conscious, but diffuse feelings about themselves (p. 54)—and what the surrounding homophobic culture thinks of them. It's about pedagogies that disbelieve in the power of the unconscious, and fail to acknowledge that "people are strange. They react not only to rational thoughts but also to illogical feelings, and do what appear to be insupportable, destructive things" (p. 54). It's about the emerging argument that "ignoring the role that homophobia plays in the psychology of AIDS . . . means ignoring an element of disease at least as powerful as biology" (p. 84).

Given all of this, who an AIDS education campaign thinks its "students" are—how it addresses its "information" to its audience—becomes as crucial to its pedagogy as the content of the information itself.

ADDRESSING PARADOX

For theoretical and autobiographical reasons such as these, mode of address is at the root of the question that shapes this book. That question is, How do teachers make a difference in power, knowledge, and desire, not only by *what* they teach, but by *how* they *address* students?

But I don't ask this question because I think that teachers can or should try to fine-tune their modes of address. I don't think that it's possible or desirable for teachers to add concerns about mode of address to their pedagogical strategies so that they can try to meet their students more directly and precisely—or change their students' social positionings more efficiently and effectively. The point here is *not* that pedagogical modes of address miss their students and that teachers should try to correct this.

The point is that *all* modes of address misfire one way or another. I never "am" the "who" that a pedagogical address thinks I am. But then again, I never am the who that *I* think I am either. The point that I try to make clear in this book is that pedagogy is a much messier and more inconclusive affair than the vast majority of our educational theories and practices make it out to be. In fact, I've been persuaded, in ways I try to explain later, that the pedagogical relation between student and teacher is a paradox. As a paradox, pedagogy poses problems and dilemmas that can never be settled or resolved once and for all.

But—and this is the real work I hope this book accomplishes—I want to show that it's worth exploring and even embracing the paradoxical nature of pedagogy. What saves pedagogy from being completely closed, permanently othering, lifeless, passion killing, and perverse in the sense of already knowing what is best for us (Phillips, 1993, p. 108), is that the pedagogical relation itself is unpredictable, incorrigible, uncontrollable, unmanageable, disobedient. As teachers, we might want to get curious about the creative and instructive ways we might put paradox to use. Instead of trying to manage and control a relation that is uncontrollable, we might ask, What might we learn from ways of teaching that are predicated, paradoxically, on the impossibility of teaching?

I'll try to make this all much more concrete by giving a number of examples of pedagogical modes of address that aren't founded on striving for and desiring certainty, continuity, or control. It *is* possible to address audiences or students in a way that doesn't require them to assume a fixed, singular, unified position within power and social relations in order to read and respond to the address being offered—in order to "learn" through it. I'm going to argue, using Felman (Felman & Laub, 1992), that the film *Shoah* does this. So, according to Felman, does the pedagogical address of psychoanalysis. And so does the academic writing of Patricia Williams (1991)—which addresses us in ways similar to those in which the literary style of magical realism addresses its readers.

The point, then, is to explore the meanings and uses of pedagogical modes of address that *multiply* and *set in motion* the positions from which they can be "met" and responded to. The point is modes of address that multiply and set in motion who they think I am as a student and as a teacher. *That's* what I think I needed in school and what I need today as a teacher. Moving modes of address that think of me as simultaneously boy and girl, black and white, in and out, queer and straight, fat and thin, learning and knowledgeable, excited and scared, capable and incapable, interested and bored, trusting and suspicious. Modes of address that take on responsibility for doing the necessary work of speaking to and about— but undecidably so.

ABOUT READING THIS BOOK

This book has ended up being a lot like the seminars I teach. For one thing, it's interdisciplinary. I turn to vocabularies and ideas from the humanities to work through questions and dilemmas concerning pedagogy. I draw on the fields of film theory and criticism, literary studies, psychoanalysis, feminisms, and cultural studies.

Making Meaning an Issue

And, as in the seminars I teach, there's a focus here on the politics of representation as they are played out in education—especially in the student-teacher relation. The notion of mode of address was invented in film studies as a way of thinking and talking about the social and political processes and stances involved in representation—in meaning-making.

In this book, as in my seminars, I turn to the humanities with questions about pedagogy. I'm saying, in other words, that pedagogy has something to do with meaning-making. And that the humanities is a powerful place to look for ways of articulating a relationship between teaching and meaning.

In the past 20 years, issues of "meaning"—how it's produced, how it circulates, and its negotiation, excesses, and articulations to power—have fueled a lot of scholarship and debate in the humanities. Look at the current theoretical discussions in the humanities about texts, language, and culture. You'll see that many of them take the shape of debates about "representation." That is, debates about what it is that texts "do," and about their relations to readers, when they are said to "mean" something.

It's not surprising that academics would be preoccupied with how meanings get constructed and read. You can't do research or teach without engaging in the construction and circulation of knowledge. And all sorts of issues are bound up in that fact—ranging from the whole matter of subjectivity and objectivity in research methods to concerns about how academic discourses and practices perpetuate or interrupt the ways that knowledge serves power and power serves knowledge.

And there are less "academic" reasons why the issue of representation is a hot one. Many scholars and cultural and political activists are convinced that the ways that things, people, and events are "made to mean" directly affects the quality and even the viability of life. AIDS activists, for example, are showing that the ways in which AIDS is made to mean are as important to their work of ending the epidemic as are the biological dimensions of the disease (Patton, 1990, Crimp, 1988, Green, 1996).

In the field of education, the politics of representation is at issue in many projects and research questions. The *terms* in which teacher and curriculum "address" students, for example, is an underlying—but often unspoken—concern in a variety of current debates. The question of address underlies educators' discussions about curriculum as text; the resistances that students and teachers put up against "official" school knowledge; the gendered, raced, and classed interpretations that students and teachers make of official school curricula; multiculturalisms; how students' and teachers' cultural positionings shape what counts as school knowledge; and the ways that the knowledges that get constructed about and by teachers and students affect their material, daily lives in school.

The point I'm trying to make here is that matters of address and the ways that meaning gets produced, circulated, negotiated, and interpreted impinge on the framing of many questions in education. They also lurk within the teaching practices that educational researchers end up prescribing. Yet you'll seldom find educational researchers dealing head-on with the processes of signification and the power of address.

Sure, education graduate students in the United States study qualitative research methods (such as interviewing, participant observation, action research, life history writing, ethnography) and methods of social criticism (such as neo-Marxist or feminist sociology, or both). These are some of the methods offered to students if they want to do research on the "social construction of meaning." But questions of meaning construction in education are almost always framed through sociological perspectives and debates that are concerned first and foremost with analyzing social structure and agency.

And so, what gets emphasized in current curriculum research is the construction of meaning *in terms of* social formation and social agency. The "problem" to be "solved," in other words, is that of how people get to be social agents even as they are shaped and constrained by social structures. This means that, unlike in the humanities, in educational research the processes of *signification, representation,* and *reading* are rarely seen as problems in their own right.

The social sciences have dominated educational research and practices—even those that are progressive or "radical." But I'm convinced that many of the questions that we ask as teachers exceed and destabilize the logics, methods, and goals of the social sciences. It seems to me that the question, How should we teach about and across social and cultural difference? is the kind that would repeatedly jam the logics of social sciences that are unable or unwilling to deal with how the meanings and uses of difference constantly overrun the categories available for analyzing them. Ask such an excessive question in terms of the social sciences, and you get stuck. Too often, when stuck, educators turn to slogans or commonsense solutions in their search for (impossible) ways out.

I'm not saying that the humanities has the answers for education's stuck and sticking questions. And I'm not saying that the humanities can plug the holes in the imperfect solutions derived through the social sciences. But I am saying that the very process of encountering current developments in the humanities can change—unfix—our theorizing and practice as educators. And this can make possible and thinkable ways of responding to pedagogical questions that have, under the social sciences, been impossible and unthinkable.

But few schools of education give or even recommend training in research methods and approaches from the humanities that could be applied to educational questions, problems, and dilemmas.

Going virtually unused and unexplored in the field of education, then, are theories and practices of "reading" from literary criticism; image, narrative, and psychoanalytic analysis from film studies; audience and reader-response studies from television studies; and interdisciplinary methods of cultural analysis that think about social agency through theories of representation and cultural production. How, for example, might research on students' readings and interpretations of particular curricula be informed by contemporary media-audience studies?

Here and in the seminars that I teach, I'm interested in provoking interdisciplinary encounters between education and fields in the humanities that also share (but differently) a concern with what it means to "make sense"—with what it means, in other words, to learn.

Moving Questions

And, as in the seminars I teach, I'm not interested here in constructing ironclad analyses, arguments, or interpretations. I do offer analyses of some educational media and practices, and of several academic texts and arguments. And there is an argument that can be traced from one chapter to the next about the importance and operations of address in pedagogy—especially about how the notion of mode of address causes trouble for the ways in which dialogue is being valorized in teaching.

But I don't intend for these analyses and contentions to be final words in an argument. I'm much more interested in using them to open up questions that make a productive difference in two places: 1) in my own practices as a teacher and 2) in the ways that students put their graduate courses in education to use as they lay out research projects and try to figure out why they should and how to be in the field of education.

Here and in seminars, I try to make possible and thinkable questions that I believe can set into motion ways of thinking and teaching that have otherwise become rigid, solidified, stuck, sloganized. The same questions and dilemmas seem to arise over and over in education, virtually unchanged, across years of effort and across various perspectives within the field.

But I'm not searching for final absolute answers or fixes for these questions and dilemmas. In fact, for reasons that I hope become clear as you read on, I think that the repeated failures of education, as a field of study, to come up with definitive solutions to its own problems is what saves it from being perverse.

But as I've said, I do have a desire for shaping my own practice through questions and modes of address that move and are moving. I'm interested in questions that shift and change what is asked and unasked by theory and practice in curriculum and teaching. Such questions can provoke an event—

rather than an answer—at the scene of address between teacher and student, researcher and researched, researcher and researcher. Here's one example of what I regard to be a potentially "moving question": Is it possible
to address "stuck places" in our work as teachers and researchers with
questions that, in the very process of their construction and articulation,
change our theorizing and practice already?

This desire for moving questions has much to do with what came to be
the process of writing this book. And that has much to do with what I
imagine it will be like to read this book. I didn't sit down at the start to
construct a hermetically sealed argument. Instead, I set out to follow my
desire to work with dilemmas in my own thinking and practice as a teacher.
And I set out to do that work with analytical tools, concepts, and ways of
reading that have been developed in the humanities.

This book offers, then, instead of a hermetically sealed argument, a
series of readings of texts and practices set in juxtaposition. Juxtaposition
is an aesthetic device in postmodern art and a rhetorical one in postmodern
theory and writing. It's an attempt to get viewers and readers to make
associations across categorical, discursive, historical, and stylistic boundaries. And juxtapositions get interesting (and political) when they provoke
associations that were never intended or sanctioned by the interests that
construct and require such boundaries in the first place.

In seminars, when I juxtapose educational dilemmas with writing from
literary theory or media studies, students are faced with complex, nonlinear, associational relations between the texts. This calls for a reading that
lets the texts be in fluid and shifting relations to one another and to the
reader. Juxtapositioning invites inconsistencies, ambiguities, and ambivalence, and foregrounds the fact that there will always be "unspoken themes"
that can't or won't be interrogated. It's a way of refusing to be contained by
linear written forms so that other nonlinear and associational modes of
address that are, nevertheless, rational, can be explored. And it's an attempt
to set in motion readings that are—for the writer as well as for the readers—
self- and cross-interrogating.

Not unlike in a graduate seminar, then, what I stage here are a series
of encounters between questions about pedagogy that I carry around as a
teacher, and various texts from the humanities that, as a teacher, I am
drawn to. Part of the work of this book is to articulate just how and why,
when I read film studies or literary criticism or feminisms *as an educator,*
stuck places in my own thinking and practice get moved, get pleasurably
and productively set into motion. Part of the work of this book is to show
what can happen in the wake of undisciplinary, unauthorized juxtapositions of questions about pedagogy and humanities texts about meaning-

making. Might what gets asked and what gets left unasked by theory and practice in curriculum and teaching become available for working over and working through in different and unexpected ways?

"Reading Through"

And so I've set out here to "read" several questions that I have about pedagogy "through" several texts from the humanities. This process of "reading through" is not a very common one in the social sciences. When I quote James Donald or Shoshana Felman, for example, I'm not only doing this to cite their authority as a way of proving or establishing a point I want to make—or to show that others agree with me. And I'm not simply borrowing their innovative, apt, or lucid uses of language.

Here's what I mean by reading through: I have a number of questions that shape my practice as a teacher who is concerned with teaching about and across social and cultural difference. Some of these are conscious questions that I can pose in language, such as, What is the relation between how we address or position our students within social and cultural difference and what they learn?

Some of these questions are less conscious. They exist as traces of thought, emotion, and sensation on a day's teaching . . . hesitations . . . forgettings . . . starting to do something and then switching gears . . . and vague wonderings, such as, Why am I suspicious of all these claims about what dialogue is capable of doing in multicultural education?

I take these vague and not so vague questions and, for example, "read them through Felman," and "read Felman through" them. I ask, in other words, What use can I make of Felman's writing in the desire and work of this question? How does the direction of Felman's writing inflect this question with a different sensibility? Given the difference I'm trying to make in my own teaching by asking a particular question, in what ways does Felman's writing offer me material to work with and to put to use in making that difference?

Reading through, then, doesn't mean that I use various texts as static, given, or known filters or lenses for each other. Reading through instead highlights the *process* of my reading and draws attention to the interests I bring to reading and to how those interests shape the meanings I construct. Reading two texts side by side can destabilize the sense I have made of each text separately, because the presences and absences in each text and in the senses I have made of them never match up. What can I learn about the reading strategies available to me or prescribed for me in the field of education by engaging in this process of reading through?

And so, you'll find some relatively long passages from other writers in this book. I use those passages as I would use a packet of readings in my seminar. They function as introductions to writers who might be unfamiliar to many in education. And I often use quoted passages as material to be worked with, worked over, worked on, reshaped to serve the pedagogical question or dilemma at hand.

Parts, Chapters, and Paradoxes

In part I, I explore what becomes thinkable and intelligible when pedagogy is taken to be a scene of address. I start in chapter 1 by introducing the concept of mode of address and where it comes from in media studies. Ultimately, mode of address is a powerful but undecidable aspect of film texts.

In chapter 2, I use mode of address to begin to rethink pedagogy. I read James Donald's (1991, 1992) discussion of the meanings of the unconscious for education through the concept of mode of address. Donald argues that because of the unconscious, it's impossible to get an exact fit between a pedagogy's address to an ideal or imagined student and an actual student's response.

And this brings me to dialogue. Donald's argument troubles the very notions that dialogue in education relies upon, namely "understanding" and "misunderstanding." Chapter 3, then, grapples with this prospect: If an exact fit between message and understanding, conscious and unconscious, curriculum and interpretation, is impossible, then teaching, as it is conventionally understood, is impossible. I follow Felman (1987) into a different version of the student-teacher relation; this version turns on their heads traditional pedagogy's assumptions of who students are, and who teachers are.

In chapter 4, I use mode of address to destabilize the assumptions underlying "communicative dialogue." By communicative dialogue, I mean a controlled process of interaction that seeks successful communication, defined as the moment of full understanding. For those who advocate it in education, communicative dialogue drives toward mutual understanding as a pedagogical ideal.

The questions I ask include, What kind of knowledge does dialogue proffer? What techniques does it use to regulate knowledge and the relationship of the teacher and students within the dialogue to knowledge and truth? I'm persuaded that dialogue, like other modes of address, is not just a neutral conduit of insights, discoveries, understandings, agreements, or disagreements. It has a constitutive force. It is a tool, it is *for* something.

And the nature of the discursive tools that speakers use — such as dialogue — dictate "the kinds of worlds which might be constituted in ways of which the speakers themselves might not be conscious" (Davies, 1993, p. xvii).

I trouble dialogue, then, as a step toward getting curious, with James Donald, about what different, less idealist, more useful conceptions of citizenship — and of education — open up when I do so.

Chapter 5 explores the possibilities and promise of a student-teacher relation that is very different from communicative dialogue. Shoshana Felman (1987) calls this other relation "analytic dialogue" (p. 126). Analytic dialogue makes use of the unpredictable and uncontrollable interaction between the teacher's and the student's unconscious resistances to knowledge and passions for ignore-ance. Analytic dialogue seeks the ways in which the very indirectness of reading — the very impossibility of understanding — can teach us something, can itself become instructive.

In chapter 6, I offer a concrete example of a pedagogy based on analytic dialogue — the film *Shoah*. I offer a reading of Felman's analysis of *Shoah* to illustrate the claims made about analytic dialogue in chapter 5. I argue that *Shoah* is a film that tries to teach through analytic dialogue — through *dis*continuity and the impossibility of full understanding.

The discontinuities that inevitably foil communicative dialogue invite us to think of pedagogy not as a representational practice, but as a performative act. As a representational practice, pedagogy tries to accurately represent the world through the conventions and politics of realism. But as a performative act, pedagogy constitutes an event in and of itself — not a representation of something else "over there." And events, according to Foucault (1977), are ruptures of continuity, of the status quo (p. 154). And ruptures, according to my argument here, *productively* prevent dialogue from having its intended educational effects.

In an attempt to arrive at some so whats for all of this, I put these first six chapters to use in part II of this book. I use them as a source of reading strategies — and I generate a series of six short readings of actual pedagogical moments, practices, dilemmas, opportunities. Given the paradoxes of pedagogy that the first six chapters expose, I try to show how the practice of teaching might be well served by a curiosity about the fecundities of paradox.

Part II, "Teaching through Paradoxical Modes of Address," then, demonstrates that the paradoxes of teaching do *not* have to leave teachers in political paralysis, moral and ethical relativism, or personal despair. Nor do those paradoxes have to be resolved, controlled, or managed (as if they could be). Far from resulting in stuck and unmoving questions or practices, embracing teaching as a paradoxical relation — allowing it its paradoxes — paradoxically, allows teaching to happen.

In exploring what this could possibly mean for actual teaching situations, I don't offer a new definition of what teaching *is* as a replacement for some old definition. Having read Felman, Donald, Williams, and others for the writing of this book, I'm convinced that setting out to construct yet another definition of teaching is the least useful, interesting, or appropriate response I could make to their work. The shiftings and rearrangements that went on for me as a teacher as I read their work are much more subtle, nuanced, complex — and involving of body, memory, desire, history — than that. As teachers, we, after all, can use language to accomplish things other than definition and communicative understanding.

And so I end not with definitions, but with demonstrations of how it is possible to constructively, positively, and creatively *respond* to the paradoxes of teaching even as they are allowed to be undecidable — even as teaching is allowed to be undecidable.

I do this in the final chapters by drawing out some productive, generative aspects of the following paradoxes of pedagogical modes of address:

- We teach, with no knowledge or certainty about what consequences our actions as teachers will have.
- At the heart of teaching about and across social and cultural difference is the impossibility of designating precisely what actions, selves, or knowledges are "correct" or "needed."
- Pedagogy, when it "works," is unrepeatable and cannot be copied, sold, or exchanged — it's "worthless" to the economy of educational accountability.
- Pedagogy is a performance that is suspended (as in interrupted, never completed) in the space between self and other.
- Pedagogy is a performance that is suspended in the time between the before and the after of learning.
- Pedagogy is a performance suspended (but not lost) in thought — it is suspended in the spaces between prevailing categories and discursive systems of thought.

In the process of working through these paradoxes of pedagogy, part II ranges across films about the Balkan "gyre" (Cohen, 1995) of war, whiteness as a mode of address that structures social relations "as white"; performance art, interaction design in new media, and magical realism as an academic writing style.

These paradoxes exceed definition, answers or solutions. They do not champion utopian moments or dreams. A switch from realist to paradoxical modes of address is not "the answer." Teaching should not become psychoanalysis. Being offered multiple, shifting, self-subversive positions within relations of power and social interaction isn't "empowerment." Nor "should" graduate students start writing dissertations in the style of magical realism.

This book comes to an end, then, not with definitions or prescriptions, but with a self-subversive turn, and therefore with a learning.

Learning, Felman (1987) says, comes "as a surprise: a surprise not only to the others, but also to the self." Learning happens, she says, when "the answer is bound in effect to displace the question" and when what "returns to itself, radically displaces the very point of observation" (p. 67).

As I began writing this book, the question I was asking in order to seek a learning grew out of my discontent with my own experiences of teaching and of being taught. It grew out of my dissatisfaction with how teaching was being talked about in the field of education. I was seeking an answer for the question, How should I teach?

What "returned" to me in reply from Felman, Donald, and others were not prescriptions for how to teach. What returned displaced my question. I heard from Felman (1987), for example, that

> it is precisely in giving us unprecedented insight into the impossibility of teaching that psychoanalysis has opened up unprecedented teaching possibilities, renewing both the questions and the practice of education. (p. 70)

Felman's assertion doesn't answer the question, How should I teach? It displaces that question. With this assertion, Felman shifts the meanings of teaching and learning so that teaching can no longer be reduced to a question of "how to do it."

Writing this book, my question, How should I teach? has been displaced by the "answer": "Teaching is impossible . . . and that opens up unprecedented teaching possibilities." This startling answer, and my attempts to respond to it as a teacher, have made teaching new and surprising again. Teaching, that is, as giving what I do not have.

PART I

Teaching as a Scene of Address

1

Mode of Address: It's a Film Thing

I DIDN'T STUDY the field of education in graduate school. I studied movies. Hollywood movies, mostly. But because I was a teaching assistant from the first day of grad school, I was also trying to figure out how to teach.

Most days in grad school, I would watch a movie like *Young Mr. Lincoln* or *Meet Me in St. Louis*. I would read and try to "get" Althusser or Lacan or Eisenstein or Kuhn or Mulvey or Barthes—folks who wrote about images and stories and meaning and desire and social change. I would try to teach a discussion section of undergraduate students how to analyze the form, style, genre, and ideology of the film they had just seen. And I would be fascinated and reinvigorated by the social, political, and aesthetic power of the movies.

I got hired out of communication arts and into a school of education to teach video production and media criticism for educators. It's been a cross-cultural experience. I didn't speak the language of educational research. I didn't know the stories or characters of the field.

Most alien and alienating of all was having to learn the theories and practices of this new academic world called "curriculum and instruction" in the complete absence of suspense, romance, seduction, visual pleasure, music, plot, humor, tap dancing, or pathos. Everything I had learned about contemporary theories of linguistics, literary criticism, semiotics, feminism, and culture was learned in the presence of—in the light of, in the pleasure of, in the wake of—some movie's story, metaphors, stars, images, mode of address.

But education wasn't like the communication arts of film or television. It wasn't in the humanities. It was more like the sociology classes I took— the ones taught through programmed workbook textbooks. The field of education was, I found out, a social science.

What I've learned most from my decade-long encounter with education as an academic field is, I don't want to teach or learn in the absence of pleasure, plot, moving and being moved, metaphor, cultural artifacts, audience engagement and interaction.

That's where mode of address comes in. It's been 20 years since I started working as a teaching assistant in an introduction to film course.

I'm 14 years into trying to figure out what people think they're doing in this academic field of education and why they've made that field into what it appears to be. And I'm thinking again about modes of address.

MODE OF ADDRESS IN FILM STUDIES

Mode of address is a film studies term with a lot of theoretical and political baggage attached to it. I learned about it in classes on film and social change. What it boils down to is this question: Who does this film think you are?

Here is a selective reading of some of the theory and politics behind this question, and behind the concept of mode of address. I'm not interested in trying to define exactly what mode of address is through this revisit to my academic roots. I'm interested in why, when I think as an educator about pedagogy these days, I keep thinking about it in terms of mode of address. I'm wondering how educators might in turn be educated by encounters with various notions of mode of address, including the one in film studies.

Film theorists have developed the notion of mode of address to deal, in a film-specific way, with some huge questions that cut across film studies, literary and art criticism, sociology, anthropology, history, and education. Those questions have to do with the relation between "the social" and "the individual." Questions like, What is the relation between a film's text and a spectator's experience? A novel's structure and a reader's interpretation? A painting and a viewer's emotion? A social practice and cultural identity? A curriculum and learning? What is the relation, in other words, between the "outside" of society and the "inside" of the human psyche? How can it be equally true that "people act in self-directed and intentional ways," and yet, the patterns that inform their actions—how they think, what they "see," what they desire—"are already aspects of social being" (Donald, 1991, p. 2)?

These are big questions. They're also key for people interested in social change. Once you figure out the relationship between a film's text and a spectator's experience, for example, you might be able to change or influence, control, even, a spectator's response by designing a film in a particular way. Or, you may be able to teach viewers how to resist or subvert who a film thinks they are, or wants them to be.

For over 25 years, film theorists have been using the notion of mode of address, in some form or other, to grapple with these issues. Here, I'm going to trace some of the meanings that this notion has had for film theorists. This selective reading starts with mode of address as a concept that refers to something that is "in" a film's text, which then somehow acts on its imagined or real viewers or both. Then there's a moment in the logic of film theory when some film theorists begin to see mode of address less as something that is in a film and more as an event that takes place somewhere *between* the social and the individual. Here, the event of address takes place in the space that is social, psychic, or both, between the film's text and the viewers' uses of it. This shift from locating mode of address inside a film's text to understanding it as event will propel my selective reading of mode of address out of film theory and into education, cultural studies, and psychoanalysis.

Who Does This Film Think You Are?

Films, like letters, books, or television commercials, are *for* someone. They have intended and imagined audiences. Now, film directors, scriptwriters, studio producers, and theater owners are often far removed from "real" or "actual" moviegoers. The distances can be economic, temporal, social, geographical, ideological, gendered, raced. And films go through many alterations between script and screening. Yet most decisions about a film's narrative structure, "look," and packaging are made in light of conscious and unconscious assumptions about "who" its audience "is," what they want, how they read films, which films they'll pay to see next year, what makes them laugh or cry, what they fear, and who they think they are in relation to themselves, to others, and to the social and cultural passions and tensions of the day.

Films have intended and imagined audiences. They also have desired audiences. Some films, like *Jurassic Park,* are produced with the desire to attract the largest possible "mass" (worldwide) audience. Others, like *Go Fish,* are produced to appeal to the people who go to the Sundance Film Festival and are made with the hope of getting bookings in small hip urban "art" theaters attended by people on ideological, sexual, racial, and political fringes.

The concept of mode of address is built on this contention: In order for a film to work for an audience, in order for it to simply make sense to a viewer, or make her laugh, root for a character, suspend her disbelief, cry, scream, feel satisfied at the end — the viewer must enter into a particular relationship with the film's story and image system.

Here is one way to conceptualize this process: There is a seat in the movie theater to which the movie screen "points," a seat for which the cinematographic effects and frame compositions were designed, a seat at which the lines of perspective converge — giving the fullest illusion of depth, movement, "reality." It's from that physical position that the film looks the best. Likewise, there is a "position" within power relations and interests, within gender and racial constructions, within knowledge, to which the film's story and visual pleasure is addressed. It's from that "subject position" that the film's assumptions about who the audience is work with the least effort, contradiction, or slippage.

For example, films intended for 12-year-old white boys who live in the suburbs are pitched to the positions that such boys are assumed to occupy (or desired to occupy by producers of films and spin-off merchandisers) within contemporary social relations, market tastes, sexual fantasy and desire, gender and racial construction. In order for those boys to "catch" the film and run with it, they have to be in the place that the film is pitched to. In order for them to become part of the structure of relations that make up the system of looks, desires, pleasures, expectations, narrative setups and payoffs that make up the film-going experience, they have to be there. In order for them to "complete" the film as its producers hoped they would complete it, they have to assume the positions offered in those systems — at least for the length of the film, at least imaginatively.

"Hey, You!"

And so, filmmakers make many conscious and unconscious assumptions and wishes about the who that their film is addressed to and the social positions and identities that their audience is occupying. And those assumptions and desires leave intended and unintended traces in the film itself. To some schools of film study, a film is composed, then, not only of a system of images and an unfolding story. It is also composed of a structure of address to an imagined audience.

The "traces" of this structure aren't visible. They don't offer themselves up for study on the screen like aspects of a film's style, such as composition of objects and people in the frame, use of color, movement, editing, lighting. A film's mode of address is more like the film's narrative structure than its image system. Like story or plot, mode of address is not visible.

Nor does someone in the film literally say: "Hey, you! You 12-year-old white suburban boy! Watch this! It'll be fun. And you'll want to buy the toy. And you'll feel older and more powerful — and taller — than you are and the whole world will seem to be centered around you. And when the film ends, you'll feel that being a white American suburban 12-year-old boy is the best thing in the world to be." Not a literal visual or spoken moment, mode of address is a structuring of the relationships between the film and its viewers that unfolds over time.

Film scholars who have focused on mode of address have come up with ways of talking about this invisible process of "hailing" a viewer into a position from which to read the film. Critics who study film narrative have borrowed concepts from literary criticism and theater and invented others so that they can name and analyze the intangible experience of story on film. These include plot, character, subtext, genre, causal links, point of view, and so on. Similarly, critics interested in mode of address have come up with concepts that name and analyze aspects of their ideas about being hailed. "Audience positioning" is one of them. Masterman (1985) describes it this way:

> [W]ithin the visual media, we, as audience members, are compelled to occupy a particular *physical* position by virtue of the positioning of the camera. Identifying and being conscious of this physical position should quickly reveal that we are also being invited to occupy a *social* space. A *social* space is also opened up for us by the text's mode of address, its setting, and its format. Finally, the physical and social spaces which we are invited to occupy are linked to *ideological* positions—"natural" ways of looking at and making sense of experience. (p. 229)

Masterman then gives an example of audience positioning in television news programs:

> As the news opens, we are addressed by a news reader who looks directly at the camera and delivers "the facts." Each viewer is given the role of direct addressee. We cut to a filmed interview. Our position changes. We are no longer directly addressed, but eavesdrop, watch and judge. The different positions assure us that some aspects of experience must be accepted (facts), whilst others (opinions) require our judgment. The highly questionable distinction within journalism between fact and opinion is sewn into the ways in which we are positioned in relation to different aspects of experience. (pp. 229–230)

What Masterman is suggesting is that in order to make sense of films or TV news *on their own terms,* the viewer must be able to adopt—if only imaginatively and temporarily—the social, political, and economic interests that are the conditions for the knowledge they construct.

An educational film's address to the student, for example, invites her not only into the activity of knowledge construction, but into the construction of knowledge from a particular social and political point of view. This makes "viewing experience" and the senses that we make of films not simply voluntary and idiosyncratic, but relational—a projection of particular kinds of relations of self to self, and between self, others, knowledge, and power.

So, part of an actual 12-year-old boy's experience of and relationship to a film such as *Jurassic Park* is a response not only to its style and story. It is also a response to the ways in which its structure of address solicits, demands, even, a certain reading from him. His experience of the film includes the conscious and unconscious one of being addressed—through, for example, camera positioning and the social space it constructs "for" him—as if he were who the film wants him to be, thinks he is, or both.

"Who, Me?"

However, he never is exactly who the film thinks he is—12 years old, American, white, suburban, boy. None of these things ever means just one thing. None of these social positions is ever a single or unified one. Maybe he's a gay 12-year-old boy. What does that do to the usual assumptions about his 12-year-oldness, his whiteness, his suburbanness, his boyness? Maybe he's a mixed-race boy who is often "mistaken" for "white." Maybe he's 12 years old and the son of an abusive parent and has never really experienced being 12 years old. Maybe he lives in the suburbs but wishes he lived in the city and goes there every chance he gets.

The viewer is *never* only or fully who the film thinks s/he is. (The viewer is never exactly who *s/he* thinks s/he is either, but we'll save that one for later.) Depending on how far off the mark the film is about who we think we are, the experience of a film's mode of address ranges from "meeting/missing" the film from two seats to the left of the ideal seat in the theater, to meeting/missing it from the front-row last seat against the wall. Both off-center seats require some reworking on the part of the viewer to bring the film into focus—some rewriting, reviewing, in order to get it from off center by imagining oneself to be at its center of address. Watching a film from front-row last seat against the side wall solicits constant perceptual translation of the image—prompts the viewer to project herself into that perfect seat in the center of the theater and imagine how much better and more pleasing it must look from the place she "should" be sitting in.

So, too, being slightly or hugely missed by a film's mode of address requires what some film scholars have called "negotiation" on the part of the viewer. What does being 12 years old and a girl mean for getting pleasure from the story of *Jurassic Park*? But this negotiation is never a simple or single thing either. Because just as the viewer is never exactly who the film thinks s/he is, the film is never exactly what *it* thinks it is. There's never just one unified mode of address in a film.

If *Jurassic Park* had been addressed strictly and solely to 12-year-old white American suburban boys, the rest of the planet would have been less likely than it was to go to see it. There was something in that film that was intended for who the filmmakers imagined me to be. (My guess is that the strong, brave, intelligent woman scientist was pitched to a part of me—even if it felt like she was put in grudgingly, and as an afterthought. And even if she was a much watered-down version of the woman scientist in *Jurassic Park*, the book.) So my negotiation of *Jurassic Park*'s modes of address was not simply a matter of having to imagine myself as a 12-year-old boy in order to get the film and enjoy it.

Multiple entry points into films is a commercial necessity. This complicates the whole notion of mode of address.

Angela McRobbie (1984) points this out in her study of how teenage girls responded to watching *Flashdance* and *Fame*. According to McRobbie, in both films, the dance scenes seem to be addressed primarily to two groups of heterosexual male spectators: those within the films' stories and those who watched the films in the theater. The musical numbers seem organized (through camera angles and placement, shot-reverse-shot editing) to appeal to the desires and visual pleasures that such an audience supposedly gets from watching women dance for them.

Yet, there are aspects of the stories of both of these films that are addressed primarily to women in the audience and to what the filmmakers consciously and unconsciously imagine to be women's desire for control over their bodies and for feeling pleasure and power in their bodies and lives. So a tension is set up *within* the modes of address of these films—a tension between who the dance numbers think you are and who the story thinks you are.

Both films' *stories* then complicate the issue of who the women are dancing "for" in the *spectacles* of the films' musical numbers. Teenage girls' pleasures in watching these films may come from reading the dancers as "really" dancing for themselves, not for the men who nevertheless are watching. Or, more complexly, teenage girls' pleasures may come from reading the dancers as "really" dancing for *both* themselves and the men watching them. The mode of address of the spectacle of the dance performances rubs up against the mode of address of the unfolding story line, and these two modes of address don't necessarily work together compatibly. Different formal and stylistic systems in a single film can have different modes of address. Multiple modes of address can be going on simultaneously.

Furthermore, once real live audiences come into the theater, a film's mode of address becomes just one among the many that make up a viewer's day. The position that a viewer "takes up" in relation to a film, and from which she makes sense of it and gets pleasure from it, shifts drastically depending on surrounding and competing modes of address. Is she watching a video of *Flashdance* with a group of girlfriends on a sleep over, in a theater with a boyfriend on a date, with her lesbian lover, as a student in a film class, as an African American woman who rarely sees other African American women on the big screen?

Mode of address in film, then, is about the necessity of addressing any communication, text, action, "to" someone. And, given the commercial interests of filmmakers, it is about the desire to control, as much as possible, how and from where the viewer reads the film. It's about enticing a viewer into a particular position of knowledge towards the text, a position of coherence, from which the film works, makes sense, gives pleasure, satisfies dramatically and aesthetically, sells itself and its spin-off products.

But, as film scholars have tried to match up the mechanisms of address in a particular film's text with the readings that an actual audience has made of that film, they have had to become more and more attentive to the complications and paradoxes of the filmgoing experience. Audiences are not simply "placed" by a mode of address. Yet, to make any sense of a film or to enjoy it even minimally, they must engage with its mode of address. However minimally or obliquely, a film's mode of address is implicated in audiences' pleasures and interpretations—even in their refusals to go see a film at all.

"Yes, You."

This is where power relations and social change come in. Mode of address is not a neutral concept in film analysis. It's a concept that comes out of an approach to film studies that is interested in how filmmaking and film viewing get caught up in larger social dynamics and power relations.

While audiences can't simply be placed by a mode of address, modes of address do offer seductive encouragements and rewards for assuming those positions within gender, social status, race, nationality, attitude, taste, style, to which a film is addressed. No one in the global audience for *Jurassic Park* is its imagined and desired 12-year-old white American suburban boy. Yet, that subject position, however much it is mythical as a norm, is linked in the film to powerful fantasies of potency, prerogative, and control.

Most film scholars have liked some of the subject positions offered in popular films, and they haven't liked others. Those working from, for example, Marxist or feminist or humanist perspectives have used the concept of mode of address to "prove" that most popular films repeatedly offer a narrow and systematically biased range of subject positions. This narrow range excludes all sorts of other social and cultural perspectives and experiences. (Where are all the coming-of-age or adventure films addressed to 12-year-old girls—of any racial or ethnic background? Why does it seem right to place this question within parentheses?)

But the sins of mainstream Hollywood films are not just sins of omission. They are also sins of repeatedly implying, through exclusion, or through narrative ridicule or punishment, that being a girl (or being black or Asian or gay or fat or Spanish speaking or being a girl *and* one or other of these) is not the thing to be. Or, being a particular kind of girl or boy or Latino/a or fat kid may be OK, but being another kind is not OK.

To ask the question, Who does this film think you are, or want you to be? then, is to pose a loaded question. It's a question formulated by film scholars who think that who particular films think you are or want you to be may contribute to unequal power relations and the unconscious formation of individuals in society. And there are some individuals—masculinist sexist men and women, racists of any color, exploitative rich and powerful people, for example—and power dynamics that some film scholars don't want to see "formed" or rewarded by films' narratives and image systems.

"Not Me!"

Some filmmakers who are convinced that social and power relations may be affected by making and viewing films have launched experiments in various kinds of "counter cinema." Some feminist filmmakers, for example, have turned Hollywood conventions against themselves. They try to both call attention to and deny pleasures of film viewing that have relied on objectifying women's bodies and repressing women's agency.

Chantal Akerman, for example, in a 3½-hour-long narrative film that she made in 1975 titled *Jeanne Dielman,* documented 3 days in the life of a Belgian woman, a petit-bourgeois widow, housewife and mother. This is how Annette Kuhn (1982) describes the film:

> Her movements around her flat, her performance of everyday chores, are documented with great precision: many of her tasks are filmed in real time. Jeanne's rigid routine includes a daily visit from a man—a different one each day—whose fees for her sexual services help maintain her and her son . . . .
> Domestic labor has probably never been documented in such painstaking detail in a fiction film; for example, one sequence-shot about five minutes in length shows Jeanne preparing a meat loaf for dinner on the third day . . . the refusal of reverse shots in the film entails a denial of the "binding-in" effect of the suture of classic cinema: the spectator is forced to maintain a distance in relation to both narrative and image, constructing the story and building up narrative expectations for herself. (pp. 173–174)

The idea is that a film like *Jeanne Dielman* is more "open" and less manipulative in its positioning of its audience than is a Doris Day film about being a housewife. It refuses to use typical Hollywood modes of address that "bind" the spectator into one way of interpreting the film.

For example, Ackerman refuses to take shots from Dielman's optical point of view. She refuses to use this convention of camera work familiar to audiences and often intended to rouse their empathy for and imaginative collusion with a character's intentions, experiences, goals. Being supposedly more open and less manipulative, *Jeanne Dielman*'s mode of address theoretically "empowers" the spectator to construct the story and build up narrative expectations for herself.

Experiments in counter cinemas have produced a whole host of strategies for addressing the audience that are seldom or never seen in Hollywood films (such as the 5-minute-long static shot of Dielman making meat loaf). Such experiments have expanded the narrative and visual lexicon—and audience expectations—available to filmmakers. And, in some cases, these innovations have changed the politics of representation that reign in Hollywood (or, such innovations have been co-opted, depending on your allegiances).

The revolutionary hope was that changing modes of address in films might change the kinds of subject positions that are available and valued in society. Films like *Jeanne Dielman* might even produce new subjects of society—new kinds of "women," for example—empowered women who construct their own stories and expectations. Such films might, in other words, produce social change for the better.

But, this hasn't turned out to be a simple or direct matter, either. Films like *Jeanne Dielman* are hard to read when you're so used to reading Hollywood films. And when hard-to-read films that deny the usual and expected (sexist, racist, escapist) fantasies and pleasures become part of an intentional political strategy, well, as one film critic put it:

> The line between estrangement as a kind of passionate and thinking detachment and estrangement as alienation in the worst sense is obviously thin. (Cook, 1985, p. 220)

In other words, some films produced in the name of counter cinema and the empowerment of spectators were difficult to read or alienating because of how they denied and negated conventional film viewing pleasures. Even worse, some of their intended audience didn't necessarily want to give up their guilty pleasures. Pleasure and fantasy may be political, but that's not all they are.

"Yes, Me (1), and Me (2), and Me (3), and..."

Judith Mayne is a feminist film scholar. She's the kind of woman viewer to whom, it might be said, many of the feminist experiments in counter cinema were addressed. She writes:

I may be an informed spectator, but that has not lessened my pleasure in what some consider inferior products, like Arnold Schwarzenegger films. Rather, the study of spectatorship has made me cognizant in quite commonplace and everyday ways, of the kinds of contradictory impulses that comprise pleasure. For as much as feminism, for instance, is fully part of my everyday life, I have somewhat peculiar (peculiar, that is, to my friends and family; not to me) regressive fantasies about male adolescence which are given perfect expression by Schwarzenegger. Spectatorship is one of the few places in my life where the attractions to male adolescence and feminist avant-garde poetics exist side by side. For Chantal Ackerman's particular approach to spectatorship, for instance, engages me in different but equally satisfying ways as Arnold Schwarzenegger's. (1993, p. 3)

As a filmgoer, Mayne is not only capable of acting against what her feminist friends and she herself would probably call her "best interests" "as a woman" in a male-dominated culture. She's also capable of desiring and enjoying such acting out even as she's doing it.

Now, that poses a big problem for people who think that mode of address can make the difference between spectatorship that is "critical," reflective and passionately detached; and spectatorship that, as Mayne (1993) puts it, "makes me act out and forget" (p. 3) and actually collude in dominant and unjust cinematic and cultural practices, pleasure, and desires. Obviously, a film's mode of address isn't all-powerful.

Some film scholars have taken up the emphasis on reading in reader-response theory, and shifted the power in meaning-making to the viewer. They have conducted audience studies to try to understand and recognize the agency that viewers have always exercised at the movies. No matter how much the film's mode of address tries to construct a fixed and coherent position within knowledge, gender, race, sexuality, from which the film "should" be read; actual viewers have always read films against their modes of address, and "answered" films from places different from the ones that the film speaks to.

This shift in focus from the text's mode of address to the viewer's response to it has raised the issue of different readings not only within the same spectator—such as in Mayne's adolescent-boy and feminist readings. It also raises the issue of different readings between different "kinds" of audiences.

Mayne and other film theorists have used black spectatorship and gay spectatorship as examples of places of film viewing that supposedly differ drastically from those addressed by mainstream cinema. How do audiences that are "black," "gay," or both, for example, read films never addressed to them?

Mayne (1993), for example, looks at this issue through James Baldwin's description of resistant black spectatorship of the film *The Defiant Ones* (1958). That film

> tells the tale of two escaped prisoners, one white (Tony Curtis) and one black ([Sidney] Poitier). During most of the film they are handcuffed to each other and through their relationship a parable of race relations in North America is told. (p. 155)

Because the film is a white myth of black and white relations, it

> contains numerous "blind spots" (to use the language of 1970s film theory) wherein Poiter's character acts, not as a black man, but as a white image of what a black man is. (p. 155)

The "truth" of Poitier's "blackness" was placed, in this film, at the mercy of the "lie" of the narrative's myth of black-white relations, its inability to "get it right." Yet, the truth of his blackness also foils the power of the narrative to completely have its way with Poitier's performance and the black audience's experience of it. To show that this is so, Mayne quotes James Baldwin's (1976/1990) description of "liberal white viewers" as cheering when Poitier jumped off the train at the conclusion of the film, "sacrificing his own chance to escape to remain with his white buddy" (p. 156). The "black Harlem audience" that Baldwin describes was, however, "outraged," yelling: '*Get back on the train, you fool!*'" (Baldwin, 1976/ 1990, p. 76).

"Who Do You Mean...'We'?"

So film theorists recognize that all audiences are not the same, and that different audiences make different readings and get different, often opposing, pleasures from the same film. But this recognition has produced its own problems. For one, an unspoken assumption of much film theory is that if the targeted social position of Hollywood movie making "is assumed to possess the attributes of 'dominance'—white, male, heterosexual, middle-class, etc." and Hollywood addresses itself to that position, then "'dominant' spectators [like the liberal white audience of *The Defiant Ones*] melt symbiotically into the screen" (Mayne, 1993, p. 159). "Dominant" spectators are assumed to "naturally" and unproblematically step into the position within the ideology and pleasure offered to them.

All "others" (like the black Harlem audiences) are considered marginal and resistant. And because resistance is not only interesting, but necessary to most political projects in film theory, audience studies have tended to focus on so-called marginal and subcultural spectators. Typical research questions include, Do resistance and difference exist in the face of Hollywood's seductive and homogenizing address? Where? Who resists? Who is different? How do they resist and maintain difference? How can we cause difference and resistance to spread?

The problem with this approach, Mayne (1993) argues, is that it sets up a "dualism of 'dominant' spectators versus 'marginal' (and therefore resisting ones)," and it "perpetuates the false dichotomy of us and them" even as it tries to alleviate it. "Defining the other as the vanguard of spectatorship only reverses the dichotomy" (p. 159).

Further, it's still not clear to those working in the field of film studies just "what" an "audience" "is." Using notions of identity and identity politics to study what various social groups supposedly do with films hasn't made things much clearer. To speak of a gay audience, for example, suggests that "all gay men and lesbians share some specific identification patterns . . . or some kind of inherent capacity to read against the grain" (Mayne, 1993, p. 166). But it's just as impossible to identify a common experience of gay male or lesbian viewing (not to mention, therefore, gay and lesbian) as it is to identify a single mode of spectatorship for blacks, women, or 12-year-old white boys. In fact, literary critics and film scholars are now arguing that there are strong homosexual currents in *all* reading and film spectatorship, and that an African American presence informs *all* U.S. cultural texts in ways that shape white readers' experiences of themselves and others (Sedgwick, 1990; Morrison, 1992). So much for the usually applied distinctions between center and margin.

Still, Mayne (1993) argues, academic writing about the "politics" of critical spectatorship usually remains locked into an either/or scenario. Either we're talking a micropolitics of the viewer or the marginal social group, where every reading is a contestatory act because the film's mode of address never fits perfectly. Or, because such localized, subcultural acts of resistant reading supposedly don't add up to social change, we're talking a "macropolitics where nothing is contestatory unless part of a globally defined political agenda" (p. 172).

As in all academic endeavors, political interests drive theories of how people view films, and how they *should* view films. As Mayne (1993) puts it, "the very purpose of academic spectatorship studies was to encourage the development of critical spectatorship, certainly to the extent that the large majority of those who write film scholarship also teach" (p. 165). By "critical," Mayne does not mean merely educated or informed spectatorship. She means spectatorship that actively resists colluding with main-

stream films in producing meanings that simply reinscribe the objectifica-
tion of women's bodies and lives, heterosexist "normality," economic
exploitation, and racist stereotypes, for example.

Many of the people studying and teaching film have wanted to better
understand how audiences read films so that audiences can be better taught
how to read films resistantly. Underlying these studies is the desire, as
Foucault (1979) might have put it, to discipline and stylize viewers' (students') uncritical readings into critical readings.

But most of us who are interested in fostering social change suffer
lapses in critical spectatorship—like those of Mayne's indulgences in adolescent boy fantasies via Schwarzenheger films. And these (pleasurable, partially welcomed) lapses point to some of the dilemmas that dog most theories of social change and trouble the political and educational strategies
launched in their names.

Mode of Address as Event

In the absence of predictable and controllable "fits" between modes of
address and spectator experience, some film theorists have stopped trying
to pin a "kind" of resistant spectatorship to each kind of (marginalized)
audience as it responds to various kinds of modes of address. They have
shifted their attention from mode of address as a relatively static aspect of a
film's text to mode of address as a more fluid aspect of the contexts in
which viewers *use* films. Mayne (1993) describes this shift in emphasis as
one away from questions such as, How do gay and lesbian audiences resist
mainstream films' modes of address; and towards questions such as, What
part does film watching play in how people and groups imagine and constitute various social and cultural identities and cultures? How do modes of
address themselves get taken up and used, along with a wide-ranging web
of texts and contexts, including rumor and gossip, in the construction of
identities, cultural practices, and organized, politicized groups? How does
camp, for example—which could be understood as an exaggeration of the
ways that modes of address miss everyone—work as a shared social pleasure within gay and lesbian communities? How does film viewing get used
in constituting lesbians and gays as a political force—such as when gays
organize as a consumer group to challenge homophobic representation in
films (p. 166)?

MODE OF ADDRESS—UNRESOLVED ISSUES

By asking, Who does this film think you are? film scholars have come up
with some pretty interesting ideas and arguments about the workings of

narrative structures and visual systems in actual films. It's hard, for example, to disagree with the claim that films speak from somewhere within currently circulating ideas, fantasies, anxieties, desires, hopes, events—and that that "somewhere" can be located by looking at the ways certain characters, voices, points of view, discourses, and actions are visually and narratively privileged and rewarded over others in the film.

It's also hard to disagree with the claim that such privileging and rewarding through mode of address is an attempt by filmmakers to anticipate and speak to a desired audience's anxieties, fears, tastes, hopes, and ways of making sense. It seems clear that by speaking *to* these, a film tries to meet its imagined and desired audience at the place of its fears and hopes. Even if the audience is never in the place that the film speaks to, the place that the film addresses does seem to exist as an abstract and shareable "there," an imagined subject position within power, knowledge, and desire that the conscious and unconscious interests behind the making of the film "need" audiences to fill. Abstractly or not, films seem to "invite" actual viewers into such positions, and "encourage" them to at least imaginatively assume and read the film from there. And viewers appear to be "rewarded" (with narrative pleasure, with happy endings, with coherent reading experiences) for "taking up" and acting from that imagined position as they interpret the film.

Yet most film theorists would agree that questions about the relationship between the abstract position supposedly assigned to the film's viewers by its mode of address, and the actual person who watches a movie, have not been resolved. Our pleasures in the movies stubbornly refuse any rigid dichotomies between simple, pure acts of highly receptive, complicit reproduction of the positions offered us on the one hand, and critical resistance to or refusal of those positions on the other.

What does seem clear to me after 25 years of film studies is that the relationships between how film texts address their audience, and how actual film spectators read films, are not neat or tidy—nor are they linear or causal. And the search for neat and tidy, linear and causal relationships is not an innocent one. As Mayne (1993) puts it, the kinds of questions about mode of address that film researchers have framed have been "haunted" questions. They are questions haunted by desires to fulfill "the possibility of spectatorship as a potential vanguard activity" for progressive political agendas (p. 172). Such desires are driven by a totalizing politics: Your interpretations of film are either resistant and therefore revolutionary or complicit and therefore reactionary. Film studies is now grappling with the meanings of the postmodern stance that a totalizing politics—even if it's intended to be progressive—is not attainable, and perhaps, ultimately, not desirable.

Film studies still hasn't got convincing answers to the questions, What difference does a film's mode of address make? Does it make a difference to who the viewer consciously and unconsciously thinks s/he is? What difference does who a viewer thinks s/he is make to how s/he acts in the world? Can different/other modes of address provoke or encourage different/other ways of being and acting in the world?

Can social change, in other words, start from or be fueled by the ways in which audiences are addressed by films, or both?

And because all education is about change, as an educator I rewrite some of these questions: Can social change or individual changes in the ways someone understands the world start from and be fueled by the ways students are addressed by curriculum and pedagogy?

Can—do—teachers make a difference in power, knowledge, and desire, not only by *what* they teach, but by *how* they *address* students?

These are unresolved questions in film studies. And they are questions unasked in education.

2

The Paradoxical Power of Address: It's an Education Thing, Too

As WE LEFT chapter 1, film scholars were changing the kinds of questions they were asking about mode of address. In the 1970s, they had framed the question of address initially in terms of spectator positioning, asking, How does the way a film addresses its audience position viewers within relations of power, knowledge, and desire? But by the 1990s, they had begun to ask instead, How do audiences take up and use the terms of a film's address, along with a wide-ranging web of texts and contexts, as material for imagining and enacting cultural and social identities?

What brought on this shift, in part, was the conclusion by film theorists that all modes of address miss their audiences in some way or other. There are no exact fits between address and response. A conclusion like this makes it pretty hard to see the power of address as being the power to position audiences and to guarantee their responses. But it has made other ways of thinking about the power of address possible.

What I'd like to argue here, then, is this: The fact that there are no exact fits between address and response has made it possible to see the address of a text as a powerful, yet paradoxical, event whose power comes from the *difference* between address and response.

Remember how Mayne (1993, p. 3) used her own "guilty" desire to watch Schwarzenegger movies as an example of how audiences exceed and spill over the "acceptable" positions offered them by, for example, "feminist" modes of address? I want to argue here that the *difference* between who an address thinks its audience is and the who that audience members enact through their reponses, is a resource available for both filmmakers and audiences as they engage in meaning-making, cultural production, and the invention of new social identities.

In this chapter I'm going to explore the meanings for educators of the paradoxical power of address. What might a teacher make of the eventful and volatile space of difference or "misfit" between who a curriculum thinks its students are or should be and how students actually use a curriculum's address to constitute themselves and to act on and within history? How can the fact that all modes of address miss their audiences in some way or another become a resource for teachers—something they can put to interesting and creative pedagogical uses?

I'm going to make three claims about the misfit or space of difference between address and response here. In the chapters that follow, I'll be exploring each of these claims in more detail, in a search for how teachers can put them to use.

They are, first, that the space of difference between address and response is a social space, formed and informed by historical conjunctures of power and of social and cultural difference.

Second, the space between address and response is a space that bears the traces and unpredictable workings of the unconscious, and this makes it able to escape surveillance and control by both teachers and students.

And third, the space of difference between address and response is available to teachers as a powerful and surprising pedagogical resource. However, and paradoxically, teachers can't control mode of address—even through pedagogical practices that are intended to regulate it. Practices like dialogue, for instance.

So, in this chapter, I want to open up even further my paradoxical contention that mode of address is a powerful thing that educators shouldn't ignore, and yet all modes of address miss their audiences in significant ways. The power of address, then, is not the power to deliver on demand predicted and desired responses from students or audiences. It is not the power to place students precisely on some desired map of social relations. The power of address is not something that teachers can harness, control, predict, or technologize.

And yet, my whole project in this book is to show that an ignore-ance of the power of address impoverishes teachers. What sense of "power" is being used here then? If the power to control, predict, and direct student responses through address is not available to teachers, then what *is* the power of address that teachers ought to explore? I'll try, in what follows, to explain what I mean when I say that in teaching, the power of address lies in its indeterminacy.

MODE OF ADDRESS AND THE
VOLATILE SOCIAL SPACE-BETWEEN

The space between a film and its audience, or a curriculum and its student as "viewer" or "reader," is a volatile space. And that space-between is what modes of address tries to manipulate. In films, the volatility of this space is acknowledged and exploited for commercial profit and entertainment value.

But Hollywood has never succeeded in guaranteeing an audience's reaction by using a particular mode of address. More often than not, it's anybody's guess whether a film will make it big. In fact, the people involved in making a film are sometimes the ones who are most surprised when a film "hits" its audience just right, making it a hit.

For example, *Thelma and Louise, Waiting to Exhale,* and *First Wives Club* are all films about which viewers and reviewers have said the following: The stories and characters are far-fetched, bordering on the fantastic, the women not at all like real women in any literal sense. And yet the terms in which these films addressed their audiences—the who they thought their women viewers were—struck powerful metaphorical chords with large numbers of women filmgoers. And no one predicted the overwhelming responsiveness of those filmgoers to these films which were never intended to be blockbusters.

Here is where I'd like to suggest a reason for the elusiveness of mode of address as a practice. It could also be a reason for the paradoxical nature of its power. It's a reason that I think can bring the notion of mode of address out from its 1970s formulations and their reliance on structuralism and its notion of fixed, knowable, locateable, and therefore addressable, social positions. Given emerging notions in cultural studies of fluid, multiple, shifting, and strategic social positionings, I think it's possible to bring mode of address into a 1990s formulation that foregrounds the play and power of *difference* in address.

Consider for a moment the ending of *Thelma and Louise.* After weighing their choices—which included being arrested for murder and imprisoned in Texas, being shot dead on the spot by the law, or driving off the cliff in front of them—Thelma says, "Hit it, Louise." And the two women drive their convertible off the cliff together.

Now that line of dialogue, "Hit it, Louise," is an element of the film's mode of address. So is the attitude with which Thelma delivered the line. So is the attitude with which Louise receives the line. So is the ending inaugurated by the speaking and hearing of this line. These are all elements of the film's mode of address at this moment in its unfolding.

But the line "Hit it, Louise" does not, in and of itself, *constitute* the film's mode of address. The film's mode of address, remember, is invisible, unlocatable, a relationship—not a thing. It's a product of the ongoing interaction of a number of aspects of a film's particular uses of form, style, and narrative structure.

So what relationship constitutes a film's mode of address at any given moment? How can we tell which relation of film elements constitutes its mode of address, and which constitutes, let's say, a particular director's visual style?

What I'd like to suggest is that the mode of address of the film at this point in *Thelma and Louise* consists in the choice of this line ("Hit it, Louise"), the attitude embodied in this line, the response it evokes, and the ending inaugurated by this line, in full light of the *difference* and *conflicts* between each of these and all the other choices available to the filmmakers, socially and historically, at the moment the film is made.

What I'm saying, in other words, is that the paradoxical power of address consists in the difference between all the other lines that *could* have been spoken and *have* been spoken in other movies, soap operas, news stories, romance novels, sitcoms—and the one that got spoken here. <u>Mode of address consists in the difference between what could be said—all that it is historically and culturally possible and intelligible to say—and what is said.</u>

This is where and how mode of address exceeds the boundaries of the film's text itself and spills over into the historical conjunctures of the film's production and reception. Mode of address entails history and audience expectation and desire.

The power of address—what an audience makes of it—rides on the difference between the filmmakers' choice of "Hit it, Louise" and all other choices that were historically and discursively possible and intelligible. And the power of address rides on this choice ("Hit it, Louise") against the backdrop of emerging but as yet discursively unavailable ways of representing and responding to the women's situation.

And it's this historical and social eventness of address that makes it impossible for filmmakers to control it masterfully, as they can, for example, control lighting masterfully. (Maybe that's why there's no Academy Award given for Best Mode of Address.)

It's intriguing to consider this: Is a film's address to its audience the thing that makes or breaks a film's popularity or cultural significance? Do some films "fail" not because their stories or actors are particularly bad, but because the mode of address is "off"—as if the film's "tone of voice" or "attitude" grated against as yet unarticulated differences that make a difference to how audiences get pleasure, who they think they are or want to be?

Similarly, maybe some pedagogies and curriculums work with their students not because of the "what" they are teaching or how they are teaching it. Maybe they are hits because of the who that they are offering students to imagine themselves as being and enacting. Maybe they are hits because of the meanings students give to the difference between who a pedagogy's attitude or tone of address thinks they are or wants them to be, and all the other whos that are circulating through power and knowledge at the moment, competing for those students' attention, pleasure, desire, and enactment. Maybe they are hits because this difference in address—this address change—moves its audience from a place they don't want to be anymore (but maybe hadn't even realized that) to a place they want to try out for a while (even without knowing for sure what they will make and find there).

Unfortunately, however, more often than not, the teacher's job is framed as one of neutralizing, eliminating, or distracting students from the differences between what a curriculum "says" and what a student gets—or understands—and the volatile happenings in that space. Nonetheless, as long as classroom relations are shaped by broader social, racial, gender, and economic antagonisms, educators cannot foreclose the space of difference between address and response. They can't ever close down the fear, fantasy, desire, pleasure, and horror that bubble up in the social and historical space between address and response, curriculum and student.

No, curriculum and pedagogy—the vehicles by which educational institutions and practices address their students and teachers—are not "natural treasures which lack all traces of human horror" (Ostrow, in Willard, 1993, p. 85). And mode of address, as an educational thing, is in part about "traces of human horror." I'll try to explain.

THE UNCONSCIOUS AND THE
VOLATILE PSYCHIC SPACE-BETWEEN

In addition to the ways that the meanings and operations of history and social difference interfere with perfect fits, there is another reason that the eruptive, unruly space between a curriculum's address and a student's response won't go away. It won't go away because it's populated by the difference between conscious and unconscious knowledges, conscious and unconscious desires.

Now that it's happened, it seems inevitable that an educator would write a book about the monstrous and education (Donald, 1992). And I'm not surprised that to write it, it took someone who was deeply involved in film studies at the time when mode of address was being developed as a critical concept. James Donald's relationship to film studies comes through his work as an educator in Great Britain's Society for Education in Film and Television. He has been using media to ask: "What sort of institution is education?"

Donald (1991) locates his discussion of the institution of education in the space opened up between the conscious and unconscious responses that students and teachers make to educational texts and appeals. He uses psychoanalysis to introduce "the idea of another locality, another space, another scene, *the between perception and consciousness*" (p. 5). This other scene is the gap, the lack of fit, the difference between, for example, the modes of address of multicultural educational materials and the actual "psychic effect of *feeling*" of a student who encounters them (p. 5).

In addition to drawing educators' attention to this other scene between perception and consciousness, Donald's work explores the significance of the claim that the boundaries of the "outside" or society (for example, a curriculum text) and the "inside" or the individual psyche (for example, the student's understanding) are "never stable or easily enforceable" (1992, p. 2).

And so Donald introduces two moments of instability. There's a lack of fit between outside (curriculum) and inside (understanding). And there are unstable, unenforceable boundaries between outside (society) and inside (psychic effect of feeling, or the individual psyche). This makes the relationship between a curriculum and a teacher's or student's "understanding" of it "neither a one-way determination, nor even a dialectic." No, it's much more interesting than that. Donald argues that the space of difference between curriculum and student understanding "is characterized by oscillation, slippage and unpredictable transformations" (1992, p. 2).

"Oscillation," "slippage," and "unpredictable transformation" are not the images usually invoked when educators talk about student understanding. Education, in its more progressive moments, is governed to a large extent by another image of how the outside gets fitted to the inside. And that's the image of mutual interaction often associated with dialogue. Donald's account of slippage, instability, and confusion, of course, "represents a less sanitized version of how we exist in the world" (1991, p. 5) than does dialogue. For Donald, in the (unspoken and unspeakable) space of difference between two participants in dialogue, "rumor, gossip, prohibition and lack bubble away" (p. 5). The gaps between self and other, inside and outside, that dialogue supposedly bridges, smooths, alleviates, and ultimately crosses, are scenes troubled by cognitive uncertainty, forbidden thoughts, unreliable and unstable perceptions. We've crossed over to dialogue's other side. (More on this a little later.)

O'Shea (1993) has taken up Donald's arguments because of the implications he saw for his own teaching practices. According to O'Shea, Donald's work shows us that even those subjectivities associated with public life (e.g., citizen, teacher, politician) can't escape the dynamics of "inner" life. Even those subjectivities engaged in the sociality of "mutual interaction" "are never disconnected from fantasies, transgressive desires and 'monstrous' terrors of the kind that surface in dreams" (O'Shea, 1993, p. 504).

And so, according to this view, sociologies of education that frame mutual interaction primarily if not exclusively in terms of public life are greatly impoverished. This is because fantasies that surface in the "privacy" of our dreams are nevertheless intimately connected with citizenship, education, and public affiliation. Those so-called private transgressive desires and monstrous terrors have force in our so-called public lives because

> we can never achieve or "complete" the identities society requires of us—"the good citizen," "the free and rational individual," "the educated and informed scholar," "the good parent," "the ideal man/woman." (p. 504)

But our failures to achieve full, complete, and seamless identities are not pathological. They're "normal." What psychoanalysis offers to teachers, according to O'Shea (1993), is "best understood not as an account of 'socialization' but of the impossibility of its success and the *instability* of identity" (p. 504).

This is where popular cultural forms come in for Donald's discussion of education. According to Donald (1992), horror films, the monstrous, the grotesque, the uncanny, the sublime, are all forms that help us to deal with the insecurity and instabilities of "our" identities. They help us to deal with "that which does not 'fit,' which cannot be satisfactorily identified" (O'Shea, 1993, p. 504). The "problem," for Donald and O'Shea, is not transgressive drives, or monstrous terrors per se. These are, after all, unavoidable and can even be productive given the impossibility of socialization and the precariousness of identity.

No, the problem is that the discourses we have used to think about and practice education hardly begin to grapple with all of this. Since the Enlightenment, O'Shea argues (1993), dominant educational discourses, "whether on the side of socialization or of liberation, have been over-rationalistic" (p. 504). By "over-rationalistic" O'Shea means that

> they ignore the fact that however carefully goals are set out, curricula designed and implemented, there is no guarantee that the knowledges and social subjectivities offered the pupils are appropriated as intended. For not only are subjectivities always only ever *problematically* occupied, but they also have to pass through "the messy dynamics of desire, fantasy, and transgression." (p. 504)

This makes for what O'Shea calls an "unruly and unresolved 'self'" (p. 504). This "self" is what is generated in "the gap between what we are supposed to be and what we have in actuality not become" (p. 504). Far from being an impediment to overcome or resolve, Donald and O'Shea argue, this gap should be embraced by educators. It is precisely this gap which "provides the space of individuation and *agency*—the resource which supports, not just brute resistance, but also conscious, intentional refusal" (O'Shea, 1993, p. 504).

The fact of the unconscious then, "explodes the very idea of a complete or achieved identity" (Donald, 1991, p. 5)—with oneself through consciousness, or with others through understanding. The failures of people to become fully identical with what social norms want us to be, or what we ourselves want to become—those failures are "endlessly repeated and relived moment by moment throughout our individual histories" (p. 4). This is because it is impossible to say everything, once and for all, in language. Any attempt to say who "I am"—to make my language become fully identical with itself and with myself—brings me up against the limits of language, up against the impossibility of language coinciding with what it speaks of, up against the gap between what is spoken and what is referred to, up against language's inevitable misfire.

Donald (1991) argues that, in fact, "at the very heart of psychic life," full and complete self-identity is not only impossible, we actually resist it. There is a resistance to identity—to the perfect fit between social norms and how we feel and what we want (p. 4). This resistance is tied to an often unconscious feeling that we are—we must be—*more* than the selves that our cultures, our schools, our government, our families, our social norms and expectations are offering us or demanding us to be. It is this resistance to the banalities of normalization that makes agency possible:

> In negotiating the self-images provided by . . . education and popular culture, the self never fully recognizes itself. It remains suspicious that there must be something more than the norms and banal transgressions on display. (p. 95)

Indeed, if perfect fits were achievable between social relations and psychic reality, between self and language, our subjectivities and our societies would be closed. Completed. Finished. Dead. Nothing to do. No difference. There would be no education. No learning.

EDUCATION AND THE VOLATILE SOCIAL AND PSYCHIC SPACE-BETWEEN

Educators just haven't dealt with questions of address in the ways or to the extent that film scholars have. This is very curious to me. It seems that the parallels and intersections between "student" and "audience" are inescapable. Students and audiences have much in common both as theoretical constructs and as actual participants in meaning-making. And with the advent of new interactive media and edutainment, the boundaries between student and audience are getting even more blurred and permeable.

As it is, both popular films and educational texts (such as textbooks, curricula, educational videos and software) make assumptions about who their audiences are—in terms of their aesthetic sensibilities, attention spans, interpretive strategies, goals and desires, previous reading and viewing experiences, biases and preferences. Very often, these assumptions are predicated on further assumptions about audience members' locations within dynamics of race, gender, social status, age, ideology, sexuality, educational achievement, geography.

For example, educational textbooks are constantly redesigning their "look" to appeal to student audiences whose reading strategies and interests are shaped in a big way by television and popular music. Looking more and more like glossy magazines or even web sites, textbooks address students' shorter attention spans and media savvy with sidebars, cross references, popular-culture-based activities (e.g., "compose a rap poem"), full color, and an abundance of choices. Educational videos, in at least their opening few minutes and in a bid to grab students' attention, often try to look and feel like MTV. Science museums are beginning to address students in ways similar to those of Hollywood action-adventure films. For example, the interactive rain forest exhibit at a Milwaukee museum unfolds mysteriously as I wind my way through a dense virtual forest, surrounded by strange sounds and smells, climbing ever higher into the forest canopy where I encounter bizarre creatures that live their entire lives hundreds of feet above the forest floor.

All of this raises the possibility of discussing educational texts (such as textbooks, web sites, educational videos, museum installations, multicultural curricula) and pedagogical practices (such as interactivity, dialogue, media use in the classroom) in terms of mode of address. What would it mean for educators to begin to acknowledge the paradoxical power of address in educational texts?

Here, I want to use the way Donald questions education, to explore what is hidden when exact or "correct" fits between educational text and student understanding are assumed, desired, sought. What gets erased and denied, and at what cost, when we act as if there is no mode of address in teaching?

Most often, teachers address students in ways engineered precisely to eliminate, minimize, or contain the messy social, historical, and unconscious stuff that might confuse "getting" an educational text, as in understanding or comprehending it. For a curriculum or pedagogy to "work," some classroom moments—and ideally all of them—have to result in a fit between what's being taught and the student's understanding. And everyone—students and teachers—has to be on the same page at least some of the time, especially when it comes to assessment. As Karen Evans put it,

Testing

this is what makes a huge difference between films and curricula—"no one's giving the filmgoers a test after the movie" (personal communication, October 25, 1996).

The bottom line for assessment purposes is for a student to get it, comprehend it, be "conscious" of it; even if she didn't want to get it, didn't enjoy getting it, or does not intend to use it—education is a success when the difference between a curriculum and a student's understanding is eliminated. We can see this formulation operating in a recent progressive book on multicultural education. One essay concludes, "That's what made it so rewarding knowing that the kids were conscious of what they were doing. I really believe that by the end of the year, almost all the kids understood having a structure for writing, whether or not they wanted to follow it" (Mizell, Benett, Bowman, & Morin, 1993, p. 46).

It's this narrow interest in understanding that makes it possible to act as if mode of address weren't an issue or factor in education. Here's where an interdisciplinary encounter with film studies can shake things up—productively, I believe.

What if, like the relationship between a film and its viewer, a student's relationship to a curriculum is a messy and unpredictable event that constantly exceeds *both* understanding *and* misunderstanding?

This perspective doesn't circulate very widely in the field of education. Nevertheless, like a student's reading of a movie, her reading of a curriculum constantly and inevitably passes through the uncontrollable stuff of desire, fear, horror, pleasure, power, anxiety, fantasy, and the unthinkable.

Film - uncontrollable
curr - controlled

Inviting audiences out to play in and with this mess is the bread and butter of filmmakers. But it's *exactly* what most educators stay up late on school nights trying to plan *out* of the next day. Classroom acts and moments of desire, fear, horror, pleasure, power, and unintelligibility are *exactly* what most educators sweat over trying to prevent, foreclose, deny, ignore, close down. Such stuff is scary to teachers with 30 or 40 kids in a room as well as to professors in seminars with 12 graduate students who are writing dissertations.

Besides . . . why would a teacher want to dwell in realms of anxiety, fantasy, pleasure, and power play? Such states are extraneous if the relation that we're really trying to make happen between curriculum and student is purely and simply one of getting it or not getting it. Sure, educators might be forced to enter such troubling realms when we encounter students and teachers who don't want to get it or who, when getting it, don't want it. But the problem of getting it is seldom perceived as some problem with the whole project of understanding per se. It's usually reframed as a matter of some onerous relation between students and their broader social and cultural contexts and constraints. In other words, students would get it if only they had the right cultural competencies, intellectual skills, or moral virtues.

This allows understanding itself to escape scrutiny. It preserves understanding and its "expression" on tests as the proper, desired, and ultimately attainable relationship that defines success for teachers.

Defining, then, the relationship between curriculum and student in terms of understanding and misunderstanding means that, in practice, most educational texts address students as if their pedagogies were coming from nowhere within the circulating power relations. By presenting themselves as desiring only understanding, educational texts address students as if the texts were from no one, with no desire to place their readers in any position except that of neutral, benign, general, generic understanding. And understanding doesn't really count as a positioning of students sought through a particular *mode* of address because, supposedly, understanding is both neutral and universal.

Even if teachers think they're addressing students with a "neutral" attitude or tone of voice, without any reference to or use of the gaps between texts and readers, the terms of their address nevertheless attempt to "place" students within relations of knowledge, desire, and power. And students in turn enact modes of address that place teachers and curricula within circulating and competing relations of knowledge, desire, and power. This is true even in the presumably "democratic" pedagogical practice of dialogue. What gets erased and denied, and at what cost, when we act as if it is possible to wipe out, through understanding, the space of difference between a speaker's text and a listener's response in dialogue?

Donald's critique of education lends itself well to this question. He bases his critique on the idea from psychoanalysis that perfect fits are impossible. A perfect fit between self and society, between social relations and psychic reality, is an impossibility (1991, p. 7). And this means that perfect fits are impossible as well between text and reading, modes of address and viewer interpretation, curriculum and learning, the ideal or imagined student and the real student, multicultural education and actual students' feelings about race.

Part of Donald's project as an educator, then, is to add the workings of the unconscious to the already circulating reasons for why educators must not see the relationship between the teacher's curriculum and the student's understandings as a relationship of one-way determination. Current ways of thinking and teaching don't offer many alternatives to this formulation, but there are a few.

Theories of student "resistance" to official school knowledge, for example, try to grasp the way students "talk back" to what they're learning. But sociologists of education seldom think of resistance in terms of what

[handwritten margin notes: "perfect fit = impossible"; "not one-way"; "resistance - talk back"]

happens in the space of difference between the outside (the social) and the inside (the individual psyche). Instead, resistance is often seen as what students do after they've *already* achieved understanding. In other words, students get what's being taught but because of social and cultural contexts of inequality that impinge on the student-teacher relation, students refuse to go along with it. Or, when students resist even before they understand what they're supposed to be learning, then resistance is often pathologized as some dysfunction or noise in their ability to understand, resulting from problems with their cognitive abilities, attention span, or motivation.

There's another alternative within educational discourses to seeing teaching as a relationship of one-way determination between curriculum and student understanding. It's the one that interests me the most because it *does* address the space of difference between the outside (the social, the curriculum) and the inside (the individual psyche, the student). In fact, it presumes to achieve understanding by eliminating that space of difference-between. I'm referring to the two-way relationship between text and student called "dialogue."

COMMUNICATIVE DIALOGUE CLAIMS: "NO MODE OF ADDRESS HERE!"

Educators constantly invoke dialogue as a means of coming to understanding without imposition and in ways more democratic than one-way determination. It's offered as a way to fulfill shared desires for understanding even if differences of opinion and power remain. Educators frequently associate dialogue with democracy. They summon dialogue as a means of ensuring that when students and teachers interact, they are being open-minded (as opposed to dogmatic), and that they are open to being changed (as opposed to being dictatorial) by the rational understandings (as opposed to unreasonable passions and self-interests) they eventually arrive at.

But what happens when dialogue as a teaching strategy — a supposedly neutral carrier of meaning and intention — is questioned about its own interests and intentions? Despite what is implied by much current literature in education, dialogue is not a natural state from which we sometimes fall and need help from teachers to regain. Nor is it the highest achievement of Western civilization, an ideal form of social interaction which Western civilization's others should strive to attain. Nor is it the royal road to communication and connection in a chronically miscommunicating world.

What escapes most discussions of dialogue in education is this: Dialogue — as a teaching practice advocated throughout the literature — is *itself* a socially constructed and politically interested relationship. It doesn't matter whether educators offer it simplistically as a conversation between interested parties seeking mutual understanding, or as a more theoretically informed means for constituting a transformative social relation among speakers. Dialogue as a form of pedagogy is a historically and culturally embedded practice. It is a socially constructed tool with intentions built into its very logic. (More on this in chapter 4.)

The point I want to make here is that when teachers practice dialogue as an aspect of their pedagogy, they are employing a mode of address. The rules and moves and virtues of dialogue as pedagogy are not neutral—they offer very particular "places" to teachers and students within networks of power, desire, and knowledge. (More on this in chapter 5.)

To deny that dialogue is a mode of address structured in history and in fact in-formed by particular interests, is to give it transcendental status. And that's just what appears to happen in many educational discourses and practices. Dialogue is assumed to be capable of everything from constructing knowledge, to solving problems, to ensuring democracy, to constituting collaboration, to securing understanding, to building moral virtues, to alleviating racism or sexism, to fulfilling desires for communication and connection.

But it's just not that easy. What happens for dialogue-as-teaching-strategy in the wake of Donald's insistence on the messiness of the space between the outside of society (of curriculum) and the inside of the individual psyche (of the student's understanding)? What happens when the supposed two-way bridge of dialogue between student and text, student and teacher, student and student, is an unsteady one that oscillates, slips, and shifts unpredictably? What happens when that two-way bridge is populated by fears, human horrors, history, and difference?

Dialogue in teaching is not a neutral vehicle that carries speakers' ideas and understandings back and forth across a free and open space between them. It's a vehicle designed with a particular job in mind, and the rugged terrain between speakers that it traverses makes for a constantly interrupted and never completed passage.

For example, who dialogue's address thinks I am, just like who *Jurassic Park* thinks I am, is never exactly who I've been or who I'm wanting to be, willing to be, able to be. Especially in curricula and conversations about gender, race, sexuality, ethnicity, the space between an address and a student's reply is a messy one cut through by history, interests, and ignoreance. When someone invites me into dialogue, they invite me into a particular practice that also exists in relation to, and is implicated in, those histories, interests, and ignore-ances. And those who initiate dialogue, no matter how "nonpartisan" or "open-minded" their intentions, cannot escape placing themselves in relation to me, to others, to history. James

Baldwin (1963/1988) confronted this in "A Talk to Teachers," when he spoke about being addressed—called—as a "nigger": "If I am not what I've been told I am, then it means *you're* not what you thought you were either. And that is the crisis" (p. 8).

If I don't answer from the place within the socially constructed and interested relation called dialogue to which you spoke when addressing me, then you are not in the place you thought you were either. And that's the social, political, and pedagogical crisis provoked if I dare to refuse to make the interests that underlie the dialogic relation my own.

TEACHING: THINGS ARE NOT WHAT THEY SEEM

What if the relationship between curriculum and student understanding can't be graphed as a linear, one-way street on which curriculum determines understanding? Nor even as the two-way street made up of those rule-governed versions of dialogue in which paths eventually meet and then happily go off in a third, mutually conceded direction? What if the relation between curriculum and students were graphed as oscillations, folds, and unpredictable twists, turns, and returns?

I'm going to pursue these questions along several different directions throughout the rest of this book. Here, I want to emphasize the productive difference between thinking that we know what we're doing as teachers—as when we prescribe various versions of dialogue for teaching about and across social and cultural difference—versus entertaining the idea that teaching is undecidable.

What I mean by "undecidable" is this: We cannot directly observe, inspect, or regulate the spaces opened up by imperfect fits between what curricula say we are supposed to be and what we have in actuality not become. What prevents teachers from achieving pedagogically prescribed goals, such as educating a virtuous individual in a good society, is the space between perception and consciousness—and this space forms "an obstacle to transparency" (Bahovec, 1993, p. 167). It is an obstacle that also (and fortunately) "prevents the possibility of total surveillance" (p. 167).

No one, Donald (1992) argues, has figured out "exactly *how* social norms inform the texture of experience or how they are transformed in the process" (p. 92). Not only is what goes on in the spaces between the social and the individual, between perception and consciousness, obscured from direct observation and control from teachers on the outside, it is also un-knowable to oneself from the inside.

But we know that the "between" of perception and consciousness is there—even if we can't see or control it:

> We "know" that cultural processes operate routinely through the unspoken, the unrecorded, through habituation and "second nature"; we know because we can both note these processes in others and catch ourselves in similarly "unconscious" cultural processes. We also know that we act against our best intentions, or fail to do what we "want" to do. (O'Shea, 1993, p. 505)

This is where, in Donald's analysis, education becomes more like a horror film than a news report.

We teachers can't directly observe the messy dynamics of desire, fantasy, and transgression that inevitably derail the knowledges and social identities our curriculums offer to our pupils—or to ourselves. The space in which these operate is not transparent.

This is why Donald (1992) studies vampire films. Wanting to address questions about what sort of institution education is, he doesn't study instructional films by the *Encyclopedia Britannica*. Instead, and along with entire fields of study and practice in the humanities—such as psychoanalysis and the criticism and writing of literature—Donald stakes his work on this belief: The unruly and unresolved dynamics of self and society that reign in that space between perception and cognition cannot be directly observed or regulated.

But those dynamics can be accessed *indirectly*. They can be engaged with and responded to indirectly, metaphorically, through literary allusion, through the *difference* between address and response, and through moments when analysis or reasoning vies with writing. They can be accessed indirectly through attention to the absences which structure what is present, through attention to that which does not fit. We can be helped toward this indirect, metaphorical knowing, according to Donald, if we pay attention to popular cultural forms—especially those, like horror films, that are made out of the jagged remnants left over after our messy attempts to fit our selves into what we are supposed to be, to fit the social into the personal.

Those bloody remnants surface (not very) metaphorically in the severed body parts and hysterical sexualized violence of films such as *Pulp Fiction,* and in obsessions with aliens, such as in *The X Files* and *Independence Day.* And in *Rosanne,* the hilarious and poignant undoings and redoings of The Family as American Institution are predicated on the desires, fears, and longings that are violently truncated by American myths of the good mother, good father, good child.

So, Donald argues, educators can learn something about education by studying popular culture—especially horror and fantasy genres. In fantasy and horror films, things are never what they seem to be. Once an educator like Donald begins to explore the meanings of psychoanalysis for education, once the idea of another locality, another space, another scene—the between-perception-and-consciousness—is admitted into conversations about knowledge, learning, and understanding; we have exceeded the hidden curriculum. We are no longer talking about the unacknowledged ideology of the curriculum which can be brought to light and decided through analysis. We are no longer asking questions that have already foreseen their own correct answers, such as Whose knowledge is taught and who benefits? We have arrived, instead, at the "inner crack" of education which "cannot be resolved" (Bahovec, 1994, p. 171). We've arrived at the impossibility of perfect fits between what a teacher or curriculum intends and what a student gets; what an educational institution desires and what a student body delivers; what a teacher "knows" and what she teaches; what dialogue invites and what arrives unbidden.

What if there is no clear, enforceable-through-the-rules-of-dialogue-or-critical-pedagogy division between "the authority of reason and its other side . . . 'as inhabited by figures of madness, sexuality, death, and the diabolical'" (p. 171)? If

> negativity does not come from the outside and cannot be done away with . . . education runs into a basic impossibility of positing a limit towards the evil, the perversion coming from the outside and the one stemming from the inside. The fragile boundary is just the one of turning the screw by which the natural becomes unnatural and supernatural, the virtuous becomes totally perverted, the well-intended and prescribed by the goals of education reveals an inner crack which cannot be resolved. (p. 171)

The unresolvable crack inside of education itself, its perennial failures to produce desired social outcomes, or to wall off young minds from their own and their society's shadows through reason, understanding, and dialogue, makes education, for Freud, one of the impossible professions. As in psychoanalysis and government, Freud observed, in education, "no one can be sure beforehand of achieving unsatisfying [or satisfying] results" (Felman, 1987, p. 70). As Donald (1992) put it:

> [I]nflated promises about both the fulfillment of the child and the development of society are endlessly broken in practice. . . . The self cannot be perfectly adapted to social norms, even through ever more pervasive techniques of education, government, or therapy (p. 3).

Donald says that he turned to psychoanalysis first hoping to find some clues for overcoming the frustrating failures of education and politics to produce desired social outcomes. But instead, what he learned was "that this 'impossibility' is less a malfunction than a sign of the *necessary* failure of identity in the psyche and of closure in the social" (1991, p. 8). Unfinished societies and individuals, and failed fits between the social and the individual are necessary if agency, creativity, passions for learning, and transgressions of, rather than conformity to, relations of power are to be possible.

What if we teachers became as curious about the *productiveness* of our continuously remodeled ignore-ances, lacks of fit, and limitations of knowing as we have been about how to achieve full and complete understanding?

> We are led out of Plato's cave through a series of disillusionments. The strong light of reason puts even our own shadows to flight. But at night, when our lives return us to dreams, who gives a hang about reason? (Willard, 1993, p. 80)

No understanding? No reason? No dialogue? No education? And yet, the people who locate themselves and work at the site of education's inner crack—dedicated and "radical" teachers such as Donald, Felman, Lacan—nevertheless teach, learn, read, write.

I am now getting curious about the meanings for me as an educator of the blurred and permeable boundaries between what educational discourses have traditionally taken to be the outside (the social, the curriculum) and the inside (consciousness, cognition, feeling). What becomes inescapable and intriguing for me is this: Our lives return us to dreams even—maybe especially—in the fluorescent lights of classroom lessons about and across social and cultural difference. And the strong light of our curricula can put even our own shadows to flight.

But as those shadows flee, they slip and fall and turn back and become ensnared and lose their way and return . . . to be folded back into our conscious daytime lives, transformed by the journey into something unrecognizable yet familiar in an uncanny way—new old material to become curious about again, to subject anew to the strong light of reason—only to be put to flight again in a new and most unexpected direction, only to return to the shadows from a place we never could have predicted or imagined.

As I entertain these notions, . . . education, as I've been taught to think about it and practice it, becomes impossible. And I've set out, as a teacher, to follow my desire elsewhere.

3

"Who" Learns? "Who" Teaches?
Figuring the Unconscious in Pedagogy

PEOPLE WHO STUDY movies aren't the only ones pursuing the questions and concerns that shape the idea of mode of address. Notions of democratic dialogue and neutral understanding are being thrown into crisis in other areas of study as well. Present in Felman's (1987; Felman & Laub, 1992) work in literary criticism, pedagogy, and psychoanalysis is the claim that each time we address someone, we take up a position within knowledge, power, and desire in relation to them, and assign to them a position in relation to ourselves and to a context. Present in Judith Butler's (1997) analysis of hate speech is the claim that "linguistic injury appears to be the effect not only of the words by which one is addressed but the mode of address itself, a mode—a disposition or conventional bearing—that interpellates and constitutes a subject" (p. 2). And similar claims inform Suzanne Lacy's (1995) work on the relation between art, citizenship, and education. Lacy, Felman, and Butler write as social and cultural critics *and* as teachers.

And there are others. Patricia Williams (1991), Peggy Phelan (1993), Brenda Marshall (1992), and Ellen Rooney (1989) all bring issues of "address" into their discussions of education—education as it relates, for example, to art, to law, to literature, to social change, to psychoanalysis, to rhetoric, to performance. Each of these teacher/scholars writes from outside of the disciplinary field of education. But she writes about the significance to education of mode of address—even if she doesn't call it by that film studies name.

Using various theoretical and critical traditions, these authors consider what is at stake in a pedagogical address. And they write about their work in ways that call attention to the pedagogy and politics of their *own* modes of address to their readers.

FELMAN AND THE IMPOSSIBILITY OF TEACHING

Felman has some pretty provocative things to say about teaching. She explores issues of address in education by offering readings of Lacan's pedagogy and of the significance of psychoanalysis in and to education.

Felman (1987) has actually said, for example, that psychoanalysis gives us "unprecedented insight into the impossibility of teaching." Then in the same breath, she says that this very insight, paradoxically enough, opens up "unprecedented teaching possibilities, renewing both the questions and the practice of education" (p. 70). She argues, "One way or another every pedagogy stems from its confrontation with the impossibility of teaching" (p. 72).

Here is a teacher who is saying out loud, with compelling and persuasive reasons, things that I've only sensed as a teacher. Finally, a teacher who is saying that teaching is impossible — and saying so in ways that don't just critique, refuse, or reject teaching. After all, Felman can't simply negate teaching, because, as she says, there is "no such thing as an anti-pedagogue: an anti-pedagogue is *the* pedagogue *par excellence*" (Felman, 1987, p. 72).

In other words, the teacher who declares that teaching is impossible is nevertheless engaging in an act of teaching — and perhaps the most profound teaching act of all:

> [E]very true pedagogue is in effect an anti-pedagogue, not just because every pedagogy has historically emerged as a critique of pedagogy (Socrates: "There's a chance, Meno, that we, you as well as me . . . have been inadequately educated, you by Gorgias, I by Prodicus"), but because in one way or another every pedagogy stems from its confrontation with the impossibility of teaching (Socrates: "You see; Meno, that I am not teaching . . . anything, but all I do is question"). (Felman, 1987, p. 72)

Felman's utterance, "teaching is impossible," isn't final or simply negative. It creates in its wake an unprecedented pedagogical situation — the situation of engaging in teaching with a full recognition of the existence and importance of the unconscious. It creates the situation of engaging in teaching in full recognition of the undecidability of pedagogy, and the indeterminacy of its address.

Given where we've been in the last chapter then, you could say that teaching is impossible because the unconscious constantly derails the best intentions of pedagogies. And addressing students as if this weren't happening — addressing them as if mutual and full understanding are indeed achievable when they're not — sets up an impossible situation between teachers and students.

In this chapter, I want to pursue an even more radical sense in which teaching can be said to be impossible. In the sense described in this chapter, teaching is impossible even when students *are* addressed with a full recognition of the unconscious. This is because once a teacher takes the unconscious into consideration, s/he must reckon with the fact that the unconscious makes impossible any final, complete moment of "having been taught." This makes both "teaching it" and getting it literally impossible. What is taught is never what is learned, and teaching is structurally incomplete: "No authority can terminate the pedagogical relation, no knowledge can save us the task of thinking" (Readings, 1996, p. 154).

Thinking about the teaching situation this way was unimaginable before the invention of psychoanalysis. And, paradoxically, the work of psychoanalysis opens up a situation of potential pedagogical "renewal." Potential, but not yet actualized. As Felman (1987) points out, the meanings of the unconscious for the practices and projects of education have not been systematically thought out or articulated. And they haven't been assimilated, grasped, or put to wide use in the classroom or in educational research and writing (p. 70).

Felman's depiction of psychoanalysis's insight into the impossibility of teaching builds across a series of essays she has written over the past 10 years. Reading those essays, over and over, I find myself to be in quite a "pedagogical situation." My interest in and questioning of my own and others' teaching practices have certainly been renewed by the ways Felman turns education on its head. For example:

> Teaching, like [psycho]analysis, has to deal not so much with lack of knowledge as with resistances to knowledge. Ignorance, suggests Lacan, is a passion. Inasmuch as traditional pedagogy postulated a desire for knowledge, [a psycho]analytically informed pedagogy has to reckon with "the passion for ignorance." Ignorance, in other words, is nothing other than a *desire to ignore*: its nature is less cognitive than performative. . . . it is not a simple lack of information but the incapacity—or the refusal—to acknowledge one's own implication in the information. (1987, p. 79)

Now, "motivation" has been an issue in education for a long time—as in, How can teachers motivate students to learn what they should or need to be learning? But admitting that learners' presumed desire for knowledge may wax hotter or colder; or may be injured and in need of healing; or may need to be guided and channeled toward socially desirable objects of knowledge isn't the same as "reckoning with 'the passion for ignorance.'" It's not the same as reckoning with refusals to acknowledge one's own implication in the information being taught.

For Felman, teaching is not a matter of convincing students that they lack certain knowledge and should therefore fill that lack. Ignorance is not a simple absence of information or a passive state of lacking the motivation to learn. It is not a passivity waiting to be enlivened by teachers and curricula. It is not a misunderstanding that can be corrected by convincing arguments, evidence, or exposure to other viewpoints through dialogue.

Rather, ignorance as it relates to the unconscious is "an active dynamic of negation, an active refusal of information" (Felman, 1987, p. 79). And the roots of an ignore-ance—that which first called it into being—are often not even known or accessible to student or teacher. They are often unconscious. The hatred or fear of one's own implication in what's being taught—about the histories and operations of racism or sexism, for example, or about the Holocaust, or about the Middle Passage—can make forgetting or ignoring or not hearing an active, yet unconscious, refusal. And the "inner resistances" that call an ignore-ance into being are stubbornly capable of maintaining it, even against the conscious intentions or desires of one who otherwise wants to learn.

In other words, ignore-ance as an active yet often unconscious refusal of information, and learning as an active yet often unintended remembering, are not opposites. Nor does one precipitate the other: Ignorance does not incite or "make room" for learning, nor does learning act back upon and cease the active dynamic of repression and refusal. Neither do ignorance and learning exist as points along some conscious/unconscious continuum. It's more like this: Ignore-ance and learning are like two sides of the same sheet of paper. The constant, daily remodeling of both conscious and unconscious selves is like taking that sheet of paper and crumpling it, twisting it, uncrumpling it, and recrumpling it again. Do that, and the two sides of the same sheet of paper enfold each other, fold over onto each other and meet each other without ever becoming each other, and separate again, so that what was inside a crease moves onto the outside surface only to be folded away again in an entirely new relationship to surface and interior. Ignore-ance and learning are mutually constitutive, equally primordial.

How are teachers supposed to address a passion for ignorance? Going from addressing a student postulated as having a desire for knowledge, to addressing a student understood as having a passion for ignorance, would seem to require quite a shift in pedagogical and curricular gears. Felman's writing about and to the profession of teaching performs just such a shift. It's a shift that has profound implications for educational modes of address. Felman enacts this shift in her own writing as a teacher. And she calls for it in her critique of pedagogies that assume a student whose passion is for knowledge.

What intrigues me about Felman's work are the meanings she makes of the unconscious for teaching and learning. Most of all, I'm intrigued by how the meanings she makes of the unconscious call up issues of pedagogical modes of address.

So I'm going to explore here some of the meanings of the unconscious and its passion for ignorance for who particular pedagogical modes of address think their students are, and for who they think their teachers are.

And I want to suggest that, by turning traditional pedagogy's assumption of a student with a passion for knowledge on its head, and assuming instead a student with a passion for ignorance, Felman engages in and makes intelligible a pedagogy that assumes and supports a passion for *learning*—for learning as "impossible," and therefore "interminable" (1987, p. 86). Her work makes it possible to think of teaching without authorities, of learning without Knowledge.

"WHO" LEARNS?

Curricula and pedagogies, like films, are *for* someone. They have intended, imagined, and desired audiences. Most decisions about a curriculum's content, structure, uses of language and image, its difficulty or ease, are made in light of conscious and unconscious assumptions about who its students are: what they know, what they don't know, what they need to know for their own good, for society's good, or both, how they learn, which curricula have worked with them in the past and which have failed, what motivates them, what is relevant to them, who they think they are in relation to themselves and to others.

Educational discourses and practices are filled with conscious and unconscious assumptions and desires about the who that a curriculum or pedagogy is addressed to. The field of education is driven by research aimed at determining ever more exactly who the student is so that s/he can be more efficiently and effectively addressed. And such assumptions, desire, and research shape education's structures of address to its imagined audiences. They are structures of address designed, precisely, to make teaching possible.

For example, Western pedagogy, Felman (1987) argues, has honed its structures of address to achieve "the exhaustion—through methodical investigation—of all there is to know; the absolute completion—termination—of apprenticeship" (p. 77). Western pedagogy, in other words, strains to make teaching possible, strains to achieve that moment of finally "having been taught."

According to humanist dreams for education, the moment of absolute completion of learning and apprenticeship is supposed to be a moment of "possibility," a moment when the mind is opened to other, previously unimagined ways of thinking and knowing. But Felman (1987) disagrees. Drawing from Lacan, she argues that if the achievement of absolute knowledge were possible, the instant of its attainment would be an instant not of possibility, but an instant when "discourse closes back upon itself" (p. 77), when language and intention are entirely in agreement with each other. In other words, if teaching could be made to be possible, the moment of having been taught would be a moment of closure, return, self-sameness, stasis, rigidity.

Fortunately, the unconscious doesn't let that happen. The one who is presumed to know by Western pedagogies as they aim at the Hegelian ideal of "absolute knowledge" (Felman, 1987, p. 77), that is, the fully conscious one whose consciousness is transparent to itself is "abolished" by the unconscious (p. 84). Felman (1987) says:

> But the unconscious, in Lacan's conception, is precisely the discovery that human discourse can by definition never be entirely in agreement with itself. . . . Indeed, the unconscious itself is a kind of *unmeant knowledge* that escapes intentionality and meaning, a knowledge spoken by the language of the subject (spoken, for instance, by his "slips" or by his dreams), but that the subject cannot recognize, assume as his, appropriate; a speaking knowledge nonetheless denied to the speaker's knowledge. (p. 77)

This presents us teachers with a who, a student, who thinks s/he knows one thing, but who really knows and thinks something else. A who who knows something but doesn't mean it. A who who knows something but doesn't want to know it. A who whose unwanted, unintended, self-subversive knowledge leaks out in her words and actions—but she doesn't realize it, can't own it or use it. A who who always says more than she knows she's saying. A who, for whom learning about the unwanted, unintended, self-subversive knowledge she already knows but has forgotten, is not necessarily pretty. A who for whom learning is often more or less traumatic, surprising, uncomfortable, disruptive, troubling, intolerable—entailing a loss of the self thought to be here and a finding of the self elsewhere, caught up in different patterns of relations to self and others.

The who who learns has an unconscious. But that doesn't mean that teachers now must, or simply can, take that unconscious into account and get on with teaching as usual. We can't just address that unconscious directly and ask it to speak or to get out of learning's way. Nor can we circumvent its passion for ignorance with new teaching strategies or curricular reforms.

The unconscious of the who who learns isn't just an irritating obstacle to her otherwise full or successful cognition. It is not "simply *opposed* to [her] consciousness," dogging the heels of her conscious comprehensions from somewhere behind. No—it's much more interesting than that. The unconscious of the who who learns "speaks as something other *from within* the speech of consciousness, which it subverts" (Felman, 1987, p. 57). The unconscious is not, Felman explains, "the simple outside of the conscious," nor is it "the difference between consciousness and the unconscious." Rather, the unconscious is "a division . . . cleft within consciousness itself . . . the inherent, irreducible difference between consciousness and itself" (p. 57).

This means that the who who learns is never identical to her consciousness of her self. She is never self-same. Her consciousness of self, of the world, of self-in-the-world has been "split," as Donald (1992) puts it. This split happens when "different desires, conducts and destinies" are coded into "the licit and the illicit, the normal and the marginal, the healthy and the pathological" (pp. 93–94). When "norms *and prohibitions* instituted within social and cultural technologies" (p.94) are "folded into" the unconscious, the "cleft within consciousness itself" that Felman describes is produced.

The unmeant, illicit desires that have been folded into the unconscious-within-consciousness-itself may be unrealized. But they haven't gone away. They are not simply a student's "forgotten or rejected bag of instincts" (Donald, 1992, p. 94). My unconscious does not exist as a rejected realm separate from that which is conscious, outside of it, under it, deeper than it. Nor does my unconscious harbor my most secret, real self. Instead, there is a *stranger within* my consciousness who speaks in dreams and Freudian slips. If those dreams and slips seem strange, it's not because they are "not me," coming from somewhere outside of myself, but because, as Donald explains by quoting Levi-Strauss, "without requiring us to move outside ourselves, [they enable] us to coincide with forms of activity which are at both at once *ours* and *other*" (p. 95). The illicit, the forbidden within myself, continues to speak as something other — uninvited but still desired — from within the licit in myself, and subverts it.

All this splitting means that a student is never answering from where we think we're addressing her. She is never answering (her teacher or herself) from where she thinks she's answering. The illicit knowledges and desires we have been split from do not speak to us directly, clearly, coherently, linearly, logically. Donald (1992) puts it this way:

> [T]he norms *and prohibitions* instituted within social and cultural technologies are folded into the unconscious so that they "surface" not simply as "personal desires" but in a complex and unpredictable dynamics of desire, guilt, anxiety and displacement. (p. 94)

Repression, then, doesn't mean that some illicit desire or knowledge has been stuffed away, somewhere deeper inside ourselves, where it exists unchanged but forgotten. Repression means that some indestructible, illicit knowledge of our desire has been changed into something symbolically unrecognizable to our conscious selves.

Prohibited from desiring what I desire, prohibited from knowing/remembering what I desire, but desiring nonetheless, I continue to "speak" my desire. But I do so through rhetorical and symbolic substitutions, displacements, replacements, transferences. I say I want x and may think I want x, but I "really" want y; I say or do x but mean to say or do y. I do not do away with my incited-but-prohibited wishes and fantasies; they remain incited. What I reject are the symbols or signifiers of my "bad" desires. And I do not reject them by isolating and burying them away deep in my unconscious. I replace them with other—usually more acceptable—symbols or signifiers.

Only, I forgot the code that I used to transform my desires from bad to "acceptable":

> Ignorance . . . can be said to be a kind of forgetting . . . while learning is obviously remembering and memorizing . . . ignorance is linked to what is not remembered. (Felman, 1987, pp. 78–79)

And I don't want to remember how and why I substituted "more acceptable" representations of desires and knowledges for bad ones, because it makes me feel guilty or anxious or afraid to remember that. I have a passion to ignore the knowledge and desire I have repressed:

> [W]hat will not be memorized is tied up with repression, with the imperative to forget—the imperative . . . not to admit to knowledge. (Felman, 1987, p. 79)

I don't want to acknowledge my own implication in the knowledge of what it is I desire, and of how and whom I have substituted for that desire. I don't want to acknowledge my own implication in all my guilty forgettings of love, conscience, and fantasy. I don't want to recognize my own desire— but I can't live without my desire, so I've translated it into something that allows me to have my desire (but not really) and deny it too (but not really).

Which means, I can't get no satisfaction. Especially if my desire is for a student "whom" I can "teach."

"WHO" TEACHES?

I started out talking about the who that "we" teachers are addressing when we teach. And I've ended up talking about "us," "we," and "I." Obviously, students aren't the only ones with an unconscious. Everything that's been said about the student's passion for ignorance can be said about the teacher's. Everything that's been said about the impossibility of mastering discourse, desire, self-knowledge, can be said in relation to the teacher. Everything that's been said about the clefting, the splitting of the student's conscious—producing intentional censorings, insistently interruptive discourses, memory lapses that are not accidental, active refusals of information, unintended and unwanted slips, knowledge that does not know itself—all this can be said of the teacher's own split consciousness.

As Felman (1987) puts it, if the student is obviously ignorant of her own unconscious, the teacher is doubly ignorant. First, like the student, the teacher is ignorant of her own unconscious, her own "suspended" knowledge—which is unavailable to her and which she can't use pedagogically. And second, the teacher is ignorant of the very knowledge she would need in order to successfully teach (in the traditional sense) her student—that is, knowledge of the student's resistances to learning, to knowing and remembering. The teacher lacks knowledge, in other words, of the student's unconscious (p. 82).

Who, then, is the who that teaches? The conscious mind of the student does not answer in the place where it is interrogated by the teacher. But neither does the question or information that the teacher addresses to the student come from the place that the teacher thinks it does within her own conscious knowledge.

With what does a teacher address the student, then, if she can't address the student with information that the student lacks about what s/he is knowing, how s/he is knowing? What might a teacher's mode of address be to a student when the teacher is not fully cognizant of her own knowledge, desire, ignorances—and cannot have direct access to the unconscious roots of the student's resistances, miscognitions, and active refusals? What's the difference, in other words, between teacher and student if it isn't that the teacher knows what the student needs to know, or what the student should know?

There is a difference between teacher and student after all, according to Felman's reading of Lacan. But it's not the difference of the teacher having more knowledge, authority, or experience than the student. Rather, the difference between teacher and student is a difference of *location* within the pedagogical structure of address that takes place between student and teacher.

What Felman asks us to consider is this: The who that teaches isn't a who at all. What teaches is a *structure of address*; it is a *relationship* that teaches:

> Knowledge . . . is not a substance but a structural dynamic; it is not contained by any individual but comes about out of the mutual apprenticeship

between two partially unconscious speeches that both say more than they know. (1987, p. 83)

? Furthermore, the structure of this relationship is triangular, not dual, be-
. cause three terms are present in it, not just *student* and *teacher*.

Now, what might I, as an educator, make of such a claim? What might be some of its meanings for pedagogy as I've known it, and for pedagogies that I haven't even imagined? What might be the point of claiming that knowledge is a "structural dynamic"—that a structure of address teaches? Might it mean that teaching is not a matter of what I say, but of how I say it and how I'm listened to?

Trying to unpack this heavily loaded reframing of the student-teacher relationship, I'll start with the part about three terms being present in the student-teacher dynamic. This should make it a little easier to come back and look at the claim that what teaches is a structure of address. But these are extremely difficult arguments to grasp, and the rest of this book will return to them repeatedly, from different angles, as I try to put them to use in my own work as an educator.

THE THIRD PARTICIPANT IN THE STUDENT-TEACHER RELATION

Psychoanalysis, Felman (1987) points out in her reading of Lacan, is about the discovery of a "third participant in the structure of the dialogue" (p. 127) between student and teacher. Psychoanalysis offers educators the discovery that a dual structure of address, or dialogue, between two fully conscious egos who learn as a result of having passions for knowledge is impossible.

This third participant in the pedagogical situation has a passion for ignorance, not for knowledge. And it is a formidable participant. Felman (1982) quotes Lacan: "*This thing speaks* and functions in a way quite as elaborate as at the level of the conscious, which thus loses what seemed to be its privilege" (p. 58). This third participant in the pedagogical situation—invited or not, recognized or not—is the unconscious that speaks, and speaks the discourse of the Other.

And so this third term—the *unconscious*—brings two complications to the traditional pedagogical relationship and its assumption of a dual structure of address between student and teacher. First, it brings a passion for ignorance, that is, resistances to knowledge and refusals of one's own implication in it—it brings forgetting.

Second, it brings a discourse that is neither the teacher's nor the student's. That is, it brings into the pedagogical situation social and cultural norms and prohibitions that have required that I and my student code knowledge and desire into the licit and the illicit. And because in the process of repression, we forget the code, this coded knowledge and desire is no longer "our own." It "belongs" as much to the social and cultural norms and prohibitions that required its coding as it does to either student or teacher. That's why it's called the discourse "of" the Other, even as it structures "our" unconscious. This capital-O Other positions us in and through norms and prohibitions, but it itself is unlocatable and cannot be directly observed. This is because its discourse is not a direct one—its language is the language of rhetorical substitutions, condensations, displacements, and transferences.

Into the ideal of the dual structure of dialogue between the teacher and student—in which it is supposed that learning develops linearly, cognitively, cumulatively, progressively, on a one-way road from ignorance to knowledge—comes a discourse that disrupts all of that. All learning and knowing takes a detour through the discourse of the Other—through the unconscious and opaque dynamics of social and cultural prohibition. And it is because of the presence of this third term that speaks not directly, but through substitutions, displacements, dreams, and slips of the tongue, that learning cannot proceed directly.

So the unconscious is the third participant. And it takes part *indirectly* in the "tri-alogue" between teacher and student. It speaks through asides, stand-in substitutions, denials, forgettings, prohibitions, feelings of fear, shame, pleasure. It returns to the teacher-student interaction the *repressed* of a society, a culture, and the individual lives lived there.

But this return of the repressed is an indirect return. It's never a simple matter. It's not enough for teachers to expect that the repressed will inevitably show up at the scene of pedagogy. Because it's not possible to take the unconscious "into account" and continue on one's way. The indirectness and encodedness of the enfoldings that make up the unconscious trouble the economy of accounting. The return of the repressed in a classroom is never as simple as, for example, the following:

> Discussing racism in a classroom brings up repressed feelings of anger, guilt, shame, privilege, erasure. And students are bound to have "Freudiam slips" in classroom discussions—moments when they didn't mean what they said, or couldn't say what they meant, or wanted to say one thing but said something else, or responded to a comment made in class "inappropriately" because it made them remember something that had been said to them on the street. So if we teachers know to expect the return of the repressed in the classroom, we can recognize

it when it happens and employ various strategies for meeting it and responding to it.

No, it's much more interesting than that. The return of memory, re-remembering what was forgotten by repression, is never symmetrical; rather, it is based on an asymmetry. Felman (1987) explains it this way:

> [T]here is an asymmetry between "the self departed from and the self returned to" when we reflect on our experience. Because all self-reference passes "through the Other," it therefore "returns to itself without quite being able to rejoin itself." This makes the return of what was repressed or forgotten "untotalizable." (p. 60)

There's always something else or Other that exceeds our abilities to remember—that escapes our conscious grasp even when the repressed returns. There's always more going on than we know or remember when, for example, "teaching against racism" in classrooms. Felman (1987) names this "something more" that's going on: "[W]hat is returned to the self from the Other is, paradoxically, the ignorance or the forgetfulness of its own message" (p. 60). When we try to remember or reflect on our own experiences, what "comes back" to us is not what "actually" happened to us. Rather, what returns to mind and body are ghostly traces of what we manage to ignore and to forget yet again because of the very way we have structured the questions we ask about our experiences.

Paying attention to these ghostly traces constitutes, for Felman (1987), "a new mode of cognition or information gathering whereby ignorance itself becomes structurally informative" (p. 60). In other words, *how* we don't know can teach us something. There's a history to what we don't know, forget, ignore. Once the existence of the unconscious is thought to make *direct* knowledge or understanding impossible, then the wheres and the whens of our forgettings and ignorings become very useful information. At what moments in the dynamic interplay of power relations do we forget? At what locations within structures of address do we ignore?

LEARNING FROM/IN PSYCHOANALYSIS

By now, this point should be very clear: The asymmetrical, triangular structure of the address that makes up the relation between student and teacher renders any unproblematic, direct, reflective, total exchange of knowledge impossible. The unconscious makes for a "knowledge that does not know what it knows and is thus *not in possession of itself*" (Felman, 1987, p. 92). It makes for knowledge that is *indirect*—and made unrecognizable by its passage through societal prohibitions and symbolic substitutions.

All this is another way of saying that once a belief in direct knowledge of the self and the world is made impossible by the discovery of a splitting, a cleaving of the self's relation to the world and to others; "knowing" the self and the world becomes an indirect matter of *interpretation*. Knowing can no longer be believed to be a direct result of observation, empathy, careful listening, objectivity, self-reflection, exchange, communication, or even (maybe especially) understanding. Felman (1987) quotes Lacan: "Interpreting is an altogether different thing than having the fancy of understanding" (quoted in Felman, 1987, p. 108).

And here is one of the things that marks education as a practice radically different from that of psychoanalysis. Educators are permitted, even encouraged, to have the "fancy of understanding." (In the last chapter, I discussed how understanding and misunderstanding have structured the terms that educators use to conceptualize the relation between curriculum texts and student.) But unlike educators, psychoanalysts have been largely prohibited from entertaining the fancy of understanding. They aren't supposed to forget the presence of their own unconscious in their relationship with their clients. Psychoanalysis has always allowed for the necessity and the power of indeterminacy in interpretation.

But with what competence does the psychoanalyst address her client/ student, if she is not allowed the fancy of mastery of her own knowledge, and if she is instead supposed to be instructed by the patient's knowledge— the meanings of which are hidden? What makes up the psychoanalyst's pedagogy?

Lacan, Felman (1987) points out, insists that the analyst's only competence lies in her "*textual knowledge*":

> Textual knowledge—the very stuff the literature teacher is supposed to deal in—is knowledge of the functioning of language, of symbolic structures . . . knowledge at once derived from—and directed toward—interpretation. (p. 81)

The psychoanalyst's job then, is to read the discourse of the Other—the client's unconscious and the analyst's unconscious—as it participates in and disrupts the "communicative" dialogue between analyst/client. And the analyst reads this discourse as if it were a work of literature or a poem. That is, the analyst does not *understand* the discourse of the Other, she offers an indeterminate interpretation of it. Felman (1987) comments on this psychoanalytic twist on the activity of knowing:

From a philosophical perspective, knowledge is mastery—that which masters its own meaning. Unlike Hegelian philosophy, which *believes it knows all there is to know*; unlike Socratic (or contemporary post-Nietzschean) philosophy, which *believes it knows it does not know*—literature, for its part, *knows but does not know the meaning of its knowledge*, does not know *what* it knows. For the first time, then, Freud gives authority to the instruction of a knowledge that does not know its own meaning, to a knowledge (of dreams, of patients, of Greek tragedy) that we might define as literary: knowledge that is not in mastery of itself. (p. 92)

So textual knowledge is not like those modern philosophies that strive to be total, universal, and noncontradictory. And it's not like those postmodern knowledges that presume to know, (ironically) with certainty, that they do not know, that, in other words, there is nothing that can be known.

Instead, textual knowledge knows, but what it knows is undecidable—it cannot be settled once and for all. This is because the process of creating and reading texts, the process of interpretation, is "inaugural, in the primal sense of the word" (Derrida, 1978, p. 11). Interpretation starts up the process of meaning-making, but it can never know or control where that process will end up. A teacher can open a book and begin to read aloud from it to students, but she can never know or control the sense that students will make of it.

Nevertheless, this textual knowledge—which is not in mastery of itself—is an instructive knowledge. Here's how: Like the literature teacher, the psychoanalyst becomes a student of the ways that language and symbolic structures function. But instead of analyzing literary texts or genres, the psychoanalyst interprets the textual processes of the unconscious.

The textual processes of a client's unconscious resembles those of a literary text in this way: A client's message or desire or memory or dream is not forgotten or repressed or returned in just any old manner. There is a complex "symbolic constellation underlying the unconscious of the subject" (Felman, 1987, p. 103). And symbolic constellations underlying the unconscious are not unlike the literary conventions that structure a novel or a short story. The idiom of a particular novelist's formal and stylistic system structures the *terms* in which certain aspects of a story are told, others are left untold, and others exist as the subtext or structuring absences of what is actually present. Similarly, the idiom or symbolic constellation of the unconscious structures the *terms* in which the client forgets, represses, or transforms into something unrecognizable and unspeakable what they know but can't bear knowing.

Instead of studying literary texts then, the analyst reads the client's resistances, stuck places, active ignore-ances, and speakings that say more than both analyst and client know. These misfires of language and intention speak the discourse of the third participant, the discourse of the Other. This third discourse structures, through an underlying complex of permissions and prohibitions, what the client and analyst remember and what they forget.

The client and analyst may forget. They may deny and repress. Yet both are constantly sending unconscious signifiers of their own inaccessible knowledge. They are constantly saying more than they know—and knowing more than they can consciously say. It is the job of the psychoanalyst to *return* to the patient the signifiers of—the traces of and pointers to—this inaccessible knowledge.

But returning these by simply mirroring or repeating or reflecting them would only hold the whole complex of forgettings and misrecognitions in place. Similarly, symmetrical reversals or simple negations of what the patient misrecognizes would only maintain the structure of her forgettings and misrecognitions. Likewise, substitutions of the analyst's own misrecognitions for those of the patient would continue to hold the patient's own structures in place. Each of these does nothing to *alter* the complex symbolic structure of substitutions, deferrals, and displacements that have now solidified into the patient's resistances, symptoms, fears, and stuck places.

And so, the analyst must return to the patient the traces of her inaccessible knowledge *from a different vantage point* (Felman, 1987, p. 82). The analyst must assume a vantage point from which to read the patient's stories, silences, and questions which won't simply mirror, reverse, or substitute the patient's—or the analyst's—own misrecognitions.

WHAT TEACHES IS A STRUCTURE OF ADDRESS

This is where the part about knowledge being a structural dynamic, and not a substance, becomes key! What vantage point will not simply mirror, reverse, or substitute the patient's—or the analyst's—own misrecognitions? What is the structural dynamic, the mode of address, that teaches—or sets the stuck client in motion—by returning a difference?

The radical pedagogy of psychoanalysis consists in this: The analyst reads the patient's questions and stories—which know more than they say—through a "literary" knowledge of how the *silences* in a text speak:

> The pedagogical question crucial to Lacan's own teaching will be thus: Where does it resist? Where does a text (or a signifier in a patient's conduct) precisely make no sense, that is, resist interpretation? Where does what I see and what I read resist my understanding? Where is the ignorance—the resistance to knowledge—located? And what can I learn from the locus of that ignorance?

How can I interpret *out of* the dynamic ignorance I analytically encounter, both in others and in myself? How can I turn ignorance into an instrument of teaching? (Felman, 1987, p. 80)

Speaking back to the patient from the position of her resistances, stuck places, active ignore-ances, sets into motion an asymmetrical dynamic between client and analyst. Addressing the client from the position of her resistances is not addressing her by way of mirroring, reversal, or substitution. It is a necessarily indirect reply to the client's questions and symptomatic stories. The analyst responds to the client's questions, *but not from the place to which those questions are addressed*. The analyst responds from the place within the client's symbolic constellation where resistance is lodged. The analyst returns to the client not an answer, but a *difference*. She offers to the client a witnessing of the gap — or the difference — between the question that the client poses and all its previous answers (Felman & Laub, 1992, p. 221). The analyst offers back to the client indications of how the client's answers do not meet her question.

Returning to the client this difference between question and answer has the potential to make a difference to the patient, because this indirect reply is an attempt to insure that the question will not go on, will not continue in the client (Felman & Laub, 1992, p. 221). The indirectness of the reply has the power to send reverberations throughout "the whole symbolic constellation" (Felman, 1987, p. 117). It can change not only what the patient "knows" — it can change how the patient knows it. It can change the patient's relation to what she knows. It can change what she does with what she knows, how she experiences what she knows, how the return of a repressed knowledge will be used to construct a (different) future.

This asymmetrical, indirect mode of address in the psychoanalytic relationship teaches then, because it is performative. The analyst returns a difference, such as the difference between what the client speaks in her stories and what she forgets or leaves unsaid, or the difference between what the client thought she wanted and the desires she actually acts out in the structure of her relations with self and others. And there is a practical effect of the analyst's return of a difference to the client's questions. That practical effect lies not in the meaning of the analyst's interpretation, but in "what the interpretation does" to the client (Felman, 1987, p. 102). The difference that the analyst returns to the client is not some fuller understanding "about" some more real or truer self, existing hidden or buried elsewhere. Rather, the difference that the analyst returns makes something happen for the client in the moment of its return. It is compelling. It has a practical effect. It has power "to elicit affect," it has "symbolic efficacy" (p. 102).

The necessarily indirect, interpretive reply that the analyst gives to the client, then,

> does not function *constatively* (as a truth report, with respect to the reality of the situation) but *performatively* (as a speech act). The success of the interpretation, its clinical efficacy, does not proceed from the accuracy of its meaning . . . but from the way this discourse of the Other situates the [client], in language, in relation to the people who surround him. (Felman, 1987, p. 114)

The analyst's interpretation does not give a different meaning to what the client said, it gives a different "*structure,* a linguistic structure by which [the client relates] himself to other human beings; a structure, therefore, in which meaning . . . can later be articulated and inscribed" (Felman, 1987, p. 114).

TEACHING THROUGH THE OTHER

Of course, the job of teaching is not the same as the job of psychoanalyzing. Teaching is not psychoanalysis. But in any student-teacher interaction, there is that third participant—just as there is in the analyst-patient interaction.

Teaching is not psychoanalysis. But consciously or unconsciously, teachers deal nevertheless in repression, denial, ignore-ance, resistance, fear, and desire whenever we teach. And in any classroom, the presence of the discourse of the Other can often become painfully and disturbingly evident and "disruptive" to goals such as understanding, empathy, communicative dialogue. This is especially so in classrooms that deal explicitly with histories, issues, and ideas that define and are defined by social and cultural difference—difference that is created through repression, through the disciplining and regulating of desire, sexuality, normativity, pleasure; difference that is created through prohibition and permission, through splitting self from other.

How does the third term in what we often suppose to be a communicative dialogue figure into the classroom? What does it do there?

Part of the training of psychoanalysts is that they themselves be psychoanalyzed. This is because, like literary critics, psychoanalysts cannot be taught how or what to interpret. They can only cultivate a familiarity with and awareness of the undecidability of readings—and of how texts manage to defer any final reading. They can cultivate a sense of how this undecidability is fecund, and enables social critique, cultural production, aesthetic surprise, individual agency, and the opportunity to fashion a different future than the one that would have been lived if everything were treated as if it were decided. They must cultivate a "third ear" that "listens to the latent contents concealed in the manifest text" that the client speaks (Bollas, 1995, p. 171).

Furthermore, the analyst must cultivate a sense of the aesthetics of the analytic process itself. Bollas (1995) writes compellingly about this:

> [J]ust as the aesthetics of literature or music have much to do with timing, pausing, and punctuational breathing, it may well be that [the analyst], too, works technically—knowing when to make a comment, what diction texture to choose, when to remain silent, what image to pick at what moment, when to use his feelings as the basis of an interpretation, or when to scrutinize a word presentation. These decisions are aesthetic choices. . . . over time [the analyst] may convey to the analysand, through care and skill, a feel for how to work in this area and, ultimately, how to live with the organized ignorance that springs to mind when one thinks of the contents of the self. (pp. 171–172)

Picture a teacher education program. Student teachers spend a great deal of time cultivating a curiosity about and analyzing their own conscious and unconscious processes of learning. They attend to those moments when they themselves learn, to what happens to and in their bodies at a moment of learning, to when learning resists, to how they think and know inside the structures of their own and their culture's ignore-ances. They make notice of when boredom sets in, when and how boredom shifts to absorption, when in what terms they remember and forget . . .

Here, student teachers are cultivating a familiarity with and awareness of the undecidability of students' readings of curriculum texts—of how each time students revisit a curriculum text, they will get it or not get it in a different way, and of the fact that this difference is a meaningful one. These student teachers are cultivating a sense of how this undecidability of teaching and learning is a most valuable resource that can be drawn upon, worked with, and set into motion for many purposes—but never with any absolute certainty of the outcome. They are cultivating a third ear that listens not for what a student knows (discrete packages of knowledge) but for the terms that shape a student's knowing, her not knowing, her forgetting, her circles of stuck places and resistances. And these student teachers are exploring the aesthetics of the teaching relation—the when of speaking; the power of tone of voice; the when and why of remaining silent; the power and timing of imagery, metaphor, humor, irony, story; the when and why of using her feelings as a basis of response . . . As they practice the aesthetics of the pedagogical relation, these teachers-in-training are watching for how and when their own students get a feel for making their own aesthetic choices, and they're watching for how and when their students become their own teachers.

Picture a teacher education program, in which student teachers learn something about teaching from reading Bollas's (1995) description of what's going on for him as a psychoanalyst as he listens to a client talk:

> When a patient tells me his dream about going to IKEA, it evokes an immediate set of associations for me: first I think of the word "key," then "I," and this sponsors an image—not immediately comprehensible—of my patient on a beach standing in the sun. Further associations occupy my more immediate thoughts while the patient continues to talk about what he did after going to IKEA. After my rather intense period of association, I recover to wonder what he then talked about, which I retrieve, since part of me was listening to him all along. (p. 17)

I like this passage. It's closer than any other description of teaching that I've read to what I experience during office hours, "as a teacher," when I listen to a student talking about their dissertation proposal, or what I experience in a seminar session when I listen to a student grappling with a course reading.

Picture a teacher education program where professors of education are teaching student teachers by offering accounts of what goes on for them as professors when they teach:

> A student comes into my office, sits down, and tries to describe her dissertation project. I listen to her words but I see that her eyes light up when she speaks some words and ideas and they go dead or somewhere else with others. I also see her hands begin to shuffle her papers when she looks down and says she really wants to write about literacy in terms of human geography, but can't. I have no idea what this "can't" is about. The way she says it makes me think it's something to do with what she thinks are the rules or expectations of academia for her dissertation—something about how the papers in her hands—her own ideas—aren't "supposed" to be arranged the way they are. This evokes an immediate set of associations for me, which take no more than several seconds to mobilize. I think of what I really wanted to do in my dissertation, but didn't think I could do, until one day a cultural event occurred that changed everything and made the dissertation I wanted to do possible intellectually, personally, and politically. I "remember" and actually feel again what it feels like in my belly when I refuse to be deterred even if I'm afraid, anxious, confused. I "remember" that from here, I know I wrote the dissertation I wanted to but there was a moment in the process when I was horribly stuck and had no hope.

Almost simultaneously with these, I feel excitement and interest: "literacy and human geography" collide in my head sending sparks of interdisciplinary cross-fertilization and cross-critique in all directions. And I think to myself (but of course not in sentences like these): I'd love to read a dissertation that violates the boundaries between those disciplines and unleashes the associations between them. This immediately sponsors an image of a multimedia project I've been planning and longing to produce myself. It involves geography too. It's a project that I'm not sure I "can do," even as I begin to assure my student that she has a great idea, she can do it, and here are some references that might help her make it happen (references I've been using to plan my multimedia project, but I don't tell her this). All the while, her desire to link literacy and human geography is rekindling my desire to get on with the multimedia authoring, convincing me that if there are two people thinking this way there must be something to it and I'm not off on a meaningless tangent. And I listen to the next thing she says, but not without a vague tenseness about the fact that I still haven't learned the computer skills I need to do multimedia, and I never will if I don't get out of this office.

Picture a student-teacher seminar. The focus is not on, What is this author saying in this required reading, what does she mean? The focus is on, What happens to my own processes of thinking, my own symbolic constellation when I read this author's words? Where, as I read this author, do I get stuck, do I forget, do I resist? Where, when I listen to a classmate's response to this reading, does my own project of "becoming a teacher" get shifted, troubled, unsettled — why there? Why now?

Picture a seminar that is less about producing a reading of a text, and more about the processes and structures of reading *"as educators."* What prohibitions and permissions circulate around reading as educators? What relationship to this text are the academy's established sociosymbolic systems trying to repeat in my own reading and writing? And what relationships between my work and myself, my students and myself, other students and myself, do these prescribed ways of reading try to structure?

Picture a teacher education program "founded" on the undecidability of teaching, on the interminable process of reading as a teacher.

4

Who Does Communicative Dialogue Think You Are?

THE CLASSROOM PRACTICE of dialogue looms large when I think about mode of address in teaching and the question of who teaches and who learns? I want to try to explain here why, as a teacher, I must take issue with the massive claims that are being made for dialogue as a pedagogical practice. And why I take issue especially, and ironically, with how dialogue is being prescribed as a way of teaching about and across social and cultural difference.

What I want to explore across these next three chapters is the difference between the dream or fancy of communicative understanding and the educational uses of interpretive or analytic knowledge. And I'm going to do this by questioning dialogue as an educational practice.

In chapter 2 I took up Donald's (1992) work on the space of difference between perception and consciousness. I used it, as he does, to trouble assumptions of a "one-way determination" and even of a "dialectic" between the "outside" of society and the "inside" of the individual psyche or student's understanding.

Remember how Donald (1992) described the relationship between this assumed outside and inside as "never stable or easily enforceable"—but rather, as one of "oscillation, slippage and unpredictable transformations" (p. 2)? He challenges the notion that there could ever be a direct, unmediated mirroring or reflecting of the outside of society or curriculum onto the inside of the student's cognition. He challenges, in other words, the possibility of full understanding.

Then in chapter 3 I offered a reading of some of Felman's work on the meanings of the unconscious for teaching as a scene of address. I tried to engage with her claim that addressing students as if the unconscious were not involved in the pedagogical situation sets up an impossible situation between teachers and students. And further, that "teaching is impossible" even when students are addressed as if the unconscious *were* involved, because once an educator takes the unconscious into consideration, s/he must reckon with the fact that the unconscious makes impossible a final, complete moment of "having been taught."

But this does not mean that knowledge is impossible. What is impossible is only that knowledge which is predicated on the one who knows, the one who believes he fully understands, the one in full possession of his own discourse. What is impossible is that knowledge which is based on assumptions that the mind can mirror the world, that language can reflect reality, that communication can be total, that curriculum is the territory it maps. Only the dream of knowledge unmediated by the discourse of the Other; only knowledge predicated on sameness, on a match, on a common tongue, is impossible.

But textual knowledge is another matter. Textual knowledge, Felman claims, is possible. Unlike full, direct understanding, textual knowledge is indirect and incomplete. And yet, it can be instructive. Felman quotes Lacan:

> Interpreting is an altogether different thing than having the fancy of understanding. One is the opposite of the other. I will even say that it is on the basis of a certain refusal of understanding that we open the door onto psychoanalytic understanding. (Quoted in Felman, 1987, p. 108)

Here, I want to lay the groundwork, in what remains of this book, for explaining what Felman's reading of Lacan's statement means to me as a teacher. I want to lay the groundwork for explaining why I think that it is on the basis of a certain refusal of dialogue and other realist representational practices, that we teachers open the door onto teaching about and across social and cultural difference.

This job calls for a couple more passes through film studies. Two notions in particular—realism and continuity editing—give me a powerful lever for dislodging dialogue from its nearly transcendent and rarely challenged status as a teaching practice capable of achieving everything from democracy to moral virtue. And so I'll move back and forth in this chapter between dialogue as a mode of address and the notions of realism and continuity editing in film studies.

"MEDIA DON'T REFLECT REALITY"

As soon as I got into grad school in communication arts, it was obvious that everything and everyone was caught up in a huge paradigm shift. Tectonic plates of theory were shifting under the fields of mass communication, linguistics, literary criticism—shaping the newly emerging academic terrain of film theory and criticism.

The first thing I learned in graduate school became something of a

mantra that framed — by its presence or absence — almost every course sylla-
bus, journal article, colloquium, professorial rivalry, and dissertation that I
encountered. You could say that my whole graduate school experience was
one long effort to understand that mantra, to try not to forget it (because it
flew in the face of "common sense"), and to search out with much excitement the ways that seeing culture and society through that mantra changed
everything. And changed everything in ways that I liked.

For people in film and television studies, that mantra was, simply,
Media don't reflect reality. For people in literary criticism, it was *Language
doesn't reflect reality.* For people in anthropology, it was *Ethnography and
ethnographic films don't reflect reality.* It was exciting to discover that
media as in *media studies* didn't mean "conduit studies." It meant something more like "mediation" studies. Media and media producers *mediated*
reality — they didn't just transmit it. They helped construct and set the terms
of culture, not just convey it.

As a teaching assistant to freshmen in the Introduction to Film course,
the way I taught the mantra was to write the word *representation* on the
chalk board as "re-presentation." Then I'd say,

> The process of representation is not a process that *reflects* reality.
> Media are not mirrors of the world. They're not windows onto the
> world. Media re-present the world. Representation presents its subject
> again, in ways that have *mediated* it through language, ideology, cul-
> ture, power, convention, desire. Media producers alter what they re-
> present in the process of re-presenting it.

Given this perspective, mode of address was one among many mediat-
ing factors in filmmaking, just as narrative mediated how a film structured
its information or expressionism mediated a director's choice of lighting
and composition.

This paradigm shift from reflection to re-presentation sent — and continues to send — reverberations through all sorts of scholarly, social, and
political practices and strategies. Let's say, for example, that films and
television programs are highly mediated versions or conventionalized social
constructions of reality — and don't simply reflect a prior reality. Suddenly
it becomes very important in social and political struggles against stereotypes and for civil rights, for example, *how* various groups' experiences and
social and historical events get re-presented. It matters how they are mediated through language, image, and rhetoric.

When we look at the world through the mantra that claims that reality
can't be reflected directly through language or film, re-presentation becomes recognizable and available as a crucial site of social, political and

educational struggles over what particular people, events, and experiences will be made to mean. Hence, the "politics" of representation and meaning-making. Hence course titles such as: Race and Racism in U.S. Popular Media; Culture and Identity in Reading and Response to Literature; Media, Representation, and the Construction of Knowledge.

THE EDUCATIONAL DREAM OF FULL UNDERSTANDING

Following this period as a grad student, I started reading educational research and literature and began teaching media in a school of education. I couldn't help noticing that there were huge areas of discussion and practice in education that seemed to be untouched by the earth-moving shift from reflection to re-presentation in other academic fields.

Of course, circulating in education are some strong and troubling challenges to what I referred to in the last chapter as the dreams or assumptions of a fully reflective understanding between teacher and student. But those challenges don't feel like a paradigm shift. They feel more like scattered reportings of anomalies.

For example, the notion of "student resistance" as it circulates in sociologies of education could be seen a challenge to fully reflective understanding. But resistance isn't usually discussed in terms of the impossibility of full and reflective understanding itself. Usually, it's seen to be more about social and cultural contexts that lead students to refuse to go along with official school knowledge after an understanding of its political and economic interests is already achieved. If students experience alienation from official school knowledge but don't understand where that alienation comes from, critical educators have the job of bringing them to that understanding.

And as I said earlier, when educational researchers don't politicize student resistance to school knowledge in terms of class, gender, or race interests, they usually see it as a clinical problem. When resistance can't be traced to some social problem, it's usually seen as some dysfunction or noise in cognition or attention which can and should be remedied to make full understanding possible.

Another one of the isolated anomalies in education as a field of research that troubles the model of a fully reflective understanding of the world, curriculum, or teacher has to do with notions of "the self." In the wake of feminisms, multiculturalisms, and postmodernisms, we are faced with a variety of multiplicities, paradoxes, and subtleties that complicate self-awareness. And this further complicates self-understanding and its implications for understanding others.

Some educational researchers are using autobiography to explore and expand these complications. Using autobiographies of school experiences, they have traced the indirect ways that students and teachers mediate the outside of the official school curriculum through their multiple and changing experiences and constructions of self. They have used autobiography to show how curriculum becomes the conflicted and irreducibly rich and nuanced inside of one's "schooled self." Mismatchings between the outside of curricula and the inside of conflicted and nuanced selves are thought to produce possibilities for agency and political change.

Student resistance to getting official school knowledge and recent theoretical and political complications of what we take to be "self-understanding" have made some noteworthy dents in the armor of assumptions that encases most educational theory and practice. Assumptions, that is, of the possibility and desirability of a reflective, "full understanding" between teacher and student.

And yet, education, whether critical or traditional, is inundated by discourses and practices that assume the possibility (and desirability) of a dual, reflective relation between student and teacher. They assume the possibility of using language to mirror, for example, the teacher's meaning, intent, knowledge (be it already achieved or in the process of being constructed). They assume the possibility of then using that mirror of language or curriculum to "show" the teacher's knowledge to the student, which the student can then "see," and "understand," and reflect back in measurable ways.

DISHONEST MODES OF ADDRESS

In film school, we had a lot of fun with films that approached us, as audience members, with disingenuous modes of address. That is, we often analyzed films that addressed us as *if* they were presenting us with *reflections* of the world. But the mantra (films don't reflect reality), of course, reminded us that this couldn't be so. So our task in seminars was often to do close analyses of such films. We'd look for the inevitable traces of mediation that marked the film's narrative structure, stylistic elements, or actors' performances.

We were detectives in a darkened room gazing intently at a (usually black-and-white) flickering screen—and we knew that things were not as they appeared to be. We searched for the inescapable and not at all innocent ways that history, culture, gender, ideology, economic interest, compulsory heterosexuality, and so on left their interested fingerprints on even the most realistic of feature films and documentaries. When we found a fingerprint—

yet another piece of evidence supporting the hypothesis that our knowledge of the world is always mediated and socially constructed—it was cause for great celebration and reward! It was what we were *supposed* to find, as students. And the more fingerprints we found, the closer we were to an acceptable dissertation. We were helping to construct the new paradigm.

And like the films we studied, this new paradigm wasn't neutral or free of vested interests itself. We weren't just detectives in search of the truth about films. We were detectives on the side of social justice. We were feminists, socialists, antiracists, gay and lesbian activists, counterculture-ists, avant-gardeists. We were angry at film modes of address that ignored, denied, or hid their own complicities in particular ways of seeing the world—ways that had a stake in perpetuating unjust social, political, and economic power relations. Any film that addressed us as if it were simply a transparent window on reality—and not a party to constructing and perpetuating that reality—became subject to the most exquisite and relent-less interrogation.

And that's what we called it. Interrogating films—forcing them to give up their secrets—forcing them to show how they committed crimes of racism, sexism, heterosexism or exploitation in the ways they used lighting, camera movement, editing, sound, or composition of frames to re-present historical events, men and women of color, white women, straight and gay people, working-class people. And then we forced them to show how they hid the evidence of their crimes under a mode of address that spoke to their audiences as if they were simply showing the world the way it was.

Whew.

After spending a good many of my intellectually formative years learning to look at films this way, it's been hard to turn off this way of seeing.

Soon after coming from communication arts to work in education, I couldn't help seeing education as a field filled with materials, discourses, and practices that addressed their audiences as if they were simply reflecting the world the way it was. Or, as if it were possible for a student's reading of a curriculum to match the curriculum text.

The primary mode of address in education appeared to be: There is no mode of address here—no mediation—here's a neutral record of reality.

The Seduction of a Realist Mode of Address

When Hollywood films address their audiences as if there is no mode of address here, it's called a "realist mode of address," and it's one aspect of a filmmaking style called *realism*. That style uses conventions of lighting, composition, editing, sound, and acting that have grown up around a belief in and a desire for the possibility and pleasures of representing the world through a transparent, accurate record of what it is, or at least, of how "we" "experience" it.

One example of a realist convention would be a use of lighting effects that has come to connote a "neutral record" of an actual event—lighting that "looks like" natural sunlight or the light coming from the lamps in the room where a scene takes place. Realist lighting conventions are very different from "expressionist" lighting conventions, for example. Expressionism as a film style employs lighting effects that are intended to comment on a character's inner state of mind through "unnatural" or "unrealistic" shadows across a face, for example.

Kuhn's (1982) description of realism was one that we often worked with in grad school:

> [W]hat is seen on the cinema screen appears to the spectator to be constructed in much the same way as its referent, the "real world." The film, that is, "looks like" the real world. This is what makes realist films easy to watch and follow: they seem to duplicate spectators' everyday ways of experiencing the world. This realistic appearance is in fact brought about not by a duplication of the "real world" referents but by certain conventions of cinematic signification. All films are coded: it is simply that certain types of films are coded in such a way as actually to seem uncoded. . . . The transparency of realist cinema then consists in the fact that the spectator is seldom actually aware in watching a film that she or he is making meanings: meaning seems to be there in the film, the spectator's only task being to sit back and take it in. This of course, is one of the pleasures of the classic realist cinema: an address which draws the spectator in to the representation by constructing a credible and coherent cinematic world, which at the same time situates her or him as a passive consumer of meanings which seem to be already there in the text. (pp. 131–132)

Realist cinema addresses us *as if* it were simply reflecting the world, and *as if* we were simply passively consuming the self-evident meanings and significance already there in the world, and in the film.

Hollywood's realist style and modes of address dominate filmmaking in the United States and most of the world. Realism as a style has established a baseline of audience expectations of film viewing. It commands vast amounts of filmmaking resources and materials, has become synonymous with "pleasure" for most filmgoers, and very nearly defines what most people mean when they speak of "the cinema."

The knowledges that I grew up on in graduate school were made possible because of a certain refusal on our part of realism's claims. We were taught to refuse to accept realism's disingenuous claims that the cinema is simply a record of the world as it is. We refused to believe that realism offered its viewers a fully comprehendible and understandable, unmediated world.

Now, as Felman (1987) points out, psychoanalysis may have contributed to abolishing the postulate of a subject presumed to know (p. 84). And it may have also contributed to abolishing the postulate that media or other forms of communication simply reflect the world. But that doesn't mean that the illusion of a consciousness—or a film style—transparent to itself has also been abolished. Most of our daily lives are lived and most of our communication and education is carried on as if we were fully conscious, and had full access to that consciousness. It's an illusion, but a prestigious and seductive one.

Felman (1987) argues that psychoanalysis may have shown that the "subject presumed to know" is a mirage—but psychoanalysis has also shown the power that that mirage has in daily life (p. 84). In fact, the prestige and affective charge of the mirage of a knowing self may be "indeed most crucial to the emotional dynamic of all discursive human interactions, of all human relationships founded on sustained interlocution" (p. 84).

Hollywood realism addresses its viewers as if they were fully knowing, coherent subjects. Realism places its viewers in the position of having privileged knowledge about the story's events, its characters, their pasts, futures, motivations, secrets. Film critics argue that the seductive pleasures of Hollywood stem in part from the ways in which watching a Hollywood film is one of the few places and times that we can immerse ourselves in the illusion of having full, complete, adequate knowledge (Cook, 1985, p. 212).

This mirage is the linchpin of realism as a film style. In film, realism requires, is constituted by, the illusion that it reflects reality and places its viewers in the position of complete knowledge of that reality. Realism may be a mirage. But it's a pleasurable and highly sought-after mirage. One people never seem to tire of. One that has helped make Hollywood the cultural broker of the planet.

But the fact that it's an illusion is something most of us get a lot of pleasure out of ignoring or forgetting. Most of us willingly and gratefully suspend our disbelief that the cinema is a window on the world, and that language is a mirror of reality, when the lights go down, or when the discussion circle forms.

Communicative Dialogue as a Realist Mode of Address

Having seen doors opened in film studies onto interpretive understanding, onto analytic understanding, I'm curious about what doors to what other kinds of knowledges might be opened to educators and students if we also gave up the fancy of full, direct understanding, and of the transparency of representation.

Here is where this passage through film studies brings me: I've spent 14 years looking at and living out the representational practices of educational materials and discourses through the eyes of film studies. I've become convinced that communicative dialogue is to teaching what Hollywood's realist conventions, such as continuity editing, are to cinema. I've become convinced that communicative dialogue is one of the central realist conventions in teaching as a system of representation, and as a representational practice.

Communicative dialogue is education's Hollywood, its dream factory. Film critics have interrogated realism in Hollywood films through questions such as, What kind of knowledge does realist cinema proffer? What techniques does it use to regulate that knowledge and the relationship of the different characters within the narrative to knowledge and truth (Cook, 1985)?

Here, I want to ask, what kind of knowledge does dialogue proffer? What techniques does dialogue use to regulate knowledge and the relationship of the teacher and students to knowledge and truth?

Let me explain.

Communicative dialogue certainly is one of those discursive human interactions, one of those human relationships that Felman describes as being founded on sustained interlocution. Like realism, it requires, it is constituted by, the illusion of the subject presumed to know. Its goal is "the fancy of understanding" (1987, p. 108). And like realism, dialogue only works when its participants suspend their disbelief. Communicative dialogue works only when we act as if its mode of address is a neutral conduit of reality, and not itself a rhetoric—not itself a mediation of knowledge and of its participants' relations to knowledge.

Many educators invoke dialogue, endlessly, it seems, as a way of coming to an understanding without imposition. They offer dialogue to teachers as a strategy capable of being more democratic than lectures and other one-way determinations by the teacher of the student's understandings. Educators constantly associate dialogue with democracy, as in, When we enter into dialogue, we agree to be open-minded and open to being changed by the process of hearing and coming to understand another's arguments, experiences, viewpoints, and knowledge. And as when dialogue is seen as a neutral means for fulfilling a shared desire for understanding even if differences of opinion and power remain.

Now, dialogue may be offered as a way of conceptualizing or structuring the relation between a speaker and listener, between the social and the individual, or between curriculum and the student. But whatever its application, and as I argued in chapter 2, communicative dialogue is itself a symbolic structure. And as a symbolic structure, it offers to those who enter into it positions within knowledge, power, desire, and history. Communicative dialogue is not a neutral vehicle that simply carries those subjects' ideas and understandings back and forth, unmediated, between student and teacher. Nor, as we've seen Donald and Felman argue, is the space between the two participants in a dialogue an empty space. It is populated by "diverse and frequently conflicting sign systems" that "coincide, and collide" (Cook, 1985, p. 246).

Dialogue is not a transparent window on its participants' realities, meanings, intentions. When someone initiates a dialogue with me, s/he calls me into dialogue's structure of relations. When I enter into a dialogic structure of discussion, or learning, I am constituted as a subject of dialogue.

WHO DOES COMMUNICATIVE DIALOGUE THINK YOU ARE?

So who does dialogue think I am? According to Chang's (1996) deconstruction of theories of communication, it assumes that I am a "solitary subject," who wants, needs, or both, to be a social subject:

> For this very reason, the theoretical challenge of communication is translated as the challenge of privacy—a challenge resulting from the encounter of multiple communicative subjects, each characterized as a disparate realm of private feelings and experiences. (p. 44)

Dialogue supposes that I am an autonomous, individual, complete subject—and that so are you. Otherwise, why would dialogue be necessary? It is our solitude that makes communication both necessary, and a big problem. How do I connect with you across the disparities in our private realms?

Communicative dialogue is intended to do this job. It sets out to transcend this privacy and singularity and to transform individuals' private beings "into a different form of cobeing . . . " (Chang, 1996, p. 44) in which difference and distance are superseded. According to the tenets of dialogue, the interplay of self and other

> occasions . . . a journey from self to the other, through which the self approaches itself *other*-wise; that is, *re*-cognizing itself anew through the mediation of an alien double. . . . Such a dialectical happening brings about a transition from individuality to sociality, from private, or lonely, existence to community/commonality. This is the telos of communication as a dialectical becoming. (p. 44)

This way of thinking about communication is so highly naturalized in Western thought, it's so tightly linked to powerful institutions and discourses, that it's difficult to see communicative dialogue as a social construct. Chang's project has been to de-naturalize communicative dialogue and question its investments in particular ways of addressing its participants.

For Chang, the problem with dialogue is that even though it says it brings about a transition from individuality to social relatedness, it doesn't. In order to make itself necessary, dialogue posits a sender and a receiver who are separate and solitary. It then offers itself as a form of mediation between sender and receiver.

But dialogue is an odd mediation. First of all, it's an asymmetrical mediation because it takes place between "that which stays the same [the speaker or sender] and that which appears to the former as different [the listener or receiver]" (Chang, 1996, p. 44). This is because as long as dialogue is thought of as the sending of a message from self to other, and then the receiving of a message from the other back to the self, dialogue doesn't really take the other into account! That is, the

> delivery or sending of the message turns out to be a return of the message, because the destination of the message . . . is determined before the sending of that message. Written by a signatory and addressed to a receiver identified beforehand, the message . . . in fact travels inside a closed circuit, inside a homogeneous space; like a letter, it moves from one address to another without ever leaving a premapped territory. (Chang, 1996, p. 46)

You can't, in other words, send a message to a place that the postal system doesn't recognize. The other has to already be on the map someplace if you're going to send a message to her. And the sender must know the address, the map, in order to send the message. This is what Chang (1996) calls the "postal principle" in communication (p. 47). It places the call to communicate inside a closed circuit, already addressed to someone whose whereabouts (within networks of knowledge, power, and desire) are already known within the premapped territory.

In other words, the call to communicate that initiates a dialogue cannot take us into territory that isn't already known. If the other responds, "Yes, I'm here, I got your message," the sender/self is only confirmed to be who s/he thought s/he was by sending the message as s/he did. But even if the response is "address unknown" or "You got me wrong, I'm not there, I'm here!" the self/sender is *still* confirmed to be who s/he thought s/he was. This is because the return message arrives back to the same place from which it was sent—confirming that place. And the onus of difference falls on the other who is either not locatable on the map, or who gets the job of having to say, "I'm different from who you thought I was."

That's what Chang means by "The delivery or sending of the message turns out to be a return of the message." And if the sending turns out to be a return, the other doesn't matter. The other doesn't need to be taken into account.

Now, if the dialogical relation does not take into account the other, the "dialectic" of dialogue becomes a

> foreclosing dialectic, eventually leading [communication theorists] to their unquestioned valorization of identity over difference, of the selfsame over alterity, of dialogue over polylogue, and most important, of understanding and the determination of meaning over *mis*understanding and undecidability. (Chang, 1996, p. xi)

To deny that communicative dialogue is itself structured in history and through interests is to give it and its participants transcendental status—and this makes dialogue a foreclosing dialectic.

This is exactly what appears to have happened in many educational discourses and practices. Dialogue in education is assumed to be capable of everything from constructing knowledge to resolving problems, to ensuring democracy, to securing understanding, to teaching, to alleviating racism or sexism, to arriving at ethical and moral claims, to enacting our humanity, to fostering community and connection.

Transcendental claims such as these hide the histories, cultural competencies and assumptions, and interested desires that communicative dialogue, as a structure of relations, requires of its participants and positions them within. It denies that dialogue circulates within premapped and closed networks of social and political relations. We may get pleasure out of ignoring or forgetting that even through dialogue, direct communication or understanding is impossible. But meanings and operations of power are also played out in that ignore-ance.

So, as film scholars have been doing with realism, I want to trouble the presumed transparency and neutrality of communicative dialogue as a mode of address to students by exploring the desire for dialogue within education. I want to do this through two questions: Who does communicative dialogue, as prescribed in educational literature, think you are? and Why does it want you to be that?

COMMUNICATIVE DIALOGUE: WHAT'S CONTINUITY EDITING GOT TO DO WITH IT?

Earlier, I said that I'm convinced that communicative dialogue is to education what Hollywood's realist conventions, such as continuity editing, are to cinema. I want to take that comparison further here, as a way of getting more specific about the interested nature of communicative dialogue as a structure of relations.

Comparing dialogue to continuity editing, I'm going to argue that the desire for dialogue is a desire for continuity: The interests of the one who calls for dialogue are interests invested in continuity. What is at stake in whether a dialogue is "successful" or not is the reinscription of particular power relations that operate in and through continuity.

So first, a few words about what film studies has to say on the power relations and knowledges that continuity editing supports.

Continuity editing refers to a codified "set of editing techniques whose objective is to maintain an appearance of 'continuity' of space and time in the finished film" (Cook, 1985, p. 212). Every new shot in a realist film threatens to disrupt the viewer's suspension of disbelief. This is because a cut from one shot to the next breaks the illusion of a unified, coherent, homogeneous, unmanipulated, "realistic" flow of time and space.

The purpose of continuity editing as a series of conventions is to bridge spaces of difference-between. Its purpose is to "'bridge' spatial and temporal ellipses in cinematic narration" (Cook, 1985, p. 213), to "efface the moment of transition between shots" (p. 208). It does this through conventions that are so familiar and pervasive that they often seem invisible.

One example is the editing technique of *match on action*. In a match on action, two shots are spliced together in a way that matches the movement and direction of the action in a scene from one shot to the next. Movement and direction are "matched" by keeping consistent the direction of the action across the shots, the speed of the action, and the angle from which we see the action.

For example: The first shot is of a woman walking from screen right to screen left toward a closed door. This is cut at the point when she begins to raise her hand to grasp the doorknob. Cut to a close-up of her hand starting in the same point in space that we left it in shot 1, as it moves at the same speed and angle from right to left toward the doorknob, which she then grasps and turns.

Techniques such as match on action make up the stylistic system called continuity editing. Continuity editing contributes to a particular mode of address to the audience. It has, in other words, a rhetorical purpose:

> The explicit objective of the continuity system is to construct—by ensuring that cuts are as unobtrusive to the spectator as possible—the appearance of a seamless and coherent narrative space and time. The effect is to make cinematic discourse—the process of meaning production—invisible. (Kuhn, 1982, p. 38)

Conventions intended to "hide the artifice of the means of representation" (Cook, 1985, p. 208) and give the appearance of seamless, unmanipulated flow of time and space, invite the viewer to accept a particular version of reality as "real." By accepting this invitation, "the spectator becomes witness to a complete world, a world which seems even to exceed the bounds of the film frame" (p. 214).

But this particular type of illusion—the illusion of a complete, whole, seamless, unmanipulated world—offered by Hollywood's system of continuity editing is not an innocent one. It's as much an argument as it is an illusion. It's an argument for the "naturalness," "givenness," and "ahistorical" nature of what is being shown, and of conventional ways of seeing.

Like a film, communicative dialogue in education is not static. It offers a series of views from constantly shifting positions within its premapped territory. Like realism in film, dialogue requires a delicate balancing act between too much change and not enough change. Both realism and dialogue must maintain a delicate poise between process and position. A dialogue that is nothing but process—nothing but constantly shifting positions—raises "the threat of incoherence, of the loss of mastery" (Neale, 1980, p. 26). But a dialogue that is nothing but the reiteration of two fixed positions raises the "threat of stasis, fixity or of compulsive repetition, which is the same thing in another form" (p. 26). Like continuity editing, dialogue works to provide a "to-and-fro movement" that provides interest and pleasure. As Cook (1985) states:

> [W]hat is needed is a perpetual oscillation between delicious instants of risk and repeated temporary returns to equilibrium. Some writers believe that the pleasurability of the cinema resides in precisely this process of limited risk. (p. 246)

The risk, to film viewers, is the threat "of the loss of meaning and control" (Cook, 1985, p. 246) if continuity editing does not successfully bridge the visual, spatial, and temporal difference between two shots—thus failing to render that difference invisible, insignificant, meaningless.

Except that it is precisely the *difference between* two edited shots that allows the story to move forward. It is the (managed) difference between shots that provides the pleasure of limited risk as understandings, beliefs, and appreciations change, but don't change too much. The trick for both communicative dialogue and for Hollywood is to keep difference a "delicious instant of risk" and not "a loss of meaning and control." The trick is to *manage* the difference between shots and the difference between speakers.

The ultimate threat to Hollywood's ability to deliver as a factory of dreams is the threat that the "sutures" of continuity editing that "hold us in place" (Cook, 1985, p. 247) as we watch a film will break. If they break, the theory goes, we will stop suspending our disbelief, our pleasures and fascinations will be interrupted, and we might just walk out in the middle of the film. Here is how Cook describes the way continuity editing "holds us in place":

> At the beginning of each shot, the spectator enjoys a secure imaginary relationship to the film, a feeling bound up with the illusion of privileged control over and unmediated access to its fictional world. A moment later, though, this illusion is dispelled as s/he gradually becomes conscious of the image frame, and hence of the fact that the fictional space is after all narrowly circumscribed. This realization stimulates the desire to see and find out more and the former illusion of the image as offering a "window on the world" yields to an unpleasant perception of the film as artefact, a system of signs and codes that lie outside his/her control. However, this recognition is soon overcome by the advent of the next shot, which apparently restores the previous condition of the spectator's imaginary unity with the images and starts the cycle off again. (p. 247)

In other words, imagine watching a film that consists of one long shot. The camera just sits there and looks at something, without moving, panning, tilting. There's no edited cut to some other perspective on the same scene, or no cut to some other space and time. Very soon, we'd become very conscious of the image's frame—of the fact that it *is* a *framed* image, constrained, limited, constructed, an artifact—and not at all a transparent window on reality. We've become keenly aware that there's more to what we're seeing than meets the eye, but we're not seeing it.

Continuity editing strives to make the next shot arrive before this "disillusionment" sets in. Through timing and matches-on action like the one I described in the example of the woman's hand reaching for the doorknob, continuity editing is designed to perpetuate a viewer's "illusion of privileged control over and unmediated access to its fictional world."

And even though a change in point of view, time, or space between one shot and another toys with chaos and incoherence, a change is needed, a difference is required—or we will lapse into stasis or repetition. The challenge for Hollywood's dream factory is to come up with a difference, a change, that nevertheless restores the "spectator's imaginary unity with the images." The difference or change provided in the potentially disruptive cut from one shot to another must be one in which the next shot is seen as another version of—is seen in terms of—the first. They share terms.

The ultimate threat to the project of communicative dialogue as a teaching strategy is similar to that of broken sutures in continuity editing. The ultimate threat arises when the listener is not just another version of the speaker. The ultimate threat arises when terms aren't shared. Remember Lacan's question and answer:

Ask yourselves what the call represents in the field of speech. It represents—
the possibility of a refusal. (Quoted in Felman, 1987, p. 118)

The call to communicative dialogue represents the possibility of a refusal—
a break in continuity. The dialogue could end. The difference could be too
great. What could be lost is a participant's ability or willingness to continue
the so-called encounter with other voices. A refusal to participate raises the
specter of a loss of coherence and control—a failure.

A break in the continuity of a film's editing calls attention to the frame
around the image—to the artifice of the world being presented, to the
illusion of reality.

A break in the continuity of dialogue—a refusal of the terms of communicative dialogue—calls attention to the frame around the premapped
nature of the territory within which the call to dialogue is addressed. It calls
attention to the illusion of dialogue's openness to *any* and *all* positions of
address.

And so just like realist movies, communicative dialogue needs its own
version of continuity editing. It needs to hold the participants of dialogue in
dialogue despite the constant changes of view and interests that threaten
coherence through difference.

And so I've gotten curious about what dialogue depends upon to hold
me in dialogue.

Pursuing this curiosity will take me into the next two chapters. In each
of them, I grapple with the meanings for me, as a teacher, of Felman's
assertion that there are (at least) two structures of address positioning
teachers and students. Each sets up a different kind of pedagogical dynamic
between teacher and student and a different order of learning experience.

She calls one of these structures of address "traditional" or "conventional." It's the dialogic structure of address in the sense in which most
educators speak of dialogue. Its goal is communication and understanding,
an exchange of information between teacher and student with productive—
possibly transformative—self-reflection by each in light of the new and
different knowledges they hear from each other. All in a dual structure of
address.

But there's another structure of address that Felman explores at length.
It's that triangular structure of address that I touched on in the last chapter.
It acknowledges and puts to analytic use a third participant in the student-
teacher relation, namely, the unconscious or the discourse of the Other.

Felman (1987) calls this triangular structure of address "analytic dialogue" (p. 83) to distinguish it from communicative dialogue or a dialogue
of exchange and understanding. Analytic dialogue, unlike communicative

dialogue, Felman argues, is intended precisely to produce and learn from
*dis*continuity, ruptures, breaks, refusals, failures.

In chapter 6, I'll offer a concrete example, in a reading of Felman's
analysis of the film *Shoah*, of the power of analytic dialogue, or the triangular structure of address, for teaching.

But first, in chapter 5, I want to argue that communicative dialogue
that strives for understanding has a dual structure of address. And that its
dual structure of address acts like the sutures of continuity editing. I want
to explore how the dual structure of address operates in teaching—and
operates as a dialectic that forecloses difference.

5

Communicative Dialogue: Control Through Continuity

WHEN EDUCATORS and others equate learning with the achievement of understanding, we are assuming that "absolute representation" is possible and desirable. We have assumed that "any thing (idea or material object) has a matching word which will make the thing present in speech" (Marshall, 1992, p. 64). And it's further assumed that if I use that matching word as I am speaking to you, and if you understand that matching word, then the idea or meaning that is present in me will also be made present in you. As Chang (1996) argues, "the correspondence between a sender and a receiver of messages stands unwaveringly at the center of the concept" of communication, with the "built-in goal" being the "trancendence of difference" (p. xi).

It is the built-in-ness of this goal that I want to explore in this chapter and the next. In what ways has the goal of transcending difference been built into the rules of communicative dialogue as it is prescribed for teachers?

Chang (1996) calls the built-in-ness of the goal of reducing difference "the ideology of the communicative" (p. xviii). He's referring to the way that theorists of communicative dialogue have reified "*understanding* as the *ideal*, the *telos*, and the *norm* of communicative activities" (p. 174). Under this view,

> to communicate is—principally—to achieve understanding, and instances of misunderstanding, of equivocation, of ambiguity, of nonsense, can be viewed only negatively, that is, as lack, aberration, or dysfunction. (p. 174)

And so communication theory makes an "implicit value judgement anchored in the primacy of understanding"—what gets valued are "certain objects or relations (such as conscious intention, consensus) to the suppression of others (such as the unconscious, desire, conflict, uncertainty, dispute, ambiguity)" (pp. 174–175). By "excluding 'disorder' at its orginary moment," Chang says, communication theory in fact helps "to legitimate the sociopolitical status quo" (p. 175).

Now, as Chang (1996) points out, my very act of writing this book embodies a desire to communicate, even if I do share with him a "deep skepticism about . . . communicability in general" (p. xi). But it's not the desire to communicate that I am resisting here. Instead, I am resisting what Chang calls the "ideology of the communicative" (p. xviii) that is built into rules for communicative dialogue as a pedagogical practice. And I am resisting the position offered to me within social relations by educational theorists who have folded the ideology of the communicative into their prescriptions for how teachers should teach across difference.

Parapharasing Chang (1996), my purpose will be served if I can manage to unsettle the relation that exists between advocates of communicative dialogue in education and their beloved practice (p. xviii). That's because I'm troubled about what the current valorizations of dialogue mean to the task of teaching about and across social and cultural difference in ways that work against assimilation. What does it mean for this task when the continuity of sameness is "built-in" to the very terms that govern the practice of communicative dialogue, and when sameness is won by excluding the discontinuity of difference?

[handwritten margin note: doesn't support dialogue?]

CHALLENGING COMMUNICATIVE DIALOGUE AS SELF-REFLECTION

Given its goal of understanding, communicative dialogue in education is said to work—it's considered to be successful—when the questions, Did that make sense to you? or, What did you think of that? or, Do you get it? are answered in a way that reflects back to the questioner what the questioner already expects. In other words, communicative dialogue has worked when the addressee is able to respond with a reiteration of what the sender meant to say, a mirroring of the sender's message.

Now, this doesn't necessarily mean that the person who answers has to *agree* with the caller's message. But it does mean that communicative dialogue as it is defined in much educational literature is working when an answer to the question, Do you understand? is a reflexive and expected answer. "Yes, I have stood under, I have taken your perspective upon myself, I can reflect it to you now in a way that you will recognize and expect—no surprises."

Given the economy of communicative dialogue's exchange, once continuity has been established, a difference can be allowed. Starting, then, by standing under the caller's position, perspective, or sense, the one who answered, "Yes, I understand," is now permitted to take issue with the caller's views. But only if s/he *starts* from a reflective understanding of that view.

In other words, what must come first in communicative dialogue is understanding—that is, a supposedly innocent, disinterested reading of the other's message. *Then* disagreement is allowed. *First*, we establish our presumed common ground of comprehension. We must find the terms we share, the things that bind us together, namely, our capacities to be impartial, to curb our passions and desires, and to act as rational interlocutors seeking an initial, neutral reading of each other's words that needs no debate. This is a reading we do not have to "agree" to through debate and persuasion, because we have "come to an understanding" of it instead.

Then, our differences, and even our "feelings," can be considered, entertained.

But now our differences or desires will never threaten the continuity of our conscious discourse, because we have already established our common ground of dispassionate understanding. Even if we subsequently disagree, we are already the *same* in the sense that we have shown ourselves to be rational interlocutors capable of an initial, unbiased reading. We already are mirrors of each other's knowledge and positions in that all-important sense.

The logic that underlies this particular structuring of relations through the rules of communicative dialogue is such that disagreeing with someone without first understanding or reflecting their view amounts to an oxymoron. I can't disagree with you before I've understood what you are saying. Granted, this moment of standing under may be fleeting. But the dual structure and necessarily continuous nature of the dialogical relation seeks to guarantee that that moment of mirroring will return again and again. When she responds, the other reverses this process and now offers me a meaning to stand under even if I want to refuse it. But this reversal does not change the structure of address itself nor its interest in holding us both in a place of sameness through alternating calls and responses.

The only thing that can break the logic of the dialogic relation is a refusal to agree to an initial, neutral, innocent understanding. Such a refusal breaks the continuity of the dialogical process. And by breaking continuity, the mechanism of dialogue's control over its participants is broken.

To repeat, then, (no irony intended): Like realism in film, dialogue requires a delicate balancing act. It requires the playing out of a tension between "process (with its threat of incoherence, of the loss of mastery) and position (with its threat of stasis, fixity or of compulsive repetition, which is the same thing in another form)" (Neale, 1980, p. 26).

But communicative dialogue as advocated by educators is not supposed to be about stasis, fixity, or a compulsive repetition of a back-and-forth call and response. Advocates argue that dialogue across differences of opinion, background, culture, knowledge, or experience can result in positive transformations in its participants. Dialogue is supposed to enable me to encounter different points of view and differing ways of seeing and knowing, leading me to reflect on my own ways of seeing "in light of" the opinions and perspectives of others. Through this self-reflection, I will be changed by my encounter with others; and as a result, learning, or in other words, a difference, will have taken place.

Felman, however, disagrees. She doesn't think that transformative learning can take place through communicative dialogue and the pursuit of understanding. That's because understanding merely adds new information to an already established way of knowing, and the way of knowing itself is only repeated and not transformed. I'll try to explain.

Felman takes issue with the idea that communicative dialogue can yield transformation of the self through self-reflection. She rejects this notion because self-reflection is always in danger of becoming just that—a reflection of the prior, same self. Communicative dialogue's call-and-response dynamic of exchange results in a "specular duality (the seductive, narcissistic mirroring)" (1987, p. 126) between two agents: teacher and student. And because it is a relationship of duality that mirrors what is already there, the knowledge that such a dialogic structure of address carries back and forth between teacher and student is reducible "to the sum total of the knowledge of each of its two subjects" (p. 56).

In this dual structure of address between two conscious egos, each is supposed to strive to successfully add the other's knowledge to her own, or her own knowledge to the other's. Or, each engages in conscious self-reflection that takes new information from the other into account in a way that leads both participants to change their previous attitudes or opinions by adding in the other's perspective.

Conscious self-reflection, as elicited by communicative dialogue is, Felman (1987) argues, "the traditional fundamental principle of consciousness and of conscious thought" (p. 61). Self-reflection is

> always a mirror reflection, that is, the illusory functioning of symmetrical reflexivity, of reasoning by the illusory principle of symmetry . . . that subsumes all difference within a delusion of a unified and homogeneous individual identity. (p. 62)

In other words, what communicative dialogue for understanding may "change," in this additive way, are conscious opinions, attitudes, beliefs, values. It may pass on and add in new information to ways of making sense that were already there.

Here's an image that might help clarify this: You're standing and facing another. Each of you holds a mirror up to the other. You position the mirrors so that each of you can see the images of yourself and of the other repeated into infinity. There's a third person standing off to the side—who is not holding a mirror. The only way that the two of you who are holding mirrors can keep your two images repeating each other is to exclude the image of the third person. You could each turn and point your mirror at the third person, but then the continuous, infinite, repetitive string of connections between you and your mirror partner would be broken.

Positioning your mirror just so, your mirror partner's face comes into view, and your own view is changed, added to. But this "change" hasn't affected *the terms or structure of your looking itself.* Something has simply been added in to your already established field of view, to what you're already looking at and seeing. Without looking outside the frame of your own mirror as it already is, you can now have the illusion of seeing something more, something else, something different. But what you're seeing is more of the same—a repetition. The other's image is framed and contained in a mirror just like yours. The field of view has not been restructured—it's only being repeated, and can be repeated infinitely.

The rules of communicative dialogue for teaching try to ensure that both participants will be practicing conscious self-reflection. As a mode of structured address, what communicative dialogue repeatedly and urgently seeks to reestablish is the continuity of *conscious* discourse. Each time someone appears to understand me, I'm allowed to operate within and perpetuate the "illusion of having a consciousness transparent to itself" (Felman, 1987, p. 84). Even new information or changed opinions reestablishes the continuity of my conscious discourse: "I understood myself, I knew what I meant, and now someone else does too!" Even if someone ends up disagreeing with me, they have had to agree (to an understanding of what I just said) before they can dis-agree. "I understand her—this is what she means, this is what I mean, and now here's the difference between our meanings . . . " The structure of address in communicative dialogue allows me to subsume whatever difference there is between us into conscious, self-reflexive understanding.

And so, what is guarded against by the rules that structure communicative dialogue is the breaking of a continuously *conscious* discourse. What is guarded against is the interruption of the unconscious, the unmeant, the unknowable, the excessive, the irrational, the unspeakable, the unhearable, the forgotten, the ignored, the despised.

Of course, all of this sameness and repetition is not at all what advocates of communicative dialogue in teaching have in mind. Advocates maintain that communicative dialogue as a process *can* result in transformative, not just additive, change in its participants. But if conscious self-reflection between two participants is to be transformative beyond the mirrored summation of the knowledge of the two participants in a dual structure of address, where would the "something else" or "something beyond" of what each participant brings to the exchange come from? How does something else enter into the infinitely repeated tunnel of mirrors without itself being simply added in and caught up in the same self-reflections? What difference would make a difference, not to what we see or understand within terms already set, but to the very terms in which we see and know?

COMMUNICATIVE DIALOGUE AND
THE POLITICS OF PLURALISM

I'm going to begin to explore these questions by reading one of the current discussions about dialogue in teaching alongside the notion of continuity editing in film studies.

Nicholas Burbules (1993) is one educator who has addressed dialogue in teaching at some length. He offers an extended discussion of dialogue in relation to teaching, and does so in a way that tries to deal with postmodern critiques of representation and their implications for dialogue as a teaching practice. An advocate of dialogue both as a teaching practice and as a way of trying to reach agreement or understanding across social tensions and difference, he says: "I do not think there is any other sustainable approach to take in the midst of a complex, pluralistic democracy, such as our own" (p. 63).

I'm going to read Burbules's (1993) detailed examination of the rules and moves of communicative dialogue in teaching through the notion of continuity editing. To do this, I chose his book on dialogue and teaching, because it addresses many aspects of communicative dialogue, and does so in the specific context of teaching and in terms that seem most widely used in education.

Continuity is a theme that runs throughout Burbules's account of dialogue in teaching. It seems that *dis*continuity of conscious discourse is as much a threat to the project of dialogue in teaching as it is to the illusion of reality in the cinematic viewing experience.

Burbules (1993) writes of tensions and dilemmas in dialogue that are not unlike those facing continuity editors in Hollywood. For example:

> While it is often difficult to communicate and understand one another across differences, this very situation stands to teach us the most, since it can bring to

our understanding the perspective, values and experiences of a contrasting point of view. The fundamental tension underlying the dialogical relation is this: *We need to be similar enough for communication to happen, but different enough to make it worthwhile* [italics added]. (p. 31)

Here, then, is the dilemma: The dialogue game requires participants or contenders who are different enough to provide sufficient tension for the to-and-fro movement to have interest and pleasure; yet when this contention comes to be seen as a struggle or battle, the enjoyment is destroyed . . . an excess of conflict is directly counterproductive to this goal [of new understandings, beliefs, and appreciations], making us *less* able or willing to encounter other voices seriously. (p. 64)

This should sound very familiar. Burbules's account of the dilemma of dialogue closely parallels Cook's account of the difficulties facing Hollywood continuity editors. Continuity editors try to provide an engaging and intriguing change in view through a cut from one shot to the next, and yet the new shot has to somehow continue the *terms* (direction of action, angle, distance, narrative causality, lighting) that were established in the previous shot.

The whole process of dialogue, Burbules implies—its continuation, its worth, its enjoyability, its significance—requires and pivots on the presence of a difference. And yet, as I read it, the literature on communicative dialogue in teaching is weakest when it tries to theorize difference and its relation to dialogue.

For example, Burbules tries to argue that dialogue whose goal is understanding can indeed be transformative. Yet more than at any other point in his theorizing about dialogue, Burbules uses "commonsense" notions of dialogue to explain the something beyond mere self-reflection that communicative dialogue is supposedly capable of producing. He says that, theoretically,

it is the nature of this dialogical relation to be able to . . . [lead its participants] beyond any intended goal to new and unexpected insights. This kind of dynamic involves more than simply combining the perspectives and knowledge of two separate individuals: Maurice Merleau-Ponty points out how "the objection that my interlocutor raises to what I say draws from me thoughts I had no idea I possessed, so that at the same time I lend him thoughts, he reciprocates by making me think too." (1993, p. 20)

Yet, whenever Burbules refers to the practice of communicative dialogue, he is at a loss to account for just where these "thoughts I had no idea I possessed" or these "new and unexpected insights" come from.

Failing to theorize where these thoughts and insights come from and how, Burbules shields theoretical commitments from analysis and allows theoretical assumptions to operate "as if in the state of nature" (Rooney, 1989, p. 36):

> Theoretical effects are never achieved so securely as when they come naturally, that is, in the form of common sense, values, or "mere" practice. (p. 36)

> The seemingly casual inscription of the colloquial within theory discloses an unexamined conjuncture, which in its turn can be read to reveal a theoretical impasse. The colloquial is a clue to the exclusions that lend theory the grounds for rigor. (p. 25)

The point I'm trying to make by bringing Rooney in here, is that when Burbules uses commonsense notions of how participants in a dialogue "make each other think," a theoretical impasse is revealed, key parts of the argument to go unexamined. The moment of resort to everyday uses of the term *dialogue* discloses the moment of an exclusion that is necessary if Burbules is going to make the otherwise unsupported claims that he does about communicative dialogue's ability to generate something more than the simple combination of the perspectives of those participating in it.

What Burbules excludes is any theorization of the *limits* of conscious self-reflection and of communicative understanding. Burbules's examination does not offer a theory of the limits of conscious self-reflection through dialogue, or of what it is that exceeds the simple combination of "the perspectives and knowledge of two separate individuals," making possible thoughts I had no idea I possessed and unexpected insights. As a result, Burbules is left to "explain" the supposed productivity of dialogue through a series of disconnected colloquialisms (as in, being "carried away," "caught up," "takes on a life of its own"). For example, Burbules (1993) writes:

> [I]t is the nature of this dialogical relation to be able to "carry away" its participants, to "catch them up" in an interaction that takes on a force and direction of its own. (p. 20)

> Once constituted as a relation, the dialogic encounter engages its participants in a process at once symbiotic and synergistic; beyond a particular point, no one may be consciously guiding or directing it, and the order and flow of the communicative exchange itself take over. The participants are *caught up*; they are *absorbed*. (p. 21)

> [T]he capacity of dialogue to involve us and carry us beyond our intentions are all aspects of the *dialogical relation*. (p. 21)

> [A]part from any specific purpose and goal, there is a point at which dialogue takes on a life of its own. (p. 64)

And quoting Gadamer, Burbules concurs with the "strong" statement that "it is generally more correct to say that we fall into conversation, or that we become involved in it" (p. 66).

Burbules continues to "shield theoretical commitments from analysis" (Rooney, 1989, p. 36) when he draws on everyday meanings of "game" and "play" to explain how "new and unexpected" insights come to the participants in dialogue. Burbules (1993) sidesteps a more specific study of *what happens and how* in actual instances of dialogical teaching practice. He claims that "play resists all analysis, all logical interpretation," and "resists any attempt to reduce it to other terms." Play has the capacity to "run away with the players." Whatever the game, the moment we play for is the moment when we "lose track of time and place; we forget the score, forget winning or losing, forget the last game or the next game, and simply *play*" (p. 51). There is, Burbules asserts, "something about the interchange that stands on its own" (p. 58):

> [A]ny game possesses a kind of continuity; . . . in a sense, the game over-
> whelms us and takes us over as a player for its own purposes of moving
> forward. Dialogue, too, has this capacity to completely involve us as partici-
> pants . . . to the point that we are unable to say whether we are steering or
> being steered by the course of the discussion. (pp. 60–61)

Obviously, if the two participants in the dual structure of communicative dialogue are to achieve more than a simple mirroring or repetition of what they already know—something else has to enter the picture. Something besides each other's already achieved conscious knowings has to interrupt what they think they already know, who they think they already are.

But for Burbules and other advocates of dialogue in the field of education to be able to theorize what this something else might be, they would have to disclose and analyze the limits of a dual structure of address. They would have to confront how and why the continuity of *conscious* discourse is not enough. Instead, Burbules employs colloquialisms that naturalize and transcend specific contexts and dialogical events. And this allows the limits of dialogue to expand infinitely—even mystically.

Begging the Question of Difference

What gets problematic pretty quickly is that all this being carried away, caught up, absorbed, taken over, overwhelmed, run away with; all this resistance to any analysis and interpretation; all this losing track, forgetting, and being played by or steered by something beyond us could easily go in more than one direction. (Just as problematic is the way these chaotic states amount to barely veiled references to processes widely associated with the unconscious—and yet the author doesn't feel obligated to grapple with the ways that current theories of the unconscious may both assist and derail his championing of communicative dialogue as a teaching practice.)

The problem here is this: Communicative dialogue's mysterious powers to catch us up beyond our conscious intentions or noticings could very well carry us away into unexpected and welcomed insights, discoveries, explorations, or connections with others. On the other hand, they could just as well carry us away to places to which we might not necessarily want to go; or to which we might want to go but "shouldn't"; have been to and didn't want to return to; thought we were going to but then we ended up someplace else. How can we be sure that after losing ourselves in communicative dialogue, when we find ourselves again, we'll be in the place (of reciprocity, deliberation, democracy) we set out to be?

What makes the difference, Burbules (1993) asserts, are moral virtues. Things go the "right" way—toward discovery, insight, and enrichment—according to Burbules, when participants play by the rules of dialogue and exercise the appropriate character traits and virtues while they play. These include participation, commitment, and reciprocity (pp. 80–83). Even without an extended explanation of each of these rules, it's easy to see that their function is to provide "consistency, predictability, and continuity" while at the same time being flexible enough to allow "spontaneity, creativity, and surprise" (p. 67).

When things start to go wrong in a dialogue striving for understanding, supposedly it is the continuity of conscious discourse that can set them right. And this is precisely why the risk of discontinuity poses an even greater threat to the interests embedded in the logic of dialogue than does the failure of the participants in dialogue to persuade each other.

Throughout Burbules's discussion of dialogue and teaching, continuity is at stake. For example, he insists that "the prime benefit of conversation is in creating and maintaining the conditions for more conversation" (1993, p. 127); "if the value of dialogue is in facilitating the possibilities of future conversations, then interactions that inhibit those possibilities must be seen as signs of failure" (p. 144). Attempting to dialogue across the "barriers" of social and political difference is imperative because "such discourse is a condition of democratic life" (p. 158):

> For dialogue, . . . maintaining the relational conditions for further discussion is frequently more important, in the long run, than settling the specific question at hand. Answers, solutions, and agreements are fleeting things in human history—while the fabric of dialogical interchange sustains the very human capacity to generate and revise those provisional outcomes. (p. 144)

In other words, unanimity doesn't matter. What matters is that "the maintenance and development of the *dialogical relation* becomes primary" (Burbules, 1993, p. 64).

Why does the continuation of the discourse, the dialogue, the conversation itself matter so much—even more than unanimity or consensus across difference?

Burbules acknowledges throughout his discussion of dialogue and teaching that agreement or unanimity cannot be guaranteed. Even if they're achieved, they're often fleeting. If the value of dialogue as a practice came down to its ability to deliver agreement on demand, it would be hard to argue for dialogue as teaching strategy.

But, according to Burbules, understanding is a different thing from agreement. Persuasion and agreement are about rhetoric and often about emotion. But understanding, it is assumed, is different. It's about information and rationality. Burbules recognizes that given deep social and political differences among participants, agreement may be too much to hope for. But, given the willingness and ability to sustain commitment, reciprocity, and participation; understanding is never beyond reach. For those who have developed the rational capacities required by dialogue, and the ability to keep their emotions in check, understanding supposedly is always a possibility. It just might take a while.

That's why continuity of dialogue is crucial. In Burbules's view, disagreements or misunderstandings are "usually" no more than temporary delays in the process that always has the possibility of reaching understanding and "respect for differences" if it's just engaged in long enough. Even if people somehow lack the skills and virtues needed to keep emotion in check, maintain open minds, and respect the other participants in dialogue; continuing on in communicative dialogue is imperative because it is by engaging in dialogue that people develop those skills and virtues. "We learn to engage in dialogue *by* engaging in dialogue," Burbules asserts (p. 165).

It follows, then, that if people give up on dialogue too soon, or prejudge its ability to bring them to some meaningful conclusion, what we have given up is "the possibility of recasting society within a more inclusive, democratic, and open-ended communicative spirit" (Burbules, 1993, p. 151); "we have given up something basic and essential about our human character," we have given up on what exemplifies "some of the highest standards of how we ought to conduct ourselves in talking with and listening to one another" (p. 66).

And so Burbules ties the willingness and ability to engage in sustained dialogue and to see it through, despite difficulties, differences, and delays, to human potentials, capacities, and moral virtues. "Our humanity" and our capacities to engage in dialogue are so closely associated, in fact, that *interesting)* giving up on communicative dialogue or failing to <u>maintain its continuity</u> <u>throws one's moral character into question</u>:

> [T]he most complex problem in the formation and maintenance of a dialogical relation concerns aspects of character among the participants themselves. For all that can be said about explicit patterns of verbal interaction, the fundamental success of a dialogic encounter springs from the personalities, values, and habits of the participants themselves, with all their strengths and flaws. (Burbules, 1993, p. 46)

Burbules does recognize that "practical communicative situations" may sometimes make elusive the habits and conditions necessary to maintain dialogue. And sometimes, "the only possibility of attaining the conditions of dialogue between persons requires a delay of dialogue among them, or a temporary avoidance of certain kinds of issues or topics within a dialogue" (1993, p. 127). But after the delay or temporary avoidance (presumably to let emotions cool and reason return) if people stick with it, dialogue will usually result, finally, in agreement, consensus, understanding, or at least a respectful agreement to disagree.

The question that Burbules's account begs, of course, is this: What does *usually* mean, as in the statement, usually dialogue's pedagogical purpose can be achieved over time given a willingness to stay with the process? What about the times when the continuity of dialogue is broken, irreparably? What about the times when someone is not willing to stay with the process, or when understanding can't be reached, no matter how long people dialogue?

Burbules's discussion of dialogue as theory and practice lacks a theorization of the limits of continuity. It lacks a theorization of discontinuity. *true?* <u>Without it, the only way we can read someone's unwillingness to stay in</u> <u>dialogue is that they have not sufficiently developed the moral virtues neces-</u> <u>sary to keep their minds "open," their emotions in check.</u> The only way we can read their failure or refusal or limits to understanding is as a failure of their rational capacities or as a mean-spirited, separatist, antagonistic and dangerous-to-everyone-who-loves-democracy refusal to honor another human being's attempt to "connect" through communication.

Part of the seductiveness of the call to communicative dialogue, and part of this call's ability to maintain its hegemonic status as *the one* process that will lead to democracy and the virtues it requires, is the way that everyday senses of the term dialogue eclipse all critique of dialogue. What Rooney (1989) claims for the colloquial meanings of "pluralism" can also be said for the colloquial meanings of dialogue.

Paraphrasing Rooney (1989) then, dialogue is an ordinary word, a nontechnical term, an integral part of ordinary language and popular consensus. In all common uses, dialogue is an honorific. The very notion of dialogue is often identified with democracy, and the American way of life as such (p. 18). Calling dialogue into question, questioning its will to power and its mechanisms of control, has the potential to cast more doubt on the one raising the questions than it does on dialogue itself.

Evading the Issue of Persuasion

Nevertheless, Rooney does call dialogue into question. In her book *Seductive Reasoning* (1989) she interrogates the unacknowledged presuppositions, limits, and exclusions of pluralism and its invitations to join in communicative dialogue. She explores the ironies that arise when invitations to join in an inclusive dialogue actually lead to intended, unintended, or unacknowledged exclusions. To her reading, claims by pluralists that they are inclusive in their invitations to join in communicative dialogue are, in fact, seductions. They are seductions that conceal the striving for power that underlies pluralism's often hidden emphasis—an emphasis not on understanding and communication, but on *persuasion*. Rooney argues:

> [U]nderstanding is never the neutral gesture pluralism requires it to be; it can never be evaluated on a simple scale of purity or accuracy. As Derrida points out: it is not a question of true or false but of the play of forces. (p.109)

Understanding, Rooney argues, is always one of two things. It can be "a reciprocal act" that comes about because the parties agree. In this case, "to understand is to be persuaded" (p. 109).

Or, instead of being a reciprocal act of agreement, understanding can actually be an act of disagreement. It can be an act of demystification—as in: Here is a text that presents itself to us for understanding (it could be a work of literature, a speaker's utterance, a curriculum, a film). This text seems to be saying one thing, but that is because it is hiding or mystifying what it's *really* saying. I'm not persuaded by its ruse. Let me show you its processes of mystification, so that you can disagree with it too.

When to understand is to disagree, the person "reading" the text "claims authority or power over" that text (Rooney, 1989, p. 109). In this case, to understand is to remain unpersuaded, and "the work of the critic seeks to interrupt the tradition [of mystification] she takes as an object of study, to initiate a break with that tradition." This second, unpersuaded understanding, Rooney says, "puts an end to 'innocent reading'" (p. 109).

Burbules, writing as a teacher rather than as a literary critic, takes great care to assure his readers that communicative dialogue in education is not *only* about successful persuasion or achieving consensus. As a teacher, he must take care to distinguish between agreement and indoctrination. And so, he allows for disagreement in and through dialogue—as long as disagreement occurs after understanding and therefore permits a continuity of dialogue. In that way, disagreement then means that we have come to an understanding of how we disagree. Or, disagreement means that we now understand the issues that are still unresolved between us.

Yet, throughout Burbules's (1993) account of communicative dialogue as theory and practice, there are many conceptual and rhetorical slippages between understanding and persuasion. For example, he argues that in the absence of a foundational, transcendental philosophy, education becomes "the means by which epistemological, ethical, political, or aesthetic 'truths' are established and justified" (p. 1). And how does education accomplish this?

> We are justified in making claims about [what is true, or good, or right, or beautiful] only when we have the means to bring others along with us to such a conclusion. While from one vantage point it might make sense to say that something is the case regardless of whether others recognize it, as a matter of practice this assertion comes to nothing unless we can back it up with an educational—argumentative, persuasive, demonstrative—effort. This effort frequently relies on a dialogical engagement. (p. 2)

So here, education and communicative dialogue are "backed up" or under-pinned by argument and persuasion. And yet, Burbules follows up this account of education with another that appears to contradict it. He also says that he is less interested in

> "giving" students certain things, "shaping" students in particular ways, or "leading" them to particular conclusions, and more [interested in] creating opportunities and occasions in which students will, given their own questions, needs, and purposes, gradually construct a more mature understanding of themselves, the world, and others—an understanding that, *by definition,* must be their own. (p. 10)

So first, there's the contradiction between this desire for students to reach their "own" understandings, and Burbules's claims that education and dialogue rely upon being persuaded and being persuasive.

And second, a question is being begged here: Whose "understanding" of what constitutes a "more mature understanding" of self, world and others will be persuasive in this teaching situation?

Such equivocations on the topic of what communicative dialogue is *for*, what its goals and objectives are in teaching (is it for persuasion, understanding, the "gradual construction" of a "more mature" sense of self in the world?) are, finally, less threatening to Burbules's account than they might be. This is possible because the desire for dialogue is less a desire for a particular outcome than it is a desire for a response—any response—because a response means the dialogue is continued.

Control Through Exclusion

By framing a discussion of dialogue in these terms, Burbules unintentionally prolongs a mystification. What is concealed in his account of communicative dialogue is the striving for power that underlies an emphasis on universal participation.

If dialogue is continuous, unbroken, and everyone is participating in dialogue, they aren't doing something else. That's power. You may not have to come to agreement through a dialogue, but you, and everyone else in a society striving for democracy and social justice, must participate in dialogue. That's because communicative dialogue supposedly exemplifies "some of the highest standards of how we ought to conduct ourselves in talking with and listening to one another" (Burbules, 1993, p.66); a "moral culture of group discussion"; a "virtue identified with the very survival and vitality of democratic society" (p. 9); "something basic and essential about our human character" (p. 163), which offers the "possibility of recasting society within a more inclusive, democratic, and open-ended communicative spirit" (p. 151).

Paraphrasing Rooney (1989), I want to ask, What does an invitation to critics and theorists of all kinds to join in dialogue constitute every participant as? No matter what her conscious critical or political affiliation, every participant is constituted as an effect of the desire to persuade to participate.

Who communicative dialogue thinks you are then, and who it desires you to be, is a *participant*. A participant, or else. A participant, or else antidemocratic, lacking in the moral virtues and character traits required of participants (because if you *had* those traits and virtues, surely, you would be participating—those virtues and traits predispose you to participation; they virtually *compel* or *obligate* participation). According to Burbules, (1993) the "play community" that supposedly forms when dialogue is going well relies on implicit agreements

> to conduct ourselves in certain ways so that the activity can go forward. . . . Hence . . . we can understand the peculiar threat that the "cheat" and the "spoilsport" pose to the maintenance of this play community, and the unified will with which they are ostracized. (p. 53)

[margin annotations: participation → obligatory; dialogue – democratic →]

So communicative dialogue thinks you are a participant who allows the activity to go continuously forward. Or else you're a "cheat," a "spoil-sport" who everyone else will agree must be ostracized. You are one of us, having the same virtues, skills, and values, the same commitment to dialogue, having already *agreed* to dialogue — and therefore already having a *common ground* with us. Or else you are different from us — and "understandably" ostracized. Ostracized by a "unified will." A will that can be unified, of course, only through the exclusion of the one(s) who threaten the continuity of the dialogue.

Chang's (1996) discussion of Serres's work on dialogue tries to make this point even more starkly:

> [D]ialogue always depends on a joint effort by the interlocutors to fight against "noise," against any third party that threatens the reciprocity between the interlocutors . . . in every communicative event, participants "must unite against some phenomena of interference and confusion, or against individuals with some stake in interrupting communication" . . . sender and receiver . . . must join forces to expel the interference, the evil demon, a "third man," namely, any party that may interrupt the sending/receiving of messages. (p. 57)

Quoting Serres, Chang arrives at a statement that defies common sense about dialogue: To communicate "*is to suppose a third man and to seek to exclude him*; a successful communication is the exclusion of the third man" (quoted in Chang, 1996, p. 57). Chang elaborates the force of this position: "[C]ommunication is fundamentally an act of exclusion, for it involves a necessary violence to silence and resist the outsider: the barbarian, the intruder, the stranger" (Chang, 1996, p. 57).

Quoting Serres again, Chang (1996) argues that because of their joint effort against a common enemy, interlocutors in action

> are in no way opposed, as in the traditional conception of the dialectical game; on the contrary, they are on the same side, tied together by a mutual interest: they battle together against noise. (Quoted in Chang, 1996, p. 57)

> To communicate in this sense is to form an alliance among co-conspirators, to create a *socious secretus* of friends or equals "who are not each Other for each other but all variants of the Same" — in short, who create a *city*, a civilized community composed of rational, reasonable, free individuals bounded together by a common project of holding back the tide of noise or symbolic pollution. . . . Although communication appears to involve only two subjects, a successful exchange of messages always presupposes the threatening presence of a third party. (Quoted in Chang, 1996, pp. 57–58)

It's like the image that I used earlier in this chapter. The third person outside the frames of the mirrors that we hold up to each other threatens the continuity of our exchange. If one of us turns to point our mirror at the "third party," the illusion of the infinite repetition and acknowledgement of self and other is broken. And if the third party isn't holding a mirror—if s/he interrupts the sending and receiving of messages and refuses to participate in the interests embedded in the rules of communicative dialogue— then the continuity of conscious discourse can't be reestablished.

Rooney (1989), too, can be joined in this effort to demystify pluralism's paradoxical effort to exclude exclusion (as in, "we are pluralists and inclusive because we are not those who would exclude"). She points to the contradiction in efforts to enforce "exclusions in defense of inclusiveness" (p. 29). Paraphrasing her argument, the "consensus" or "unified will" of those in the "play community" of communicative dialogue to ostracize the one(s) who would break or rupture the continuous flow of dialogue, masks "a deeper consensus concerning the correctness of the status quo" (p. 29). Pluralism is threatened, Rooney argues, by the contradiction it raises when it says it invites all participants into dialogue—and yet is committed to "essential *exclusions,* in particular, the exclusion of exclusion, and . . . of those who would exclude" (p. 62).

The ideology of the communicative, in other words, can supposedly tolerate the one(s) who say(s), "Our differences are so great, you cannot persuade me." But that tolerance comes only because communicative dialogue asserts that there is actually a difference between persuasion and understanding. Persuasion may not be possible, but understanding always is. Even in the presence of disagreement, there is a possibility—a moral and democratic obligation!—to continue the dialogue in search of understanding.

But understanding is not a neutral gesture. To understand *is* to be persuaded.

What communicative dialogue cannot tolerate, what it *must* exclude, is the one who says, "Our differences are such that you cannot understand me, and I cannot understand you." This one ruptures the continuity of communicative dialogue, breaks its coherence and control, and fractures the ideology of the communicative. This one forces the "recognition of the irreducibility of the margin in all explanations," this one foregrounds "*interests,* with *exclusions* as the inevitable and clearly articulated consequence" of interests (Rooney, 1989, p. 63). The one who refuses to answer communicative dialogue's call to participate in its continuation, and refuses on the grounds that there's been a rupture, a break in common ground or common interests—that one must be excluded. That one has broken the rules of reciprocity, commitment, and participation—the rules of continuity. That one has refused the authority of communicative dialogue.

Now, Burbules (1993) claims that "to my way of thinking, an authority that is not in some sense working toward its end runs the risk of taking its own status too seriously" (p. 34). But by this, he does not mean that he is working toward the end of the authority of communicative dialogue. He is not working toward the end of a "deciding authority" founded on the "ultimate possibility of the decidable" (Chang, 1996, p. 174). Because, after all, Burbules (1993) asserts, some decidable standards and deciding authorities are necessary. Granted, they must be flexible and "inclusive within a broad range of possible values and perspectives." But they must also have "sufficient substance to exclude at least some possibilities (otherwise [dialogue] could not serve as a *standard* at all)" (p. 18).

Burbules chooses to ground the standards for communicative dialogue in teaching on individuals' communication skills, character traits, and moral virtues. This, of course, individualizes, personalizes, and psychologizes the grounds for communicative dialogue. In this way, he perhaps unintentionally insures that the question, Who is excluded when standards are decided? will *not* be framed as a question of history, power, desire, or social and political interests. And this insures that if the continuity of communicative dialogue is broken—if understanding is not achieved—then it is the personal "fault" of one or more participants.

THE THREAT OF DISCONTINUITY

The hegemony of communicative dialogue as described by Burbules in education and other civic enterprises is such that when someone rejects the claims made for dialogue, it's not at all clear what the alternatives might be. What other structures of address are there? Isn't dialogue what we're all doing all the time? Isn't it just the way we communicate? I'm going to argue that there are plenty of productive alternatives—and *they* are what we are doing all the time.

For example, once the sutures that hold the continuity of communicative dialogue's sending and receiving of messages are broken, once the limits of understanding and persuasion are admitted, the possibility of "partial" readings, of "partial understandings" is opened up. Partial in the sense of incomplete, and partial in the sense of invested and having interests at stake.

A partial reading or understanding is one that steps out of the place appointed to me by communicative dialogue's dual structure of address. In a partial reading, I don't try to understand what I have heard; rather, I put

[handwritten note: how do you put to use something not understood?]

it to use—I "extract from it what I want" (Rooney, 1989, p. 60). But this is what everyone does anyway, even those who embrace communicative dialogue. To pretend that any reading is innocent of such partiality is to claim to be reading according to a universal, transcendent standard. It's to claim a moment of pure, decontextualized reading. But such a moment is impossible.

Breaking the sutures of continuity of the dual structure of communicative dialogue, I have not answered from the position I have been called to. I do not reside at the address spoken to in my name. I have not answered as the who I have been addressed as by the call. A partial reading "asserts discontinuities" (Rooney, 1989, p. 60). The one who leaves or breaks off communicative dialogue by asserting discontinuity can "follow her desire elsewhere" (p. 59), and enter the process of interpretation from a different angle, with other purposes in mind.

And this is at the heart of communicative dialogue's concerted effort to master discontinuity. What if I follow my desire elsewhere, leave communicative dialogue and engage in some other structure of address? What if I engage, for example, in the triangular structure of address that makes up what Felman calls analytic dialogue? What if I engage in the triangular structure of address that includes, welcomes, indeed relies upon, the intrusion of "noise" or the third man that communicative dialogue excludes at its orginary moment? What if I put my mirror down and turn toward the third party who has constituted noise in communicative dialogue? What if the unconscious is invited to play this game?

Then, the exclusions that lend to dialogic theory the grounds for rigor (Rooney, 1989, p. 25) might suddenly become visible from this new angle. Stepping out of the place appointed to me by communicative dialogue, I might look back at dialogue from within a different structure of relations. That different structure of relations might foreground, rather than conceal, the exclusions that are required to maintain communicative dialogue's illusion of understanding; the exclusions that sustain dialogue's rhetoric of inclusivity even as it excludes; the exclusions that allow communicative dialogue to frame its socially constructed and politically interested project as one driven not by interests, but by the highest universal human aspirations and values.

A number of theorists and critics are currently asking the question, What sort of institution is education? Several have stepped out of the place appointed to them by dual structures of address and communicative dialogue. Theories about the limits of the continuity of conscious self-reflection and of understanding are multiplying. Felman's (1987; Felman & Laub, 1992) work on teaching and the unconscious explores the desire for ignorance and the limits of self-knowledge. Donald's (1991, 1992) work on the education of the democratic subject explores the limits of the normative practices of education when they meet the uncanny, the fantastic, and the abject of popular culture. The work of a number of postmodern cultural critics such as Marshall (1992), Phelan (1993), and Trinh Thi Minh-ha (1989) explore the limits of representation as a technology of knowledge, and the political and educational uses of that which exceeds representation and rationalization. Chang's (1996) deconstruction of communication theory argues against the tendency of theorists to value understanding over misunderstanding, order over disorder, success over failure, decidability over undecidability.

These scholars do not mystify and celebrate the moments in dialogue when context is lost, when, as Burbules puts it, we "lose track of time and place," "forget the score," "the last game or the next game," or "our intentions." Instead, they consider the meanings and operations of dialogism as a practice that is never confirmed by actual historical and social events of communication (Chang, 1996, p. xii). To each of these scholars, discontinuity is viewed *not* as a matter of personal failure, incomplete education, misunderstanding, flawed character, or a mysterious something that is beyond us. Instead, they see discontinuity as a necessary (and in many ways desirable) matter of history, power, knowledge, and desire.

PARADOXES OF DEMOCRACY

In her review of Donald's book, *Sentimental Education* (1992), educational theorist Bahovec (1994) writes:

> [A]t the very heart of the logic of democracy, there is, as Claude Lefort put it, indeterminacy, and at the very heart of forming a democratic public and educating democratic subjects, there is a paradox because such an idea is not simply congruent with the concept of democracy itself. (Even the idea of teaching independence of mind is in a way paradoxical, since it can actually mean thinking "as I tell you."). (p. 168)

Is it democratic to insist, as many educational theories of communicative dialogue do, on participation in dialogue — even if the participation is in a supposedly democratic dialogue? Is it democratic to insist that participation in a democracy necessarily requires participation in communicative dialogue?

If "what" democracy "is" and how it is achieved and practiced must remain indeterminate (as in, open to criticism and even antagonism, open to citizen input and revision, open to historical and cultural change), then how can anyone claim to have found the logic or the educational practices (such as dialogue) which lead to or support democracy? Once someone defines or tries to determine classroom democracy or prescribe democratic classroom practices, those practices are no longer democratic. And yet, while democracy is supposed to be about *self*-determination, what the self determines can't be just *anything*. And yet again, how can you "teach" or form someone into a democratic subject when democratic subjects are supposed to be *self*-determining and to have *independent* minds (that is, independent of their teachers' minds or of those of the larger community or nation)?

Donald (1992) tightens the screw of this paradoxical twist in the logics of both democracy and education. He points out that being a "citizen" in a "modern liberal democracy" means that I have to be two things simultaneously. First, I must be "a member of the imagined community of the nation." Simultaneously, I must be "a self-conscious and self-monitoring ethical being" (p. 2).

My relationship to this first self, the self that is "a member of the imagined community of the nation" is a kind of "pedagogical" relationship, because the community claims to "tell me who I am." But who the community is trying to teach me that I am "is always put into doubt" by this second, self-monitoring ethical self. It is put into doubt by the fact that as a citizen of a democratic nation, I must be author of my own utterances and actions (Donald, 1992, p. 2).

That is, who the imagined community of a democratic nation thinks you are or ought to be *can't* be who you are or become — because then it would be determining you in a very undemocratic way. So who the discourses of liberal democracy think you are is always at risk, as you "independently" go about making yourself into a member, into a kind of participant who may or may not map onto those discourses. My pedagogical relation to "the community" (it teaches me who it thinks I already am) is put at risk by the *performativity* of my self-conscious self-monitoring.

This is the paradox that Bronwyn Davies (1993) found herself working within when she studied primary school children and the ways that gendered knowledge is constructed through the teaching of reading and writing. Using her research with children in schools, she restates this tension between having to learn the who already prescribed for me as a citizen of democracy on the one hand, and, on the other hand, having to be the author of my own actions in order to be considered a subject of democracy:

> To achieve full human status [in modernist Western culture] children must therefore achieve a sense of themselves as beings with *agency*, that is, as individuals who make choices about what they do, and who accept responsibility

for those choices. At the same time those choices must be recognizable as "rational," that is, as following the principles of decision making acceptable to the group and inside the range of possibilities understood by the group as possibilities. (Davies, 1993, pp. 8–9)

When children appear obsessed with what one ought to do, this need not necessarily be interpreted as something "natural" to children (that they like rules and categories), but rather as stemming from the fact that effective claims to identity require a knowledge of how to "get it right." At the same time, "getting it right" does not mean behaving exactly as everyone else behaves, but rather it means practicing the culture in an identifiably individual way. (p. 9)

The process of subjectification, then, entails a tension between simultaneously becoming a speaking, agentic subject and the co-requisite for this, being subjected to the meanings inherent in the discourses through which one becomes a subject. (p. 22)

Bahovec, Donald, Davies and others see these logics, processes, and practices as paradoxes at the hearts of democracy, education, and individuality. They refuse to see these paradoxes as accidents. These incongruities are not caused by bumps in the road to real or full or radical democracy— bumps that can be smoothed by pedagogies that are ever more critical or dialogical. The discontinuities that plague communicative dialogue when it is put in practice are not merely "deviations from an ideal." Rather, Bahovec (1994) argues, "inequalities, conflicts and incommensurabilities are . . . indicative of an inner impossibility, 'an index of corruption' inherent in the process of education" (p. 169).

But educators seldom regard "inequalities, conflicts, and incommensurabilities" as inherent in the process of education. Instead, the gap between what is promised by a democratic education and what actually occurs in practice is usually taken to be, as Donald (1992) puts it, "the measure of the oppressions and injuries of capitalism, of patriarchy, of racism and of other social divisions" (p. 134). Educators seldom entertain the idea that in addition to being correctable deviations from some achievable democratic ideal, social inequalities and injuries can also be indicators of "inner impossibilities" inherent in the very processes of democracy and education. Donald asks:

What if one starts instead from the problem of how social relations are instituted in a field where such antagonisms are an inherent feature rather than an accidental one, and then asks how the social relations thus established act on individuals and groups? Then different, less idealist conceptions of citizenship open up. (p. 134)

Here, meaning and understanding are disrupted *not only* by historical and material conflicts, but also by the very structures of the language and logic we use to fabricate democracy and education, and which we naively think we control (Chang, 1996, p. 187).

Inner impossibility? Inherently corrupt education? How could education and democracy be corrupt at their hearts? Why would a teacher *want* to "start instead" with the notion that social injustices and inequalities are *inherent* in the structures and logics of democracy and education; that such disturbing things inform the very textures of American democracy, communicative dialogue, and pedagogy? Why would a teacher want to start with the limits of dialogue—with its exclusions instead of with its inclusions?

Toni Morrison (1992) offers some good reasons, I think. And she does so not necessarily because she *wants* to:

> The need to establish difference stemmed not only from the Old World but from a difference in the New. What was distinctive in the New was, first of all, its claim to freedom and, second, the presence of the unfree within the heart of the democratic experiment—the critical absence of democracy, its echo, shadow, and silent force in the political and intellectual activity of some not-Americans. The distinguishing features of the not-Americans were their slave status, their social status—and their color. (p. 48)

> How could one speak of profit, economy, labor, progress, suffragism, Christianity, the frontier, the formation of new states, the acquisition of new lands, education, transportation (freight and passengers), neighborhoods, the military—of almost anything a country concerns itself with—without having as a referent, at the heart of the discourse, at the heart of definition, the presence of Africans and their descendants?
>
> It was not possible. And it did not happen. What did happen frequently was an effort to talk about these matters with a vocabulary designed to disguise the subject. . . . But the consequence was a master narrative that spoke *for* Africans and their descendants, or *of* them. The legislator's narrative could not coexist with a response from the Africanist persona. (p. 50)

I'm persuaded by Morrison's point, that some narratives of the world cannot coexist. For an educator, it's a hard point to get, because nearly everything about the institution and field of education, including the practice of communicative dialogue, tells me that the job of a teacher who teaches about and across social and cultural difference is to make diverse narratives of the world coexist. At the same time, as an educator, I can't pretend that my own teaching practices haven't been troubled by the paradoxes and impossibilities of communicative dialogue, of democracy, and of teaching itself.

As a teacher, I'm confronted, then, by paradoxes. There is the paradox that Bahovec (1994) names: "Even the idea of teaching independence of mind is in a way paradoxical, since it can actually mean thinking 'as I tell you'" (p. 168). And there is the paradox that Morrison (1992) describes: Within the heart of the democratic experiment there exists "the presence of the unfree . . . the critical absence of democracy, its echo, shadow, and silent force in the political and intellectual activity of some not-Americans" (p. 48). And this inner crack at the heart of the democratic experiment means that the "legislator's narrative could not coexist with a response from the Africanist persona" (p. 50).

These paradoxes cause deep trouble for the educational logics and practices that make communicative dialogue their centerpiece. Communicative dialogue has been elevated to a master strategy for accomplishing everything from teaching children how to read to ending racism. I want to trouble communicative dialogue as an educational practice, listen to its "echo," follow its "shadow," hear the "silent force in the political and intellectual activity" of those excluded from dialogue. I want to visit the other side of communicative dialogue.

I'm persuaded that dialogue, like other modes of address, is not just a neutral conduit of insights, discoveries, understandings, agreements, or disagreements. It has a constitutive force, it is a tool, it is *for* something. As Davies (1993) put it, "*the nature of the [discursive] tools* [used by speakers dictate] the kinds of worlds which might be constituted in ways of which the speakers themselves might not be conscious" (p. xvii). I want to trouble communicative dialogue because I'm curious about what different, less idealist, more useful conceptions of citizenship—and of *education*—open up when I do so.

Like, for example, those initiated by Felman's discussion of analytic dialogue.

6

The Power of Discontinuity: Teaching Through Analytic Dialogue

ANALYTIC DIALOGUE isn't like communicative dialogue. It doesn't strive for or desire an economy of exchange, continuity, or understanding. What might be the mode of address of a teacher who believes communicative understanding to be impossible? What might a film version of the structural dynamics of Felman's "textual knowledge" and "analytic dialogue" look and feel like? How would it address its viewers? Would it have continuity editing?

Here I want to offer a concrete example of a film whose pedagogy refuses communicative dialogue and continuity. The film is *Shoah* (1985), a ten-hour-long film by Claude Lanzmann made up of his interviews with survivors, ex-Nazis, and bystanders of the Holocaust. It's a film that teaches through analytic dialogue—through *dis*continuity and the impossibility of full understanding.

Felman offers a detailed analysis of *Shoah* in *Testimony: Crises of Witnessing in Literature, Psychoanalysis, and History* (Felman and Laub, 1992). In this book, she argues that traditional educational ways of accessing and narrating human experience (through communicative dialogue predicated on representation) fail to encompass and account for traumas of history such as the Holocaust, Hiroshima, and Vietnam. Yet, we must speak about these events if we are to address and respond to their ruptures of history. How can we teach the Holocaust, Felman asks, when it is impossible to represent, to comprehend, to understand, the Holocaust?

The impossibilities of representation, comprehension and understanding that Felman points to across her work as an educator do not stem from the extremity of the Holocaust. They are present in all events and practices that pivot on the designation of "insiders" and "outsiders"—on the social construction of difference that then gets taken up in ways that make a difference in opportunity, safety, and status. Felman's analysis of *Shoah* and her discussion of testimony in relation to pedagogy is pertinent to all teaching situations that grapple with social and cultural difference.

I'm going to read Felman's analysis of *Shoah* side by side with her essays on Lacan's pedagogy and the pedagogical power of analytic dialogue. Felman doesn't discuss *Shoah* explicitly in terms of analytic dialogue. And she doesn't discuss *Shoah* or analytic dialogue in terms of mode of address.

That's the job I've set for myself here: I'll be reading her analysis of *Shoah* in light of her arguments for analytic dialogue; and I want to read both her account of *Shoah* and of analytic dialogue through the concept of mode of address. I'll be trying to make explicit the particular teaching practices and ways of addressing audiences and students that become possible and thinkable for the maker of *Shoah* and for Felman as they break with teaching as a practice of communicative dialogue and of representation.

Felman's extended, eloquent, and astounding discussion of *Shoah* in relation to her theory of testimony and pedagogy is something that I would not try to recapitulate, summarize, or retell. Instead, I want to put it to use here, as a way of inviting educators to get curious about how we might teach in and through the daily moments where representations don't map the world and representational certainties are "always undermined by the insistent operations of desire and terror" (Donald, 1992, p. 119).

How might we teach in and through the oscillating, slippery, unpredictably changing morass of determinations that meet us in the spaces between historical events and our knowledge of them? How might we teach in and through the permeable borders of self and other, self and self? How might we teach in and through the leaky edges of the "social outside" of the curriculum, and the "individual inside" of the psyche? How might we teach in and through the discontinuities and ongoing cultural and personal silences that personal and social histories introduce into our very beings? How might we do this without denying those silences and histories, and without canonizing them through irresponsible—that is, non-responsive—assertions of understanding and continuity?

First, I'll use Felman's analysis of *Shoah* to offer concrete examples of the discontinuities in knowledge, understanding, desire, address, learning, that confront those who would try to "teach" the Holocaust. What are these discontinuities? Where do they come from? Where and how do they produce misfires in communicative dialogue? How might they be turned into pedagogical material to be productively worked through and worked over by teachers?

Then, reading Felman's analysis of *Shoah*'s educational significance through the notion of mode of address, I'll offer explicit examples of how Lanzmann's *Shoah* structures a pedagogical relation through discontinuity. How and why does *Shoah* constitute its viewers as subjects of analytic dialogue? How and why does it offer us textual knowledge as it refuses full understanding?

Finally, this extended example of *Shoah* will bring me to a discussion of the power of address in this film's teaching and learning. How do the lessons of this film pivot on the terms of its address—on who it thinks we are, and wants us to be, as viewers?

SHOAH AND DISCONTINUITY

Shoah is a film that, Felman (Felman & Laub, 1992) claims,

> acutely shows how the Holocaust still functions as a cultural secret, a secret which, essentially, we are still keeping from ourselves, through various forms of communal or personal denial, of cultural reticence or of cultural canonization. (p. xix)

According to Felman, Lanzmann desires to return to the Holocaust, but not so that he can mirror it, grasp it, control it, or know it through re-presentation—through making it present again. His interviews are not intended to reveal the ongoing cultural secret that is the Holocaust. And his interviews are not communicative dialogues intended to understand witnesses' stories and then re-present them in film so that viewers could have knowledge of the Holocaust.

Rather, Lanzmann returns to the Holocaust through necessarily ruptured and fragmented memories and testimonies. He desires a return of the forgettings and of the failures of comprehension—but not so that broken memories can be completed or made full and adequate to a comprehensive understanding or portrayal of the Holocaust. Rather, Felman argues, Lanzmann returns to fragmented memories and testimonies in order to perform

> the historical and contradictory double task of breaking of the silence and of the simultaneous shattering of any given discourse, of the breaking—or the bursting open—of all frames. . . . The film is the product of a relentless struggle for remembrance, but for the self-negating, contradictory, conflictual remembrance of—precisely—an *amnesia*. The testimony stumbles on, and at the same time tells about, the impossibility of telling. (Felman & Laub, 1992, p. 224)

Lanzmann's encounter with the Holocaust, its history and its ongoing nature, is necessarily an encounter with and through discontinuities: loss, fragmentation, silence and silencing, self-negation, amnesia, cultural reticence. His purpose in returning to the Holocaust, according to Felman, is to provoke a "return of a difference" (Felman, 1987, p. 82)—that is, a paradoxical and simultaneous "breaking of the silence," "shattering of any given discourse," and "bursting open of all frames" that have been offered for understanding the event.

I'm going to list some of the discontinuities that, according to Felman's discussion, prevent the question of the Holocaust from being "settled." Lanzmann structures *Shoah* through these discontinuities, and these discontinuities structure the Holocaust as an ongoing event. They are the discontinuities that Lanzmann points to and puts to use as he struggles to respond neither with denial and repression, nor with "answers" or "understanding"—but by returning a difference.

There is the discontinuity between any one witness's testimony and the testimonies of every other witness. This is because each unique, situated testimony is constituted by the fact that "like the oath, it cannot be carried out by anybody else" (Felman & Laub, 1992, p. 206).

The result is the discontinuity of the "*differences* between heterogeneous points of view" (Felman & Laub, 1992, p. 207) in the testimonies of those that Lanzmann interviews. But this heterogeneity is not simply about a diversity of points of view or a diversity of degrees of implication and emotional involvement in the event. The discontinuity between testimonial stances of the Jews, the ex-Nazis, and the bystanders is "the *incommensurability* of different topographical and cognitive positions, between which the discrepancy cannot be breached," which can "neither be assimilated into" nor "subsumed by, one another" (pp. 207–208).

There is, in other words, the radical discontinuity between "inside" the Holocaust—the camps, the victims, the ghetto, the loss; and "outside"—the countryside, the perpetrators, the bystanders. "From within," Felman writes,

> the inside is unintelligible, it is *not present to itself*. . . . In its absence to itself, the inside is *inconceivable* even to the ones who are already in. . . . the inside is *untransmittable*. . . . The truth of the inside is even less accessible to an outsider. . . . Since for the outsider . . . the truth of the inside remains the truth of an exclusion. (Felman & Laub, 1992, pp. 231–232)

The inside and the outside "are qualitatively so different that they are not just incompatible but *incomparable* and utterly *irreconcilable*" (p. 236). In other words, narratives of the inside and the outside cannot coexist. How, then, to teach the Holocaust to those outside? And, how to teach the Holocaust to those who "survived" the inside precisely because their witnessing of that inside has been repressed or symbolically murdered? Felman says:

> Lanzmann's problem becomes how to speak about—and *from inside*—erasure, without being reduced to silence, without being oneself erased; how to be *heard* about—and from inside—erasure; how to make a film from inside anni-

hilation that would speak with equal force, however, *both to insiders and to outsiders*. (p. 250)

And there is also the discontinuity between the event itself and memories of it that become unknowingly tainted with fantasies (Felman & Laub, 1992, p. 265); in a churchyard scene, described below, we watch memories become tainted by myth and self-delusion.

Further, there is the discontinuity that is the "splitting of the eyewitness" by the "blinding impact of the event" (Felman & Laub, 1992, p. 219) that reduces its witnesses to silence. This is of course the historical discontinuity produced by the literal deaths of millions of witnesses to the Holocaust.

But also, the eyewitness is split and testimonies are made discontinuous by the symbolic deaths of individual witnesses. "The desire not to read, and not to talk, stems from the fear of hearing, or of witnessing, oneself. The *will-to-silence* is the will to *bury* the dead witness inside oneself" (Felman & Laub, 1992, p. 225).

The event of the Holocaust, in other words, had empirical witnesses—people who saw. But "cognitively and perceptually" it was without a witness because while people saw and heard, they did not *look*, did not understand and, indeed, can never understand (Felman & Laub, 1992, p. 211). In the space of difference between "seeing" and "looking," there was an "incapacity of seeing to translate itself spontaneously and simultaneously into a meaning" (p. 212). The experience of the Holocaust was a radically foreign experience that could not be translated.

And there is the discontinuity, the rupture in *history* caused by both the actual and the symbolic murderings of the event's witnesses. Felman calls the Holocaust "an event which historically consists in the scheme of the literal *erasure of its witnesses*" (Felman & Laub, 1992, p. 211). And, as an ongoing cultural silence, it is an event that is reenacted and repeated in continuing acts of silence and silencing, of deception and self-deception.

Felman's discussion of this particular discontinuity—the ongoing cultural silence created by self-deception and the symbolic murder of its witness—is one that I will risk summarizing here. Then, I'll use the moment when cultural silence is repeated and reinscribed in history and in the film to show how Lanzmann structures a pedagogical relation through the discontinuities of analytic dialogue.

The Discontinuity of Cultural Silence

Lanzmann ends *Shoah* with a scene in a churchyard. Simon Srebnik, a survivor, returns to the site of a concentration camp in Poland. There, as a young boy, he had sung songs for guards. Doing this delayed the day of his death. When that day came, he was shot in the head and left for dead, but the bullet did not kill him.

Srebnik returns with Lanzmann to the Polish village where the camp was located, and where the villagers remember him for his singing. Srebnik "concretizes . . . allegorically, a historical return of the dead witness" (Felman & Laub, 1992, p. 257) on the scene of the event-without-a-witness.

But what "materially and unexpectedly *occurs*" that day of filming,

> what the film shows us here, in action, is the very process of the *re-forgetting of the Holocaust*, in the repeated murder of the witness and the renewed reduction of the witnessing to silence. The film makes the testimony *happen*— happen inadvertently as a second Holocaust. (Felman & Laub, 1992, p. 267)

This repetition of "re-forgetting" the Holocaust "appears spontaneously before the camera" (Felman & Laub, 1992, p. 268) when Lanzmann asks the villagers, the bystanders to the Holocaust who are now standing in a semicircle around Srebnik, why they think all this happened to the Jews. In response, the church organist "finds his way out of the crowd . . . and pushing himself in front of the camera, overshadows Srebnik and eclipses him" (p. 263). He answers Lanzmann:

> The Jews there were gathered in a square. The rabbi asked an SS man: "Can I talk to them?" The SS man said yes. So the rabbi said that around two thousand years ago the Jews condemned the innocent Christ to death. And when they did that, they cried out: "Let his blood fall on our heads and on our sons' heads." Then the rabbi told them: "Perhaps the time has come for that, so let us do nothing, let us go, let us do as we're asked." (pp. 263–264)

Hearing this in translation, Lanzmann asks the interpreter, *"He thinks the Jews expiated the death of Christ?"* The interpreter replies, "He doesn't think so, or even that Christ sought revenge. The rabbi said it. It was God's will, that's all" (p. 264).

According to Felman, the organist has thus given unwitting testimony to a self-deception. He intended his testimony to endow "the Holocaust with a strange comprehensibility and with a facile and exhaustive compatibility with knowledge" (Felman & Laub, 1992, p. 264). He, and the cultural myth he retells, has dehistoricized the Holocaust by subsuming it under the prophetic knowledge of the Scriptures. This, Felman argues, amounts to the organist and the other Poles gathered in the churchyard "literally washing their hands of the historical extermination of the Jews" (p. 264). They have testified to a murder which they "go so far as to call suicide" (p. 265). By doing so, the bystanders "unwittingly begin again to dream reality and to hallucinate their memory" (p. 265). And the church organist, "in forging, so to speak, the rabbi's signature so as to punctuate his own false witness and authorize his own false testimony . . . disavows responsibility for his own discourse" (p. 265). Felman writes:

> The collapse of the materiality of history and of the seduction of a fable, the reduction of a threatening and incomprehensible event to a reassuring mythic, *totalizing unity of explanation, is in effect what all interpretive schemes tend to do* [emphasis added]. [The church organist's] satisfied and vacuous interpretation stands, however, for the failure of all ready-made cultural discourses both to account for—and to bear witness to—the Holocaust. (p. 266)

Srebnik thus, "in returning back to history and life, is once again *reduced to silence*, struck *dead* by the crowd" (p. 267).

By the enactment of this "second Holocaust," because of this "repeated murder" and re-forgetting, the same cycle of discontinuities is set in motion in that churchyard yet again. In this single scene, each of the discontinuities that Felman identifies in her analysis of *Shoah* comes into play again.

For example, the churchyard that Srebnik returns to becomes a scene of discontinuous testimonial stances—his as victim, theirs as bystanders— each marked by symptomatic blindnesses. It becomes the scene of the repeated splitting of the witness and the burial of the dead witness inside oneself—as Srebnik stands silent in the face of the organist's story. It is the scene of the repeated splitting of the witness by the failures of the bystanders' comprehension before an incomprehensible event. It is the scene of the discontinuities and limits of historiography itself—the limits of the organist's recourse to an "historical event" as explanation of the Holocaust. Historiography relies on and produces knowledges that will always be only partial; and historiography itself is used consciously or unconsciously by historians who desire to forget or deny. It is the scene of the radical unintelligibility of the inside of the Holocaust from both the inside and the outside. It is the scene of enacted discontinuities between memory and fantasy.

And then, finally, the churchyard becomes the scene of a newly cut rupture of personal and cultural response-ability. The return of a witness, Srebnik's return, does not result in his testimony and presence being "met" or "encountered" by the villagers. It does not result, that is, in the "return of a difference"—of a different reply to the question, Why did this happen to the Jews? What is needed, but what is missing, is a reply that will not authorize or make intelligible past and future Holocausts.

And so Srebnik's return does not result in reassessed implications of changed selves in their own and others' memories and histories. It does not result in the villagers producing another, different way of responding to the return of Srebnik and of his presence being again in their midst. Rather, it results in the repetition of the same, of the Holocaust as ongoing event, through the ritual murder of the witness returned from the dead.

And yet, Felman argues, through *Shoah*'s structure of address, a difference *is* returned. Yes, the villagers may be trying to close these various discontinuities by offering a final reading of history that grasps, understands, explains, answers, the Holocaust. And not accidentally, it is a reading that would absolve them of any implication. But the villagers' narrative simply cannot coexist with Lanzmann's project and its return of Srebnik to the village. Lanzmann's job is not to construct a film that closes discontinuities or erases them through truth telling or even through a "correct" reading of history based on Srebnik's version of events. Instead, Lanzmann's work as a filmmaker and educator is to highlight, underscore, and aggravate the discontinuities between the villager's reading of history and Srebnik's. His job is to construct a filmic mode of address capable of "placing" his audience within the interminable process of encountering these discontinuities. These discontinuities are constitutive of the Holocaust, of the Holocaust as an ongoing cultural secret.

The Impossibility of Communicative Dialogue

The discontinuities that Felman identifies cannot be bracketed from the dialogical process or game, as if they only accidentally trouble the possibility of communication, comprehension, empathy, trust, or respect. These discontinuities are not troublemakers intruding from outside of the structure of dialogical relations. History, politics, religion, personal or social prejudices, tradition, are not outsiders. They do not arrive, uninvited from elsewhere, to derail the efforts of those who would otherwise be able to commit to the ongoing process of coming to an understanding—through dialogue—of the diversity of points of view, experience, implication, and involvement in that village.

These discontinuities are not mishaps in some otherwise able-to-be-continuous, unbroken matching of conscious discourse among participants in the churchyard. They are not produced by the failures of those in the churchyard, bystanders and victim alike, to learn and live by particular values, or to exhibit particular character traits required of participants in democratic dialogue.

These discontinuities, rather, are what *constitute* all attempts at communicative dialogue between Lanzmann and the villagers whom he interviews in the churchyard, and between the villagers and Srebnik.

Srebnik stands silent as the church organist recites his "false witness" that, once again, makes the Jews responsible for the Holocaust. Srebnik stands as "a ghost which, as such, is essentially *not contemporaneous* . . .

with the voices of the crowd which surrounds him, nor even with himself—with his own muted voice" (Felman & Laub, 1992, p. 267). Srebnik is, in other words, unable to respond in the moment to what is happening around him, just as the villagers are unable to respond contemporaneously to Srebnik's return. They are capable only of repeating what had gone before.

Is this because Srebnik has not learned and used particular rules of the game of dialogue, or that he lacks the commitment to take part in the sometimes necessarily long and ongoing process of communicative dialogue? Is this because the damage to his and the villagers' communicative abilities has not been adequately healed, yet, but could be, if they only participated long enough in dialogue with one another?

Felman argues that ready-made cultural discourses, including discourses about dialogue, moral values, communicative competencies, and character traits, fail to account for—and to bear witness to—the Holocaust. The Holocaust, and all attempts to represent it in dialogue, film, curriculum, or testimony, are *constituted* by these discontinuities, ruptures, losses of voice, failures of language, self-deceptions, and repeated splittings of the witness. In this case, when these discontinuities are not admitted, "like a hall of mirrors, the church scene is a hall of silences infinitely resonate with one another" (Felman & Laub, 1992, p. 266).

And beyond this, in addition to the particularities of the Holocaust, all ready-made cultural discourses will fail to account for the discontinuities of human subjects and their knowledges. The Holocaust is not the only event of which human subjects and their knowledges are not fully conscious, self-aware, self-same, singular, unitary, homogeneous, or joined by common interests. These very discontinuities are not mere obstacles to overcome on the way to successful communicative dialogue. Rather, they mark the limits of sameness. These very discontinuities are what make up the material and the process—and the *difference*—of what Felman calls analytic dialogue.

STRUCTURING A PEDAGOGICAL RELATION
THROUGH DISCONTINUITY

Back to the question of mode of address, then. What might be the mode of address of Felman's "textual" knowledge and "performative" pedagogy? Who does Felman's pedagogy of analytic dialogue think I am?

Using Lanzmann's film and Felman's discussion of it, I want to come at these questions from two directions. First, I want to look closely at the way Lanzmann addresses his audience, and does so through the structure of relations that Felman calls analytic dialogue.

Second, I want to show how the structure of Lanzmann's film itself traces the indirect, discontinuous routes of reading that its witnesses have performed in order to give the testimonies that they do. As we engage with the film through this structure, questions are raised for us as viewers: How *will* we read the discontinuities that are *Shoah*—and the Holocaust? How *will* we read the discontinuities that are our selves as we encounter the Holocaust as ongoing event?

Lanzmann does not take all the discontinuities that Felman locates, and then edit the interviews he has filmed in a way that has the interviewees speaking to each other across those discontinuities—as in communicative dialogue. Lanzmann could have structured the film in a point-counterpoint fashion—similar to the structure of CBS's *60 Minutes*. This convention positions discontinuities between divergent testimonies: One interviewee speaks from one side of a discontinuity, the next interviewee speaks from the other side, and the discontinuity they speak across becomes an indicator that someone's not telling the truth, or is ignorant of the truth.

But this is not the structure of address that Lanzmann employs. If he did that, he would be repeating the very dual structure of address that allowed the organist in the churchyard to "kill" the witnesses—in himself, and in Srebnik—once again!

The radical pedagogical innovation of psychoanalysis, according to Felman, is that the triangular structure of analytic dialogue between analyst and analysand places both participants on the *same side* of discontinuity. Not face to face, but side by side, both the teacher and the student are positioned on the same side of the splitting of language, of the unconscious, of, as Felman (1987) quotes Lacan, "a speech which comes from elsewhere and by which [they are both] traversed" (p. 137). Both the analyst and the analysand, both teacher and student, must define their identities and knowledges "against systems of pre-existing cultural relations" (Cook, 1985, p. 246). For both teacher and student, this means that "the chief constraints at work in the evolution of the subject lie beyond [their] conscious control" (p. 246).

This means that there are never just "two" participants in a dialogue. There is always a third participant—namely, those constraints within the culture as a whole and arising from the splitness of my own psyche. These lie beyond my conscious control. All readings of self and other must inevitably pass through them.

The radical "educational" intervention that *Shoah* makes is to address its viewers (students) in a way that invites them into the ongoing predicament of the Holocaust. It invites its viewers into the predicament of having no "other side" of discontinuity. There is no continuity, no understanding, no comprehension, no end of the Holocaust to cross over to, to speak back to the audience from, and to settle into through communication or through referential knowledge.

Lanzmann takes up the discontinuities that Felman locates and puts them to use as the material and the process of the film's structure, of its address to its viewers and of its unfolding in time. Lanzmann's strategic necessity as a filmmaker and as an educator is to *not* foreclose these discontinuities or to resolve them into "knowledge" or "understanding." His task is, in other words, to refuse to do what the church organist did in the village churchyard. His task is to use these discontinuities instead to provoke something else into happening—something other than the return of the same old same old forgetting, denial, framing through ready-made interpretations, fantasies of complete understanding, and dehistoricizing, silencing, splitting, refusals of difference.

With this shift from pedagogy as a representational act to pedagogy as a performative act, we've left the business of communicative dialogue and of realism in education.

So what, then, does a mode of address that takes up discontinuity as its material and process look like on film? How does the structuring of analytic dialogue play out on film? What does Lanzmann "teach" in the face of the impossibility of representing the Holocaust? And who does Lanzmann's way of teaching the Holocaust think you are?

Analytic Dialogue: Accounting for a Route of Reading

Unlike communicative dialogue, which seeks and requires continuity and understanding, analytic dialogue seeks the ways that the very indirectness of reading—the very impossibility of full and complete understanding—"can teach us something, can become itself instructive" (Felman, 1987, p. 79).

Because meanings of the world, events, and our experiences of them cannot be read directly off of the world or ourselves, the meanings that we do make are the products of interpretation—of particular routes of reading. They are not products of absolute representation or direct understanding. And this is why the processes and routes of our acts of interpretation become so crucial.

What gets "analyzed" then, in analytic dialogue, is the route of a reading. How did you/we *arrive* at this interpretation, without knowing it— maybe even without desiring it? How have your/our passages through history, power, desire, and language on the way to this interpretation become integral parts of the very structure of the interpretation—of our knowledge? How can the indirect routes taken through history, power, desire, and language be (partially yet usefully) reconstructed through the symptomatic traces they have left behind in our interpretations—traces of forgettings, fears, denials, guilty pleasures, vested interests, unconscious detours?

Analytic dialogue produces what Felman calls, following Lacan, textual knowledge (Felman, 1987, p. 81). It is knowledge of the necessary and productive indirectness and disconnectedness of the routes we use to read the world and texts. It is knowledge of how any single route of reading can never be travelled the same way twice; of how routes of reading are suggested or discouraged by particular literary or representational devices and conventions as well as by particular power relations; and of how literary and other representational devices have been invented and employed in order to encourage some routes of reading and disallow others. Textual knowledge is knowledge of how routes of reading are always multiple—there can always be another, different route from the one I've taken. It's knowledge of how particular routes are foreclosed by personal and social repressions. Of how there is always more to read along a route—no route covers the whole territory—and of how no matter what route we take, our interpretations always read more into the text than is there.

And textual knowledge is knowledge of how the routes of reading have significance and consequences over and above the interpretations arrived at. It is knowledge of how the routes and the reasons for reading have to do with power, history, and desire. It is knowledge of why and how one route or interpretation has been taken repeatedly, and not others. Of which routes have been possible and intelligible with certain texts, readers, contexts—and which have remained impossible and unintelligible—with what consequences. Of how institutions, practices, and performed social identities have attached power to some routes and not others—authorizing those routes and deauthorizing others. Of where and how texts, events, experiences, stories of selves and others have become stuck, fixed, silenced, resisted. Of how and why some groups of readers have changed their routes of reading, producing new and unexpected interpretations that have surprised and disturbed, and sometimes informed, events.

If reading is always an indirect and strategic act, then, and never a simple mirroring of a text in an understanding reader, reading will never be finished or complete. One reading will never be the "correct" one, the "ethical" one, or the "just" one—because any reading already has done the inevitable violence of excluding other possible readings, and, therefore, other readers.

But readings _can_ be more or less useful or practical or "just" or effective, given what a particular reading is _for_. And Lacan's "quintessential service to our culture," Felman (1987) argues, is to enact a way of reading that keeps systems of signification open to _other_ readings (pp. 15–16).

But the claim that analytic dialogue remains open to other readings does not mean that those who practice analytic dialogue escape the responsibility to read—to assign meaning to events and experiences. Rather, Lacan's intervention in "our culture" is to keep this "open" question of response-ability ever before us: Which reading will I/we perform, after all, in this situation? Why this reading instead of that reading? These are open and undecidable questions because constitutive discontinuities between self and self, and between self and other, render inaccessible any "higher authority" such as the Truth, Knowledge, or even understanding of the correct, right, moral, best, or final reading. And as a result, these questions cannot be escaped.

The responsibility for meaning-making, in other words, cannot be laid at the door of what Rooney (1989) calls "the religious myth of expression and of reading at first sight . . . the transparency of the text, the *giveness* of the object of knowledge" (p. 46). Instead, meaning and its effects become a social and historical achievement.

This is a very important point. Lanzmann does not presume to locate, through Srebnik's return, the Truth of the events in that Polish village. In fact, it is the will to Truth—the claim to Truth—that allows the villagers to "miss" the opportunity to "meet," to "be contemporaneous" with Srebnik's return. Meeting Srebnik would, of course, necessarily disrupt the Story, the Truth, that the organist retells in front of Lanzmann's camera. This is because the organist's story and Srebnik's cannot coexist.

If these discontinuous stories can't coexist, and if claims to Truth are themselves part of the problem, then on what grounds are we to choose between these competing stories? If Srebnik's story isn't "more true" than the organist's, then on what basis can we justify rejecting or disagreeing with the organist's? If the discontinuities that constitute all encounters with the Holocaust make understanding or comprehension of the Holocaust impossible, on what basis can I decide which of the stories is "better" or "worse"?

What analytic dialogue does "to" communicative dialogue is to radically and profoundly shift the terms of discussions about truth and about the role that understanding takes in how we come to "warrant" "desirable" social relations. With analytic dialogue, the question is not, What does this text or event mean, truly and really? And with analytic dialogue, warrants for action do not follow "logically" or "morally" or "ethically" from the determination of that truth or reality.

Analytic dialogue poses a question of a very different order, namely, In what ways does the world rise or fall in value when a reader or groups of readers perform and let loose in the world this particular meaning or reading of a text or event? (Phillips, 1995, p. 45). This question is not "about"

truth or establishing warrants for action. This question is about the necessity, the right, and the responsibility of participating in the ongoing, never
completed historical, social, and political labor of meaning-construction.
"What counts" as a "rise" or "a fall" in the value of the world becomes a
historical and social achievement—not a transcendental given waiting to be
discovered.

Let's say that, as I watch *Shoah*, I count Lanzmann's reading of the
Holocaust as one that makes the world and my own life rise in value, and I
count the organist's explanation for why the Jews were exterminated as one
that makes the world and my own life fall in value. My "judgment" or
"choice" has been made possible, thinkable, intelligible, because of ongoing
intellectual, political, cultural, emotional, aesthetic, social, and physical
labors of tens of thousands of people across decades. My choice of Lanzmann's reading over the organist's is a social and historical achievement. It
is a historical and cultural "fact" that to many people today, remembering
the Holocaust is "valued" over forgetting; encountering its discontinuities is
valued over denial and ignore-ance. The fact that this way of responding to
the Holocaust is available and intelligible to me at all is a result of countless
actions of individuals and groups performed and let loose in the world. And
the fact that there are cultural spaces in which Lanzmann's reading is valued
over the organist's requires the concerted and ongoing efforts of many
groups and individuals to renew, restore, and extend those spaces. By being
loose in the world—by its circulation and availability—this way of responding to the Holocaust has made similar responses possible and thinkable in
other sites, times, and situations only barely related to the Holocaust.

Is this reading true or false, right or wrong, good or bad? is a question
that drives toward closure, stasis, and the fixing of knowledge. But the
question, What has this reading performed or let loose in the world? sends
us out on an exploration. It sends us on an exploration of what Lanzmann's
reading of the Holocaust—a reading that refuses to offer any final or complete interpretation or understanding of the Holocaust—lets loose in the
world. Exploration of meaning-making and its consequences, unlike truth
finding, "does not entail an end." Any ostensive ending "is but a promise
that another ending will come" (Chang, 1996, p. 227).

If readings of texts and events are never finished, complete, direct, or
closed—if reading as a constant "struggle to become aware can never reach
a term," then, Felman (1987) asserts, "the route itself—a route of reading—
might be as important as the insight to which it hopes to lead" (p. 15). *How*
we read, in other words, the uses to which we put reading; the strategic
difference it makes to read this way compared to that way; what we include
and exclude as we produce our reading; which silences we are aware of
and which we ignore or forget—the route of a reading itself—might be as

important as the "insight to which it hopes to lead." Analytic dialogue asserts the political and social gravity of routes of reading. The concept of pedagogical modes of address asserts the political and social gravity of the structuring of routes of relations between teacher and student.

Far from condemning me to boundless relativism then, the assertion that there is no Truth to arrive at as a final discovery opens up for exploration an entire landscape of human labor that shapes and is shaped by intricate networks of routes of reading and routes of relations. Each route has its own specific, situated, and material consequences, weight, and force. Each intersection sends inflections of meaning along the intersecting routes. And yet none of these routes or its consequences is final or decidable, none has a term.

The challenge for Felman as a literary critic and as a teacher, then, becomes to write and teach in a way that gives an account of, owns up to — takes social responsibility for — a particular, strategic route of reading. The challenge for Lanzmann as filmmaker and educator is to give social and semantic form to the *specificities* — not the relativities — of routes of reading. Lanzmann attempts to give social and semantic form to the *difference* it *does* make to the value of the world when individuals or groups take one route or reading rather than another.

The Gravity of Routes of Reading in *Shoah*

Lanzmann takes up this challenge by structuring his film as a tracing of the indirect, discontinuous routes of reading that witnesses have performed in order to give the testimonies that they do — and in order to silence or exclude the testimonies that they do not give. And Lanzmann traces these routes of reading in a way that lays open the question he poses to his viewers: How *will* you read and respond to the discontinuities that are *Shoah* — and the Holocaust?

For example, Lanzmann structures his three roles in the film as three (sometimes overlapping, contradictory, self-subversive) routes of reading the testimonies that he films. He functions as narrator of the film, interviewer of the witnesses, and the artist-inquirer "on a quest concerning what the testimonies testify to" (Felman & Laub, 1992, p. 216).

In his role as narrator, Lanzmann must ironically "abstain from narrating anything directly in his own voice . . . the narrator has no voice" (Felman & Laub, 1992, p. 217) in *Shoah*. This is because the stories of the witnesses

> must be able to *speak for themselves* if they are to testify, that is, to perform their unique and irreplaceable first-hand witness. It is only in this way, by this

> abstinence of the narrator, that the film can in fact be a narrative of testimony; a narrative of that, precisely, which can neither be reported, nor narrated, by another. (pp. 217–218)

And yet, paradoxically, in his role as interviewer and inquirer, Lanzmann "is a transgressor, and the breaker of the silence" (Felman & Laub, 1992, p. 218). When Lanzmann does speak in the film, he speaks as interviewer, not narrator. But the questions he asks are not merely factual inquiries geared toward building a story. They do not seek to "endow the Holocaust with a . . . comprehensibility, and with a facile and exhaustive compatibility with knowledge" (p. 264).

And here is a key difference, as enacted in *Shoah,* between analytic dialogue and communicative dialogue!

Lanzmann speaks with the witnesses and asks his questions—but not to understand. Not to elicit information. Not to gather material from witnesses in order to construct representations of the Holocaust. Not to close the gap in knowledge, perspective, experience, memory, between himself (and his viewers) and those he interviews.

Rather, throughout the interviewing process, Lanzmann "is at once the witness of the question and the witness of the gap—or difference—between the question and the answer" (Felman & Laub, 1992, p. 221). Lanzmann struggles to record on film not the interviewee's answer/knowledge/understanding—but the *indirectnesses* and *discontinuities* of the route between question and answer. He witnesses the detoured passages through power, fear, terror, loss, implication, desire, and forgetting. These detours produce the gap between the place within language, power, history, fear, from which the question was asked—and the *different* place within forgetting, desire, loss, implication, to which the answer was, inadvertently, returned.

Here's an example of how this actually plays out in the film. Throughout the film, Felman explains, Lanzmann replies to what a witness has just said

> by merely recapitulating word by word a fragment of the answer, by literally repeating—like an echo—the last sentence, the last words just uttered by the interlocutor. But the function of the echo—in the very resonance of its amplification—is itself inquisitive, and not simply repetitive. (Felman & Laub, 1992, p. 221)

This echo produces, according to Felman, a "*question* in the very answer, and [enacts] a *difference* through the very verbal repetition" (p. 222).

This happens in the churchyard when the Polish villagers tell Lanzmann of the screams they heard as the Jews were being gassed:

Lanzmann's repetitious echoes register the unintended irony of the [Poles'] narration:

[Lanzmann:] *They heard screams at night?*

[Interpreter:] The Jews moaned. . . . They were hungry. They were shut in and starved.

[Lanzmann:] *What kinds of cries and moans were heard at night?*

[Interpreter:] They called on Jesus and Mary and God, sometimes in German . . .

[Lanzmann:] *The Jews called on Jesus, Mary, and God!* (Felman & Laub, 1992, p. 221)

Here, Felman argues that Lanzmann, by remaining silent as a narrator, by not commenting upon or trying to explain for us, the viewers, what the Poles are telling him in the churchyard, allows the "*question* of the scream" (p. 222) to persist.

And so does the *difference* of what the screams in fact call out to. Here as elsewhere in the film, the narrator is, as such, both guardian of the question and the guardian of the difference. (p. 222)

Lanzmann's "inquisitive," nonrepetitive echo is a way of refusing to close the question of the scream — a way of protecting it from being made continuous with an answer. His echo is a way of reopening the question in the face of the bystanders' "answer," and reopening it in a way that refuses to close the discontinuity between the Poles' accounts of the screams and the "*difference* of what the screams in fact call out to" (p. 222). Lanzmann's echo refuses to forget the difference,

the Nazi overall design precisely of the framing — and of the enclosure — of a difference, a difference that will consequently be assigned to the ultimate enclosure of the death camps and to the "final solution" of eradication. (p. 221)

The Poles' answer "*does not meet* the question, and attempts, moreover, to *reduce* the question's difference" (p. 221). But the question of the screams, and the explanation's attempts "at the containment (the reduction) of a difference — perseveres" (p. 221) both in Lanzmann's speech as the interviewer and in his silence as the narrator. The narrator, through his silence, is there "to insure that the question will *go on* (will continue in the viewer)" (p. 221). He is there to ensure that the viewers will not become self-satisfied by a fancy of understanding.

Analytic Dialogue—The Return of a Difference

The weapon used by the villagers in the churchyard to repeat the murder of Srebnik as witness, was, precisely, continuity. History came full circle in the churchyard. The organist's telling of the Story about the SS men and the rabbi came around again and met itself completely and directly. That Story got told by the organist the same way it was told to him, and for the same reasons it has been told over and over. It got told for the purpose of doing the same work of not responding to, of murdering the witness in both the organist and in Srebnik, as it was intended to do the first time around. The Story marked a return of the same—the same inability to encounter the Holocaust, to respond to it—the same denial, repression, forgetting, silence. The Story marked the same inability and unwillingness to see Srebnik, and to *look* at him.

In the wake of the symbolic murder carried out through the assertion of continuity, the political act that Lanzmann needed to perform was an interruption of continuity. The villagers' symbolic murder of Srebnik as witness—and of themselves as witnesses—was a murder performed *through* an assertion of *continuity,* of sameness, between myth and memory, denial and looking.

Lanzmann's strategic imperative was to refuse this continuity. Lanzmann's film thus becomes a documentation of the undocumentable, of what it is that breaches documentation. It becomes a documentation of silences, of the particular and repeated erasures required in order for continuity—for understanding, for explanation, for representation—to be asserted. Lanzmann documents the silence required in order for the organist's story to be told again, the same way it always has been, despite the discontinuity that threatens the organist's explanation when Srebnik returns—from the dead! with a filmmaker!—to the scene of his murder.

And now Lanzmann's tracings of indirect routes of reading lead . . . to us, the viewers.

Srebnik's return to the churchyard, to a missed encounter with the villagers, occurs in the last scene of *Shoah*. His return is a double return because it is also a return appearance of Srebnik in the film itself. Ten hours earlier, *Shoah* begins with Srebnik returning to the site where he had been shot, and singing the song that he sung in order to delay the day of his death.

That first singing, for the viewers of *Shoah*, is, according to Felman, an apparently "innocent" singing that "introduces us into the soothing notes and the nostalgic lyrics of a Polish folk tune" (Felman & Laub, 1992, p. 269). But by the time Srebnik sings the song again at the very end of the film, Lanzmann's project is to ensure that we, as viewers, cannot hear it the same way. It is to ensure that we encounter Srebnik's song as a question, and not as something already familiar, already known, settled, and comprehended:

> The whole film, which ends only to begin again with the return of the song, testifies to history like a haunting and interminable refrain. The function of the refrain—which is itself archaically referred to as "the burden of the song"—like the burden of [Lanzmann's] vocal echo which, as though mechanically, returns in the interviewer's voice the last words of the discourse of his interlocutors, is to create a difference through the repetition, to return a question out of something that appears to be an answer. . . . The echo does not simply reproduce what seems to be its motivation, but rather puts it into question. Where there had seemed to be a rationale, a closure and a limit, the refrain-like repetition opens up a vacuum, a crevice, and through it, the undefined space of an open question. (Felman & Laub, 1992, p. 277)

The vacuum of silence, the crevices of repression, denial, false testimony, forgetting, and ingore-ances—none of which can be "shown" directly on film—are what Lanzmann struggles to render tangible for viewers, by having Srebnik return at the end of the film. By positioning Srebnik to sing his song again in the film's last scene, Lanzmann positions us to hear it *through* what has come between the two singings. He urges us to hear it through the difference that marks the contexts or textual positionings of the first and second singing. He works to insure that we can no longer hear Srebnik's song "directly," or literally, as we might have thought we heard it the first time—we cannot hear it "innocently." Lanzmann's structure of address poises us to hear the song differently, that is, through our textual knowledge of the vacuum, of the crevices created by the "odd community of testimonial incommensurates" (Felman & Laub, 1992, p. 279) that form the body of the film we've just seen.

The echoed return of Srebnik's song puts into question the apparent harmony and innocence of the first time we hear it at the beginning of the film, just as Lanzmann's echoing of an interviewee's response, given to his question, puts the apparent harmony and innocence of the answer into question. This "refrain-like" structure creates a difference through repetition—returns a question out of something that appears to be an answer.

But it is not simply the repetition that turns the answer into a question. It is the return to the apparent answer *through* the splittings of language, through the crevices formed by the splittings of the witness by denial, repression, forgetting; through the vacuums formed by the impossibility of comprehension. A difference is created, a difference is returned, when the apparent answer, the apparent closure, the apparent innocence of understanding, is returned to, revisited through the third participant: through the unconscious—the limits of understanding, of comprehension, of knowing, of accessing.

By the end of *Shoah,* in other words, while the organist "knows" what *he* means by his story about the rabbi and the Jews, it is both Felman's and Lanzmann's project that we viewers will not be persuaded. The organist's *interpretation can be given another reading.* Felman quotes Lacan:

> In analytic discourse, you presume the subject of the unconscious to be capable of reading. This is what this whole affair of the unconscious amounts to. Not only do you presume him to be capable of reading, but you presume him to be capable of learning how to read. (quoted in Felman, 1987, p. 22)

Who does the mode of analytic address in *Shoah* think you are? In *Shoah,* Lanzmann presumes his viewers are capable of learning how to read—how to read symptomatically. He presumes his viewers are capable of learning how to see through testimonies and interpretations to the indirect routes of reading that produced them. He presumes his viewers are capable of reading the discontinuities and indirectnesses of their own routes of reading, and capable of taking different ones. He presumes viewers are capable of re-reading their knowledges and histories, and thereby re-reading their futures. He presumes viewers are capable of participating in the ongoing, immediate, situated, and consequential labor of cultural production.

Analytic Dialogue—Neither Continuity nor Boundless Relativism

Felman concludes her discussion of *Shoah* with these words:

> In much the same way as the testimony, [Srebnik's second performance of his song] exemplifies the power of the film to address, and hauntingly demands a hearing. . . . Srebnik, though traversed by a bullet that has missed his vital brain centers by pure chance, reappears from behind the threshold of the white house to sing again his winning song: a song that, once again, wins life and, like the film, leaves us—through the very way it wins us—both empowered, and condemned to, *hearing.* (Felman & Laub, 1992, p. 282)

The task of encountering *Shoah* is infinite, interminable. The haunting returns of the witnesses and their fractured, fragmented, and incommensurable testimonies address us, demand from us a hearing. Felman claims that if we don't go somewhere else, to some other time and place in our memory or desire—if instead, we become contemporaneous with and able to respond to the shock, displacement, and disorientation of hearing—we will be, paradoxically, both "empowered" and "condemned."

But our "empowerment" will *not* consist in Knowledge and understanding. Rather, we will assume what is an infinite and necessary task of responding to the Holocaust as ongoing event. We will be condemned to a hearing and to an interminable, irreparable predicament of encountering an event that will never be settled. The empowerment of analytic dialogue condemns us to shocking displacements of our fancies of understanding the world and of knowing ourselves and others. What we take to be our understanding will always require another reading—a different reading from the one we have settled ourselves and our interpretations of others into.

Yet, even as we are condemned to an interminable reading, what is won, according to Felman, is life. In analytic dialogue, what is won is a structuring of relations capable of setting the stage for becoming contemporaneous with the meanings and enactments of Srebnik's return and the villagers' repeated murdering of the witness. What is won, what we will be empowered with, is the ability to situate our processes of interpretation and meaning-making in a frame of reference that is not informed solely *either* by repression, denial, forgetting, ignore-ance—*or* by certainty, Knowledge, and understanding.

We have won, in other words, the ability to change—to change answers we have into new questions—and to change the routes we take to arrive at an interpretation; so that we do not repeat the symbolic murder of ourselves as witness to the consequences of various routes of reading.

We have won, in other words, the ability to learn—by "hearing" the discontinuities in our own, and others' speech, knowledge, and memories—how to give what we already know another meaning.

But not just any "other" meaning or route of reading will do. Because the meanings we make are never "relative." They are always made *for* something. They are always made to *do* something. And that making and doing will always have material consequences for ourselves and others.

Now, there's a crucial difference between the two questions, How will I respond? and On what grounds will I choose between this meaning or reading of the world and that one? Like communicative dialogue, the question of how to choose which competing story or meaning (Srebnik's or the organist's, for example) is *better, just, true, moral,* or *right* is a question that drives toward continuity. It drives toward a fit between question and answer. For example: Srebnik's story is true and the organist's is false because . . . Srebnik's story is the one we must choose because it is congruent with our beliefs and values . . . We must choose Srebnik's over the organist's because Srebnik's conforms more closely to our shared vision of social justice . . . or to the available historical record.

On the other hand, I've been trying to show here how, instead, analytic dialogue supports our arrival at and engagement with the interminable question, How will I respond? What I have tried to do in this chapter is to insist on the inescapability of that question without sewing up the discontinuities of that question. I've been trying to indicate how this question can be used to refuse to close or make continuous the difference between itself and all "answers" we might arrive at. In other words, within the structure of relations of analytic dialogue, "I will respond by . . . " is not an *answer*.

Let me explain. The question, How will I respond? is inescapable because we are both empowered and condemned to meaning-making. We cannot *not* communicate. We cannot *not* respond to the events and stories that in-form us. Even not responding is a response — it has its consequences for myself and for others.

And yet, as Lanzmann demonstrates in *Shoah*, the third participant in analytic dialogue insures that there will always be a difference between the question and its answer. I cannot not respond, and yet parts of my responses will be unintended, the consequences of my responses can't be predicted or controlled, and I will never know their outcomes or the full extent of their unanticipated effects.

And still the question, How will I respond?

I can't answer that question with: "I will respond by doing x and that will fulfill obligation y by accomplishing z" — because as we've seen, even if I say I'm going to do x, I can never do exactly x. And obligation y can never be completely and finally fulfilled. And outcome z can never be controlled or predicted.

And still the question, How will I respond?

How I respond is an inescapable yet unfinalizable question of history, power, and culture. It is not a question of choosing between prior, individualized moral stances. It is not a question of re-presenting already known and knowable, decided-in-the-past virtues or answers, in an attempt to suture the discontinuities of a less controllable here-and-now situation. Rather, How will I respond? foregrounds the question of performativity. It confronts pedagogical practices (such as communicative dialogue) which pivot on re-presentation, continuity, and control through sameness with what they have had to systematically ignore in order to maintain their logics and interests. How will I respond? raises the question of the performativity of pedagogy.

As Donald (1992) argues, in the "unrecorded but resourceful improvisations of everyday life . . . cultural norms are transgressed and reworked in the very moment they are instituted" by individuals (pp. 2–3). Our "practices of everyday life" (p. 3) are inaugural, they are not re-presentations of already achieved and decided Truths. Our improvisations are performative, they are culture-in-the-making. All the pregiven norms and prescriptions called up by the question, How will you respond? are both enacted *and reworked* in my response. There is a performative aspect to any response I give, and that prevents my response from being an answer, from being settled.

And so when I act in response to the question, How will you respond? — my action is not *continuous* with that question. Any response I make, inasmuch as it produces actions and constitutes operations "cannot be logically true or false, but only successful or unsuccessful, 'felicitous' or 'infelicitous'" (Felman, 1983, p. 18), in relation to a socially and historically in-formed intention.

How will you respond? is a question that repeats interminably and that I will encounter over and over, in new forms, with each new instance, each new action, that empowers and condemns me to yet another response. What I have learned from Felman's teachings about analytic dialogue is that a most impoverished form of response is repetition — whether it be in the form of a repeated ignoring, or in the form of the duplication of some model behavior that "worked" at other times or "made sense" in some other context. Repetition *is* a response, but it's not a response that is contemporaneous with the unique and inaugural aspects of the *difference* of this event happening right here and now.

Read in this way, the question, *How* will you respond? insists on the consequences of difference, discontinuity, and the performative to pedagogy.

It also insists that the question, What is your standard for choosing between action *a* or *b*? *not* be allowed to remain the only question supposedly capable of shielding us from "boundless relativism." The contention that boundless relativism is kept at bay only when there are *some* things that are decidable, settled, and answered once and for all (of us) is itself a social and historical construct. Its own logic is bound up in interests, intentions, fears, and desires. Its advocates, too, must be held accountable for the route of reading that they took to produce and authorize this question at the cost of displacing others.

The question, How will you respond? then, both empowers and condemns us to participate in the ongoing cultural and social struggles over which meanings will be valued and why — which meanings will be available to serve which intentions. Empowered to participate, but never as The One with the "right" Story. Empowered to participate, rather, as one among many. Condemned to a participation that has material consequences for lives lived — consequences that, even as a participant, I can never fully know, understand, or control.

The next part of this book follows Felman, Phelan, Williams, and others as they move, as productive and provocative teachers, out of the representational, and into the performative, out of continuity, and into paradox.

PART II

Teaching Through Paradoxical Modes of Address

ALL OF THIS reading of teaching and learning through the notion of mode of address has produced quite a few paradoxical claims and situations:

- The unconscious makes teaching impossible, and yet we teach and we learn.
- The teacher's "authority" lies in textual knowledge — and yet she has no mastery over it: Textual knowledge knows but does not know what it knows (Felman, 1987, p. 92).
- The only "instructive" form of self-reflection doesn't reflect the self at all. It returns to the self but does not meet self; it's self-subversive (Felman, 1987, p. 60).
- Teaching about and across social and cultural difference is not about bridging our differences and joining us together in understanding, it's about engaging in the ongoing production of culture in a way that returns yet another difference.

The thing is, as a teacher, I don't see any threat of paralysis or nihilism coming from these paradoxes. There's no need to panic or despair. When I find myself despairing as a teacher, it's not the paradoxes of my profession that have brought me down. Usually, what leaves me feeling hopeless is the way that the culture of teaching manages to ignore, deny, or bull its way past its own ironies and impossibilities.

In fact, the fecundity of teaching lies precisely in its paradoxes and ironies. That's because the paradoxes of teaching aren't like logical incongruities in philosophy or in syntax — which can indeed lead to paralysis. Computers, for example, lock up and seem to spin in place in response to self-contradictory glitches in programs or in the sequence of commands you just entered.

But there are other senses of the term paradox that don't necessarily suggest paralysis, nonsense, or futility. These other senses of paradox bring us up against history and cultural production.

For example, according to the *Oxford English Dictionary*, paradox can mean "contrary to received opinion or expectation . . . being discordant with what is held to be established truth . . . a conclusion contrary to what the audience has been led to expect . . . a phenomenon that exhibits some conflict with preconceived notions of what is reasonable or possible."

Given these meanings, the paradoxes of teaching suggest something like this: It's been assumed that the question of teaching is decided, settled—and along comes some opinion, expectation, conclusion, or phenomenon that sets in motion again what counts as an answer, a truth, a preconception. The issue or question is not decided or settled at all.

It's this more historical and political sense of paradox that informs some postmodern approaches to language, literature, and film studies. There, paradox is understood in terms of undecidability.

For example, those who practice deconstruction in literary criticism work to overturn the hierarchies that history and power have constructed between binaries, such as the teacher-student binary. And then, deconstruction must resist what Chang (1996) calls "the ever present desire to reestablish a new hierarchy" (p. 42)—the ever present desire to *decide* what each term really means and which one will have power and authority in the teacher-student relation.

To deconstruct the teacher-student binary then, is to refuse its hierarchy—but not so that *student* can now become the privileged term, as happens in pedagogies where the student supposedly becomes the teacher. Instead, the ongoing work of deconstruction is to trouble every definition of teaching and studenting arrived at.

And so reinscribing *teacher* and *student* means keeping "both the old and new hierarchies off balance" (Chang, 1996, p. 143). Rewriting the teacher-student relation this way means refusing to let the question of the teacher-student relation be settled. It means working in and through the oscillating space of difference between teacher and student as positions within a structure of relations. And it's in that space of difference-between that a new concept of the teacher-student relation erupts. But paradoxically again, it's a new concept that refuses to settle into any single meaning.

In what follows, I'm going to explore a particular "new concept" that erupts when we try to keep both old and new hierarchies of teacher and student off balance. That new concept is this: The teacher-student relation is undecidable. The teacher-student relation is something that can't be named.

By "undecidable," I don't mean enigmatic, equivocal, ambivalent, or romantically rich in inexhaustible meanings. No, undecidability here refers to the way in which the values or meanings of the terms teacher and student "both urge choice and prevent that choice from being made" (Chang, 1996, p. 144). They urge us to choose: Am I a teacher or a student? Who am I "as" teacher, who are you as student, what do I do as teacher, what do I want from you as student? The terms teacher and student urge me to choose among the many answers currently circulating and competing for these questions.

But the impossibilities and paradoxes of teaching prevent me from making any final, absolute, authoritative choice. When I take them to be undecidables, teacher and student "signify the 'between' that at the same time is the two poles"; they vacillate "between two poles of the opposition *without ever constituting a third term*" (Chang, 1996, p. 145). Who I am as a teacher is *both* teacher and student, and who you are as a student is both student and teacher—but this new concept of the "teacher-student" must never be constituted as a third (additive) term, because we must continue troubling every definition of teacher-student that is arrived at. Because teaching is interminable, no knowledge about the practice of teaching can save us the task of engaging in the ongoing cultural production of teaching. Reading teacher and student through the unconscious or through historical events that exceed simple binary opposition is one way of resisting the illusion of full and complete understanding of the "teacher"-"student" relation.

As a teacher, I don't feel stuck in the face of the undecidable terms and relations that have brought me this far in this book. Not at all. I'm convinced by what Chang (1996) says about the process that got me here: "Strategic, parasitic, and seductive, deconstruction is apparently nihilistic, but, at root, it is affirmative—without, however, being *thetic*" (p. 147). It can be affirmative, in other words, without having an already known referent for what it affirms. What is affirmed in deconstruction—in the insistence that the teacher-student relation is undecidable—is that teaching is "the name over which arguments take place . . . in heterogeneous idioms" (Readings, 1996, p. 161). "Any attempt to say what [teaching] should be must take responsibility for itself as such an attempt" (p. 160). Teaching is, in other words, a continuing and never finished moment of affirming and engaging in ongoing cultural production.

What I want to affirm here are the strategic and moral necessities to participate in attributing meanings to "teaching." But not in a way that produces a transcendent meaning for teaching, not in a way that arrives at a meaning of teaching that "can be worshiped and believed in" (Readings, 1996, p. 161). By claiming that teaching is an undecidable, we throw "those who participate in pedagogy back into a reflection upon the ungroundedness of their situation, their obligation to each other and to a name [teacher] that hails them as addressees" (p. 161).

This is how I see the paradoxes of teaching, then: as calls to action—as calls to participate in the ongoing, interminable cultural production that is teaching. What will we, as teachers, do with this paradoxical calling? What will we make of it?

In the last part of this book, there are two things I want to do with several paradoxes of teaching. I want to take some of the paradoxes that emerged in the first part of this book, and get a little more concrete about them. I want to do this by revisiting them through actual moments when they erupt into teaching practices.

At the same time, I want to resist getting *too* concrete about these paradoxes — because that risks inflaming desires to turn them into pedagogical strategies or technologies. And so I want to explore and preserve the uncontrollable fecundity of paradoxes of teaching by using examples that (productively) intensify their incongruities.

The paradoxes that I take up here include:

- The paradox of social agency, as in the taking of action that is affirmative without positive reference, without knowing what good the action taken will do
- The paradox of authority and power in the pedagogical relation
- The paradox of the pedagogical event, which leaves no *visible* trace of its happening
- The paradox of pedagogy as performative — as a taking of action that is, nevertheless, always suspended in the space between self and other
- The paradox of pedagogy as a performative act that is always suspended in the undecidable time of learning

And, drawing on the meanings and usefulness of magical realism as a mode of address in academic research and writing, I end with a discussion of the paradox of pedagogy as a performative act that is always suspended in thought. "[N]o knowledge can save us the task of thinking" (Readings, 1996, p. 154).

7

A Paradox: Teaching as the Taking of Action Without a Positive Reference

IN A RECENT review of films "spawned by the wars in what was Yugoslavia" (Cohen, 1995, p. 1), Roger Cohen describes Milcho Manchevski's *Before the Rain*. It is a film about "the smoldering hatred between ethnic Albanians and Orthodox Christian Macedonians in a fragile, newly independent state born of Yugoslavia's dismemberment" (p. 24). In the film, the hero, Aleksandar Kirkov, "is shot dead for his effort to bridge the gap between the Albanians and the Macedonians" (p. 25). Cohen writes:

> Before returning to Skopje, [Kirkov] had quit his job as a war photographer because, simply to provide him with a powerful photo, a camp guard in Bosnia shot a prisoner dead. By quitting, Mr. Manchevski says, [Kirkov] has abandoned "a morbid voyeurism and life of moral emptiness."
>
> Does [Kirkov's] gesture [of quitting his job as a war photographer] make any difference? Although the structure of Mr. Manchevski's film is circular, its last words are "The circle is not round." (p. 25)

Acts of representation that start out with the intention to mirror the other, refer to the other, understand the other; but end up referring to the self, to the act of representation itself, to the act of killing (unconsciously? inadvertently?) something in order to get a better picture of it, a better understanding of it, a better grasp of it—in order to know it.

Self-reflection that returns to the self without meeting the self . . . Circular structures that are not round . . . Analytic dialogues that follow indirect, elliptical routes through a third participant before they return (a difference) to the self . . .

Kirkov may believe he is outside of the structure of relations in the prison camp. He may believe he is representing—re-presenting—through photography, what is already there. He may think he is helping to alleviate the situation by giving the silenced other a voice through his photographs. He may think he is giving an objective, innocent reading of the camp "as it is" in order to educate others outside about what is going on inside there.

But the crisis of representation comes home for Kirkov when he realizes that he and his picture taking do not operate somewhere outside of the structure of relations of the camp or of the war. A prisoner is shot so that Kirkov can have a more powerful picture.

The crisis of representation is the crisis of living out the consequences of the theoretical claim that any particular interpretation or "reading is . . . neither true or false, but practical under certain political and theoretical conditions . . . " (Rooney, 1989, p. 37). Readings of the world, photos of prison camps, are always going to be *for* something. Readings and representations are always intended to make something happen, and to keep something else from happening.

While the war photo was intended by Kirkov to be referential—to refer to something other than himself, other than his act of taking the picture, other than his desire to photograph the camp—the act of picture taking, of representation, is by its very nature self-referential. It is an illusion that the self-referential act of taking the picture is really *about* something else or refers only to something other than the uses and intentions that Kirkov has for the representation *he* makes, and that his audiences desire.

And it is an illusion that the "truth" of the camp can be grasped by a properly objective photograph of fact, a report—or that a photograph made virtuous because of its truth could eventually set the prisoners free. This is an illusion because Kirkov's making of the photograph is not an act of informing or describing. It's an act of participation in the ongoing structuring of relations in the prison camp. The photograph, inasmuch as it produces actions and constitutes operations "cannot be logically true or false, but only successful or unsuccessful, 'felicitous' or 'infelicitous'" (Felman, 1983, p. 18).

Kirkov is engaged then, not in an act of representation, but in a performative act. That is: an expression "whose function is not to inform or describe, but to carry out a 'performance,' to accomplish an *act* through the very process of [its] enunciation" (Felman, 1983, p. 15).

Leaving the realm of the true or the false representation, entering the realm of the successful or unsuccessful act of enunciation, Kirkov leaves the logic of universal or transcendental guarantees. He enters instead a history of antagonisms, of power relations, of the constant, interminable struggle over what meanings will be made and how they will be used.

Photographing the prison camp, in other words, "is in no case tantamount to knowing, but rather to *doing*: *acting* on the interlocutor, modifying the situation and the interplay of forces within it" (Felman, 1983, p. 27). Taking the photograph in the camp "is performative and not informative; it is a field of enjoyment, not of knowledge. As such, it cannot be qualified as true or false, but rather quite specifically as *felicitous* or *infelicitous*, successful or unsuccessful" (p. 27).

Here is Kirkov the photographer making and using photographs as if they were representations. And there is the camp guard who does not read the photograph in terms of representation or truth, but who *uses* the photo-

not knowledge? then where does know- ledge come from?

graph to modify the interplay of forces within the situation of the camp and the war. What transpires between the two is an untranslatable dialogue in two languages: "a dialogue between two orders that, in reality, do not communicate: the order of the act and the order of meaning, the register of pleasure and the register of knowledge" (Felman, 1983, p. 31).

Kirkov's crisis begins when he realizes that he too is engaged in performing actions by taking photographs. He is not merely or innocently recording or discussing the truth. As social actors, both the guard and the photographer "literally escape the hold of truth" (Felman, 1983, p. 31). They can no longer appeal to Truth or Falsehood as a way to establish whether their actions are just or unjust, good or bad, moral or immoral. Actions can only be judged successful or unsuccessful, felicitous or infelicitous according to some purpose. Whether the purpose "is" just or unjust, good or bad, then becomes not something to be discovered, but something to be produced, constructed, achieved, through social and political action (Flax, 1993).

At the moment the guard kills the prisoner in order to give Kirkov a more powerful photograph, Kirkov can no longer deny, repress, or "forget." He is awakened to the historical fact that his desires and ignore-ances are implicated in the "knowledge" that he constructs "about" the war through the photographs that he makes. He is not outside the structure of relations of the prison camp or of the war, simply representing what he sees there. He is a participant. The questions become, How will he participate, how will he respond to his implication in that structure of relations?

Before the Rain has a circular structure. But by quitting his job as a war photographer, Kirkov tries to ensure that the circle is not round.

Instead of producing the same-old-same-old photographs of war — even more repetitions of the thousands of photographs that exist of this and other Balkan wars — Kirkov quits. He returns to Skopje to work toward "bridging the gap between the Albanians and the Macedonians." Kirkov himself is then shot and killed for this "gesture." And Cohen asks, "Does his gesture make a difference?" Does his gesture, in other words, prevent the circle of repression, desire, forgetting, hatred, from being round, from meeting itself again exactly, from cutting the same groove of Balkan history deeper and deeper?

Does his action result in a return of a difference?

ELLIPSES RETURN A DIFFERENCE, CIRCLES DO NOT

According to film reviewer Cohen (1995), circular structures dominate a number of other films about what he calls the "Balkan gyre of war." Images and structures of vortices abound:

Grievances, passed down through generations, return, distorted by the passage of time but still strong enough to encircle the Balkans and hold the area in a grip of violence. History is palpable and untamed. It is alive in the psyches of families and nations and in the repeated attempts to settle old scores. (p. 1)

Cohen describes Zafranovic's film *Decline of the Century*:

In a flat tone, using mainly old black-and-white documentary footage, [Zafranovic] shows the joy of the Croats as the Nazis arrive in Zagreb in 1941; the horror of the Croatian Jasenovac camp, where Serbs and Jews, among others, were massacred; Serbian babies with their skulls crushed; bodies floating on the Sava river; massacred bodies being exhumed at Bihac, a northwestern Bosnian town that has been the scene of recent fighting.

Elsewhere in Europe, such history has been told and confronted. But Communist Yugoslavia did not allow it. Tito, the Communist monarch, left the rancor and the fear to fester in people's souls.

The former German Chancellor Willy Brandt went on his knees in the Warsaw ghetto. Tito never went to Jasenovac. . . . Thus a place representing what Mr. Zafranovic calls "man's greatest fall" remains unredeemed, still charged with the power to foment new killing. (p. 25)

Is Brandt's gesture of going on his knees in the Warsaw ghetto a gesture that "makes a difference"? Would a gesture by Tito of going to Jasenovac, of telling and confronting the history of the Jasenovac camp, the Sava river and Bihac have made a difference? Can such gestures act performatively rather than representationally, and resituate the events of places such as Jasenovac within a different structure of relations and thereby rob them of the power to foment yet another killing?

"In a world that is fundamentally without guarantees," Felman (1983) writes, "one cannot be sure of anything at all, not even of infelicity. In a theater of radically diabolical performances, one cannot really count on anything, not even—especially not—on the act of failing." "The 'fallible' is not itself infallible" (p. 140).

No social theory or theory of representation can guarantee that Kirkov's gesture of quitting as war photographer will make a difference—prevent the circle from being round. Certainly, the consequences and significance of his action cannot be predicted beforehand. Likewise, Felman (1983) argues, no one can guarantee that his gesture *will not* make a difference:

Thus radical negativity is not simply "negative," it is—in a very complex way—positive, it is fecund, it is affirmative. . . . Thus negativity, fundamentally fecund and affirmative, and yet without positive reference, is above all *that which escapes the negative/positive alternative*. (p. 141)

Felman (1983) uses the metaphor of the ellipse, or elliptical "revolutions" to describe occurrences that escape "negative/positive," good/bad, right/wrong alternatives. Unlike the circle, which is either complete or broken, either meeting itself or missing itself, continuous or disjoined; the ellipse breaches the circle from within. An ellipse "displaces, corrodes, unmakes" a circle (p. 139) through a "non-return" that is *both* "subversive and self-subversive" (p. 138).

This brings us back to the distinction that Felman draws between two meanings of the word revolution: revolution "as subversion, an epistemological break" (1987, p. 67); and as "almost the exact opposite"; as "the very movement of turning round, of revolving, of endlessly returning to the same place, of repeating" (1983, p. 67). An epistemological break — originality, change, difference — Felman argues, can be visualized in terms of an ellipse. Self-subversion — or "learning" — is

> precisely the way in which a reflexive movement, in returning to and upon itself, in effect *subverts itself* — finds something other than what it had expected, what it had set out to seek; the way in which the answer is bound in effect to displace the question; the way in which what is revolving, what returns to itself, radically displaces the very point of observation. (1987, p. 67)

THE ELLIPTICAL MOVEMENT OF ANALYTIC DIALOGUE

In analytic dialogue then, learning happens when the self has been subverted — it happens when "self-reflection" describes an ellipse, rather than a circle. Learning happens when the very question we asked in order to seek a learning has been displaced by the return of a difference, a surprising, unexpected, interfering encounter with the ignore-ances of one's "very point of observation," of one's very point of asking.

In relation to many of those pedagogies that set out to liberate, emancipate, self-reflect or create democratic classrooms through dialogue; the self-subversion that Felman desires is truly excessive. Most practitioners of liberatory pedagogies seek to subvert teaching, questioning, or selves — up to a point. Self-subversion must stop at the point at which that subversion *meets* or *matches* the desired "revolutionary subject," "feminist subject," "liberated subject," "critical thinker," "subject committed to and skilled in communicative dialogue."

As I said in chapter 4, what can't be subverted by the dialogical process is communicative dialogue itself. What can't be subverted by dialectical thinking is dialectical thinking itself. What can't be subverted by "feminist" teaching is the desire for and of a feminist subject herself. There is an endpoint to each of these pedagogies: the democratic classroom, the femi-

nist student, the critical teacher, the moment of social and economic justice—or at least, some kind of decidable ongoing process that liberates.

What makes analytic dialogue "unique," according to Felman (1987),
is that it has no such endpoint—it is interminable. Further, it is "interminably self-critical":

> Lacan's amazing pedagogical performance thus sets forth the unparalleled ex-
> ample of a teaching whose fecundity is tied up, paradoxically enough, with the
> inexhaustability—the interminability—of its self-critical potential. (p. 90)

As a teaching practice then, according to Felman (1987), analytic dialogue is *invested* in taking the measure of the ignore-ances of its own questions. It is invested in asking, How can I interpret *out of* the dynamic
ignorance that I analytically encounter, both in others and in myself? How
can I turn ignorance into an instrument of teaching" (p. 80)? It is invested
in raising, "through every answer that it gives, the literary question of its
nonmastery of itself" (p. 96).

All understandings or stories of ourselves are actings-out of the unconscious (Felman, 1987, p. 153). All understandings or stories of ourselves
are stories "of, precisely, the acknowledgement of the misrecognition of the
story by itself" (p. 153). Stories and teachings do something through the
telling that the telling fails to account for (p. 154). It's like Kirkov's photographs—by taking the photograph of the murdered prisoner, Kirkov does
something, he acts within and on relations of power, but that something is
not and cannot be represented in the photograph itself. Krikov discovered
the difference between the photo as a representation and the photo as
performative act.

It's in this way that analytic dialogue is like an ellipse. It turns back on
itself, but does not meet itself. And the turn that analytical dialogue takes to
return to its own incomprehensions, to its riddles disguised as knowledge, is
an ironic turn. Because it returns a difference, it has a performative dimen-
sion and force—"always somewhere subversive"—always circling back to
and from elsewhere, never describing the same path in the way a circle
does. And because its return is ironic, it shows a "residual smile (always
somewhere self-subversive)" (Felman, 1983, p. 143).

> Does [Kirkov's] gesture make any difference? Although the structure of Mr.
> Manchevski's film is circular, its last words are "The circle is not round."
> (Cohen, 1995, p. 25)

Kirkov's gesture did make a difference. His gesture prevented the circle
from being round. But, at the same time, his gesture poses a riddle. Under
the guise of Kirkov's "knowing" that by quitting his job as a war correspon-

dent, he will make a difference, there is an uncertainty. There is no guarantee, there is no certainty, there is no theory that can predict that his actions will be "positive or negative."

But his action *is* fecund, it is affirmative "without positive reference," without *knowing* what might be positive about it, without knowing the nature of its fecundity. His action is fecund and affirmative without *knowing* what *must* be done, without knowing the sure and direct route to liberation from the Balkan gyre of war. Kirkov knows that he has made a difference in the structure of relations, but, as with all textual knowledge, he doesn't know what difference he has made.

> The hero of Mr. Manchevski's *Before the Rain* is shot dead for his effort to bridge the gap between the Albanians and the Macedonians. But he dies with a smile on his face. (Cohen, 1995, p. 25)

Is his smile the smile of self-satisfaction, of self-knowledge, of completion, of a happy continuity between intention and outcome? Or is his smile the ironic smile of self-subversion and of knowing one's own self-limitation—of knowing that he has made a difference, *and* even had he lived, there would have been no way of knowing finally, completely, and certainly, what difference he has made?

8

A Second Paradox: The Paradox of Power and Authority in Teaching

IN HER BOOK *Teaching the Postmodern: Fiction and Theory* (1992), Brenda Marshall says that if an author's writings

> alter our perception of history, and thus, of reality, then the writer has taken on great authority. On the other hand, it is the nature of postmodern discourse . . . to simultaneously assign responsibility to the reader. (p. 154)

Postmodern authors, according to Marshall, assign responsibility to the reader for what meaning s/he makes out of the multiple interpretations any encounter with a text makes possible. And the reader is assigned responsibility for her/his evasive silences as well.

Marshall (1992) comes to these assertions: "The [postmodern] narrator-author challenges the reader to participate in creating the picture. And the reader must comply, if only in the attempt to make sense of the text" (p. 153). "A paradox emerges: the writer takes control and manipulates the reader into the position of taking on responsibility" (p. 154).

And I back up to re-read these assertions through the residue of the daily practices, dilemmas, and interests that confront me as an educator. A teacher's "taking of control" in order to "manipulate students into taking on responsibility" for the meanings they make—for the knowledge they construct—is a paradoxical gesture. Like all paradoxes, this one doesn't "make sense."

It might not make sense, but when I think about Marshall's point with pedagogy in mind, it makes a difference. Suddenly, solidified positions and repetitious prescriptions that, for me, have dulled much of the talk among educators about pedagogy and authority, are set in motion.

As a paradoxical mode of address to students, "manipulating students into taking on responsibility" is *not* yet another version of, The teacher empowers students by exercising her own power and authority. It's not, The teacher empowers students by giving up her authority. And it's certainly not, The teacher empowers the student by practicing reciprocal, dialogical relations that equalize power relations among teachers and students. "Manipulating students into taking on responsibility" exceeds these formulations; it can't be contained by any of these resolutions. Yet it can be enacted. It can be performed in the classroom.

What would constitute a pedagogical mode of address that tried to manipulate students into taking on responsibility for the knowledges they construct? I want to explore this paradox with the following story.

WHITENESS AS A SCENE OF ADDRESS

In 1994, C. Carr wrote an article for the *Village Voice* called "An American Tale: A Lynching and the Legacies Left Behind." She begins her essay:

> I was an adult before I ever saw the picture. But even as a girl I knew there'd been a lynching in Marion [Indiana]. That was my father's hometown. And on one of many trips to visit my grandparents, I heard the family story: The night it happened back in 1930 someone called the house and spoke to my grandfather, whose shift at the post office began at three in the morning. "Don't walk through the courthouse square tonight on your way to work," the caller said. "You might see something you don't want to see." There was laughter at the end of the story—which puzzled me. *Something you don't want to see*. Then, laughter. (p. 31)

As Carr's story unfolds, it becomes clear that just as *Jurassic Park* was "pitched" to a particular position within discourse and power (remember how I used the example of *Jurassic Park* to explain mode of address in the first chapter?), the terms of address in Carr's family story assigned her a place in the theater of U.S. race relations. The mode of address of her family's telling of the story of the lynching in her hometown offered Carr two positions within the structure of family relations from which to enact whiteness each time the story was told. If she's "white," she either laughs at this lynching story (whether or not she finds it funny), or she keeps silent and goes numb about what it does to her to hear it.

The problem with these two seats is that they position her as either above the meanings of whiteness (she laughs with her family at the story) or an agency-less victim of its meanings (she goes numb and silent with guilt, denial, or shame).

Carr's essay performs the intellectual, cultural, and personal labor necessary to refuse the terms of address of her family's story and to construct for herself another position to act from within the theater of U.S. race relations. The work of her essay is to re-tell the story of the lynching

without positioning the students of her re-telling in either of the two locations offered her by her family's telling.

I'm going to focus on just one aspect of how Carr re-structures the
address of her family's story. It's the aspect that deals directly with the
paradox of authority in the teaching relation—the paradox of attempting
to manipulate readers into taking on responsibility for the meanings they
make. I want to argue that in her essay, Carr achieves a paradoxical mode
of address that does manipulate her readers into taking on responsibility for
the meanings they make.

At the moment in which Carr (1994) writes her article, the context of
learning about whiteness and of learning to act white that she needs to
break out of, to leave, is held in place by her own silence and numbness. It
is also held in place by the fact that "somehow a survivor hadn't made it
into the family story" (p. 32). Carr learns that there was a survivor of the
lynching in Marion. While two other black men were hanged until dead in
the courthouse square that night, James Cameron survived, living to author
what is probably the only written record of a lynching by a survivor. After
the lynching, Cameron's accuser admitted that Cameron had had nothing
to do with the shooting involved, and that no rape, previously alleged, had
taken place.

So Carr does the work of creating, moving into, and acting from another context of learning—and this includes going to Milwaukee to meet
James Cameron and to witness *his* own work of creating, moving into, and
acting from another context of learning—namely, the lynching museum he
has struggled to establish. Carr re-structures the address of her family's
version of the lynching by breaking her own silence and by re-reading her
family's story through Cameron's.

There's a way that Carr's re-telling of her family's story echoes one
particular aspect of the story Cameron has been telling since 1930. What I
want to argue here is that what gets echoed makes the difference between,
on the one hand, an address that positions me as one who laughs or goes
numb—and, on the other hand, an address that paradoxically manipulates
me into taking on responsibility for the meanings I make of these stories.
Ironically, what both Cameron's and Carr's stories echo in each other is a
silence. And it's that silence that, in these stories, paradoxically teaches.

Let me explain.

TEACHING WITHOUT A POSITIVE REFERENCE

The pivotal moment in Cameron's version of the lynching story comes as
the noose is being tightened around his neck. In the midst of the noise of
the mob, he hears a woman's voice call out:

> Suddenly a woman's voice called out, sharply and clearly. "Take this boy back! He had nothing to do with any raping or killing!" (Carr, 1994, p. 33)

The crowd falls silent. In his book about the lynching, Cameron writes that "hands that had already committed murder, became soft and tender, kind and helpful," and he saw many heads bowed as he staggered back to jail (Carr, 1994, p. 33).

> In the years since the lynching, Cameron has spoken to many white people who were present in the square that night. And no one heard any voice. No one but him. "You were just lucky," they tell him. But something stopped the rampage cold, and Cameron knows he didn't imagine the voice. Sometimes, he can still hear it. (Carr, 1994, p. 33)

Neither Cameron (as quoted by Carr) nor Carr as researcher of this story offer explanations for the woman's or the crowd's actions. We don't know who "the woman" was or why she did what she did. We don't know if she "really" existed. We don't know what motivated the crowd to stop its rampage cold and remove the rope from Cameron's neck. Cameron doesn't know who called out and saved him that night. He offers no theory for her motivation, conversion, or reasoning.

Just as Cameron is silent about what "made" the white woman call out and the crowd to stop its rampage cold, Carr (1994) is silent about why she takes up the work of this essay — of re-structuring the address of her family's story. What she does say is that she wondered for years whether she should write about these family things. After mentioning this to her brother, he sent her a newspaper clipping about Cameron's lynching museum. Ironically (symptomatically?), after rereading the article many times, she "lost it at some point along the swing shift of my ambivalence. Even so, I knew I would have to meet this man or regret it for the rest of my life" (p. 32)

But we never hear about where Carr's knowing came from. What kind of motivation is this alternating knowing and forgetting, this swinging ambivalence, this finding and losing? What is it that she would regret and why?

Why she takes up this work, what motivates her to leave the field of her family's storytelling, is not the focus of her article. Yet most educational literature and practices aimed at ending racism seem preoccupied with identifying, inciting, and proliferating discrete turning points in students' attitudes, understandings, and behaviors towards race and racism. Carr's rewriting of her family's story departs from other teaching stories, in part, because it frustrates desires to know *what* "changed" her. Her story is not one of conversion, enlightenment, empowerment, or emancipation. It does not present her self as turning from ignorant to knowledgeable, from complicit to absolved, from apathetic to committed, from racist to anti- or nonracist.

Let's imagine that an author of a multicultural textbook came upon Carr's and Cameron's stories. Given current structures of address in multicultural and antiracism pedagogies, how might s/he frame Carr's and Cameron's stories? Many multicultural and antiracism curricular texts (at least implicitly) address students as if they also inhabited one of the two "seats" offered by Carr's family story. The who that multicultural texts think their students are includes the who who has been socialized into racist ideas and attitudes just as Carr's family was, and who laughs along with them at the story. And often, the who that multicultural texts think their students are includes the one who already knows that laughing at the story is wrong but—like many others—is silent or doesn't act on that knowledge.

And because I'm imagining an educational use of Carr's story, I'd imagine that the usual third position would also be referenced, namely, maybe you're not necessarily racist or afraid to speak up, maybe you're just ignorant, and if you just knew what your laughing or acquiescence meant, you'd stop.

And because I'm imagining an educational use of Carr's story, I'd expect that the typical fourth position would be offered—the one desired by the project of education itself—the one held out as the position of knowledge, and therefore of virtue. This fourth position would be the prescribed position—the remedy: Who you are should be like the woman who called out to stop the lynching. If you're sitting in one of those three "bad" seats of racism, acquiescence, or ignorance, you need to move into that "good" seat that's a little higher up in the theater, floating above the rest. You need to be like Carr and the woman who called out.

But Carr refuses to give us any information about the woman, and about what "made" Carr change, or remember and find that newspaper clipping again, or want to work to change her family's telling of the story. We don't know, after reading Carr's essay or Cameron's story of the lynching, who we *should* be. We can't *be* the woman. There will never be another night that exactly replicates that one in Marion. Anything we might be is going to have to be responsive to the shifting meanings and operations of whiteness and racism as we encounter them from situation to situation. As new situations arise, our performances of whiteness can certainly be informed by Cameron's and Carr's stories—but not in ways that we can specify, prescribe, guarantee, or predict. To specify a locatable, decidable, particular who that we should be as we read and respond to these stories is to take up an "orientation toward autonomy, an assertion that knowledge involves the abandonment of a network of ethical obligation, to have knowledge is to gain self-sufficiency" (Readings, 1996, p. 156). No individual can *be* just, Readings argues. Justice is not something you are, it is something you do within a specific historical and cultural network of social obligation. "To do justice is to recognize that the question of justice exceeds individual consciousness, cannot be answered by an individual moral stance" (p. 162).

And yet, both Cameron and Carr address us by their stories. Who, then, does Cameron's and Carr's address think we are?

TEACHING TO THE MULTIPLE WHOS WITHIN US

Cameron refuses to address us, the readers of his book about the lynching or the audience of his lynching museum, as if we "were" black or white, or as if we occupied any particular fixed and locatable positions within blackness or whiteness.

> [O]ne day while Cameron was out in the town Anderson, he saw a man on a bicycle, riding with a little blond girl perched on the handlebars—both of them laughing. Suddenly Cameron realized that this was one of the raging men who had grabbed him in the Marion jail [the night of the lynching] and pulled him out into the street. And he felt a flicker of intense anger, but mostly he felt confounded by the purely human mystery of it. How could it be that this "happy-go-lucky man with that equally happy child had been capable of doing the things I knew he had done?" (Carr, 1994, p. 34)

Never the same thing twice, whiteness can be performed by the same man "as" a member of a mob pulling Cameron into the street to his death by lynching *and*, at another time and in another circumstance, a laughing, loving father giving his daughter a ride on bicycle handlebars through the same street, as Cameron looks on.

With images such as these—of multiple and shifting enactments of whiteness—both Carr and Cameron try to reframe whiteness from identity to social relation. By framing whiteness(es) as performances that are never just one thing, and never the same thing twice, Cameron and Carr show whiteness to be historically framed and situated. Each use of the socially and historically produced meanings and consequences of whiteness takes place within a particular time period and place, and within particular relations of power. What whiteness can and will mean, how it can and will be performed, and with what consequences to relations of power and dynamics of social interrelation can't be specified before any particular performance, or projected to other times and places.

This doesn't mean that generalizations about social dynamics, such as "racism," are impossible and no longer useful in constructing knowledge about events or in organizing political work. What it means is this: If whiteness is always more than one thing, and if it is never the same thing twice, then refusing to perform the racist work associated with any one enactment of whiteness must be seen and staged as historically situated and context specific.

Neither Carr nor Cameron address their stories to some locatable, identifiable, fixed seat of whiteness within the theater of race relations. They don't address all of their audience members as if they were, or as if they wished them to be, the white woman who called out that day to save Cameron's life. Because neither Cameron nor Carr knows who she was or why she did what she did, it's impossible for them to construct a structure of address that would try to (re)locate the rest of us in her position. Cameron refuses to tell the woman's story of conversion, commitment, knowledge, or individual moral stance. Carr refuses to tell her own. But they don't have to provide their readers with "models." Instead, they have constructed a paradoxical mode of address that uses the terms of their storytelling—what gets included and what gets excluded—to manipulate their readers into taking on responsibility for the meanings they make. Here's how:

Cameron's address, for example, is pitched to an array of seats in the theater of U.S. race relations. And those multiple seats are moving. Sometimes they overlap and threaten to burst the seams of any single social position. Sometimes individual seats divide and threaten to split a reader in two. This makes it impossible for me as a reader to inhabit, fully and completely, any of the single positions that Cameron addresses. Like the white man on the bicycle, moving through time and space, my whiteness inhabits a number of positions within power and history simultaneously. Like Carr, with her swings of ambivalence, forgetting, and losing—and then finding, committing, and acting—I am capable of many contradictory and fallible performances of my whiteness.

Carr echoes Cameron's paradoxical address in her essay. By telling the lynching story differently, she wants and needs to reposition her family's address to her as a white daughter/audience of family stories—and thereby reposition herself-within-relations-of-whiteness. And yet, *she* is not who she thinks she is. So to what position within whitness would Carr redirect the terms of her family's address? Much of Carr's essay traces the complicated and contradictory terms in which the historical, economic, and political meanings and uses of whiteness were constructed in Marion, Indiana. Her family laughs at the lynching story, and yet her grandfather's house was the only one of Carr's relatives' homes in which she "ever saw black people—women from my grandma's Sunday school class" (1994, p. 35). Her family laughs, and yet her grandmother herself "was one-quarter Indian" (p. 35).

The result of Carr's effort to restructure the address of her family's story is a story that keeps open the possibility of exploring with students how the ongoing constructions of selves within and through and against racisms may mean that we can be simultaneously ignorant *and* knowledgeable; resistant *and* implicated; committed *and* forgetful, committed *and* ambivalent, tired, enjoying the pleasures and safety of privilege; effective in one arena *and* ineffective in another.

By denying her readers an account of an originating moment that incited her to take action, Carr's story remains open to exploring with students the ways that, as Williams (1991) puts it: "Nothing is simple. Each day is a new labor" (p. 130). Each day of work against racisms requires new forms of labor and changed analyses of changing circumstances. Each day confronts new forms and terms and sites of denial and ignorance.

The who that Carr's and Cameron's stories think you are is a structurally incomplete who. The question of what would constitute justice that night in Marion is a question that exceeds the individual consciousness of the woman who spoke out. If she had spoken out and no one else in that courtyard square had listened, would *justice* have been done?

Justice exceeds individual moral stances and necessarily entangles groups, communities, institutions, in the interminably, repeating question, How will we respond? By refusing to offer us a single, fixed, locatable, decidable position from which to respond to their stories, Cameron and Carr paradoxically manipulate us into taking on responsibility for the positions we construct, take up, and act from in response to their stories. They paradoxically manipulate us into taking on responsibility—that is, into seeing reading as well as storytelling as a social relation and site of cultural production, a "site of obligation that exceeds an individual consciousness of justice" (Readings, 1996, p. 154).

9

A Third Paradox: Teaching as a Performance Suspended in the Space Between Self and Other

PEGGY PHELAN'S (1993) study of the politics of performance art and of the differences between representation and performativity suggests a third paradox of teaching. It's a paradox that hinges on the lived time and space of teaching. It's the paradox of teaching as a suspended performance (p. 174).

Teaching is a suspended performance in the sense that it is never completed or finished. And it is suspended in the sense that we, as teachers, must stop ourselves if students are to take on responsibility for the meanings they make.

Teaching is suspended also in the sense that our performance as teachers takes place on what Phelan (1993) calls the "rackety bridge between self and other" (p. 174). Phelan's bridge is a suspension bridge. It spans what Readings (1996) has called "the abyssal space of reading by the other, the fact that we never know to whom our words may speak" (p. 156). That abyss is opened up by the fact that the who to whom we address our teaching is never the who who replies. We pitch our teaching into an abyss between self and self, self and other. And yet something, and hopefully not a repetitive echo, but an inquisitive, ironic echo—a difference that makes a difference— returns.

And teaching is suspended also in the sense that no matter how we try or how good our intentions, both I and the other must perform our lives somewhere along the rackety bridge. Neither of us ever crosses to one side or the other—neither of us ever fully meets our selves or the other.

Following Phelan's thoughts onto that rackety bridge between teacher and student, I'm intrigued by the view, by the danger, by the constant oscillating motion that throws me off balance and then lets me regain balance again, only to lose it again . . . I'm especially intrigued by how, on this bridge, teaching another is not a matter of meeting another face to face and closing the abyss between us.

Rather, on this bridge, teaching might come to mean something more like standing nearby another as we both face the abyss, and getting curious about what suspended performances each of us might make so that each of our passions for learning might be entertained here.

TEACHING AS A PERFORMATIVE ACT

And so following some of these thoughts onto that rackety bridge, I find myself entertaining these ideas:

What Phelan says about the interaction between the art object and the spectator can also be said about the interaction between a curriculum and a student's taking on of responsibility for the meanings s/he makes of that curriculum. That is, the interaction between student and "new information" is essentially a performative act of memory and description. A student's activity of remembering, restaging, and restating new information is a generative act of recovery and memory. It passes through the student's personal and social meanings, associations, and histories (Phelan, 1993, p. 147). It is not an act of repetition or reproduction. Different students' readings of any given text will vary considerably, even wildly. And if you ask the same student over and over, across time, about the same text, they will describe a different text (p. 147).

And so the quality of all learning, knowing, and seeing is, Phelan (1993) implies, performative. And that makes it unrepeatable (p. 149). That is, any event of a return of a difference — any screening of *Shoah* that results, for the audience, in a return of a difference — is unrepeatable. Surprising and productive interferences of the unconscious or of history can never be command performances.

And further, the performativity of teaching makes teaching unrepresentable. You can't film a return of difference and you can't re-present it in language. That's because what gets changed by a return of difference is both invisible and that which escapes language. What gets changed is our *relationship* to the meanings that circulate and vie for authority around us. What gets changed is the way we are implicated in the silences that make language possible.

The notion that teaching is a performative event that is unrepeatable and "leaves no visible or speakable trace afterward" (Phelan, 1993, p. 149) raises some pretty serious implications for reigning educational practices. That's because teaching is most widely practiced as an act of reproductive representation. A multicultural curriculum that would try to turn the woman in James Cameron's story into a model for us to imitate, would certainly *not* try to manipulate students into taking on responsibility for the meanings they make. It knows already who its students should become, and it would transform the paradoxical mode of address of Cameron's story into an address predicated on full and complete understanding—on getting students to occupy and repeat the same social and political position occupied by the woman.

Phelan argues that because a performative act cannot be imitated and mass produced, performativity clogs the smooth machinery of reproductive representation necessary to the circulation of economic capital. Phelan (1993) sees performance art's independence from mass reproduction—technologically, economically, and linguistically—as its greatest political strength (p. 149).

But, at the same time, performance art is vulnerable to charges of valuelessness and emptiness, Phelan (1993) says. Because only rarely in this culture is the "now" to which performance addresses its deepest questions valued. Performance dares to honor "the idea that a limited number of people in a specific time / space frame can have an experience of value which leaves no visible trace afterward" (p. 149).

For pedagogy to be performative, that is, for the teacher to paradoxically manipulate the students into a position of taking responsibility for the meanings and knowledge they construct, it must be situated within its specifics of time and place. It must be related to the network of relations and "ethical obligations" (Readings, 1996, p. 157) that make meaningful what will count in that context as the taking on of responsibility. Performative pedagogy's only life, therefore, is in relation to its context and moment.

And yet, social, political, and educational discourses consistently and insistently construct and use teaching as a representational practice. That is, as a language-based practice of describing or representing things in the world in ways that strive to be truthful and accurate across contexts and moments. As a result, the performative aspects of teaching and learning that exceed questions of truth and accuracy have barely been explored by educational researchers. Meanwhile, across a number of academic and social discourses and practices, confidence in language's ability to deliver truth and accuracy has been shaken.

Phelan (1993) describes a current critique of authoritative representation this way: Representation follows two laws. One, it always conveys more than it intends to convey, and the "excess" meaning conveyed by representation creates a supplement. This supplement makes multiple and resistant readings possible, and prevents the reproduction of the same meaning or sense from one reading of a text or event to the next. And two, representation is never totalizing—it never gives a complete, exact picture of what is being represented, it always fails to reproduce the real exactly. Therefore, representation also produces ruptures and gaps, making a full, complete, or adequate understanding of the world impossible (p. 2).

Phelan (1993) argues that the widespread belief in the possibility of sameness, commonality, and recognition—that is, widespread belief in the possibility of full understanding and representation that reproduces the real exactly—

> has committed us, however unwittingly, to a concomitant narrative of betrayal, disappointment, and rage. Expecting understanding and always failing to feel and see it, we accuse [ourselves or] the other of inadequacy, of blindness, of neglect. The acceleration of ethnic and racial violence may be due in part to the misplaced desire to believe in the (false) promise of understanding. . . . perhaps the best possibility for "understanding" racial, sexual, and ethnic difference lies in the *active* acceptance of the inevitability of misunderstanding.
>
> Misunderstanding as a political and pedagogical telos can be a dangerous proposition, for it invites the belligerent refusal to learn or move at all. This is not what I am arguing for. *It is in the attempt to walk and live on the rackety bridge between self and other—and not the attempt to arrive at one side or the other—that we discover real hope.* That walk is our always suspended performance—in the classroom, in the political field, in relation to one another and to our selves. (p. 174)

For Judith Butler (1993), as well as for Phelan, this "failure of the mimetic function"—this failure of any author or text to "stand for and explain," or fully reflect or know the complexities of the world—"has its own political uses" (p. 19). This failure, in other words, can be productive. In the absence of the possibility of a complete and adequate master text about the world, or knowing of the world, the production of partial texts "can be one way of reconfiguring what *will count as the world* [emphasis added]" (p. 19).

It is precisely the imperfect fits and slippages in the space of difference between text and world, knowledge and the real, and the intended and unintended audiences and fields of reading that make it possible, Butler (1993) claims, for writers and cultural activists to deviate "the citational chain . . . to expand the very meaning of what counts as a valued and valuable body in the world" (p. 22).

TEACHING WITHOUT KNOWING WHY

As a strategy in educational and cultural activism, producing partial texts with the intent of deviating citational chains is at odds with communicative dialogue and other representational practices that dominate current conceptualizations and practices of "critical pedagogy," for example. Partial texts and discontinuous citational chains are not about making rational sense, or achieving understanding or a match between the text, the world, and the readers' shared interpretations.

Performative pedagogy makes claims not to Truth and validity, but to viability and efficacy in relation to a particular audience and intention within in a particular situation. It strives not for Truth, but political and social response-ability, credibility, and usefulness-in-context, and in relation to its particular "audience" of students.

In his analysis of "the university in ruins," Readings (1996) insists on thinking of pedagogy as a scene of address. He insists on thinking of pedagogy, that is, as a lived time and space in which teaching positions students and teachers both physically and discursively, and creates terms for social relationship through modes of address. For Readings, thinking of the activity of teaching as a scene of address gives an ethical weight to teaching. This ethical weight jams the supposedly smooth machinery of representation. This is because

> justice involves respect for an absolute other. The other speaks and we owe the other respect. To be hailed as an addressee is to be commanded to listen, and the ethical nature of this relation cannot be justified, we have to listen, without knowing why, before we know what it is we are to listen to. To be spoken to is to be placed under obligation, to be situated within a narrative pragmatics. (p. 162)

According to Readings then, our reason for listening is not that we hope to finally understand and know the other. Disagreeing with Burbules, Readings argues that the ethical obligation entailed when I am hailed as an addressee cannot be justified on the grounds that communicative dialogue leads to understanding; to bridging the gap between self and other or between self and self; or to establishing common ground for taking "right" action. My ethical obligation to respond to being hailed is not, according to Readings, the obligation to try to understand the other, know the other, or find our common ground.

Rather, Readings refers to an obligation to respect an absolute, unknowable other. He describes a scene of pedagogical address in which I am obliged to listen without knowing why, without understanding, and before I know what I will hear. In this scene, I speak and listen not because I recognize myself or aspects of self reflected in the other (whom I therefore find respectable)—but because I owe respect to an absolutely different other, an unrecognizable other, an other irreducibly different from myself. The ethical nature of the relationship between speaker and listener is undecidable, forever unsettled and unsettling. And yet, to be spoken to, and to speak to another, is to situate self and other within a scene of address that carries an obligation. Chang (1996) puts it this way:

> Communication cannot not take place. This is the paradoxical freedom of communication, the unbearable freedom that one cannot not comunicate, even if one chooses not to do so. . . . As a result, we, the communicating subjects, are both autonomous and other-dependent — free to receive as well as to reject the other and yet bound to play this double role by the contractual force of an *an-archic* [authorless] imperative. (p. 227)

When Phelan writes of the rackety, uncrossable bridge between self and other in an afterward entitled "Notes on Hope — For My Students," she offers her students the paradox of pedagogy as a necessarily suspended or authorless performance. In hope, she offers her students the conclusion that a teacher's performance is never in full possession of herself, of the student, or of the texts and meanings that she works with. She does this in hope of shattering the illusion of arriving at one side or the other of this suspended bridge — an arrival that, if it were even possible, would stop the performance, end the movement, solidify and fix the teacher and the student and knowledge into the selfsame.

As Felman (1992) demonstrates in her reading of *Shoah* and Lacan, and as Phelan (1993) argues in her words to students, it is only in the walking and living in the rackety space of difference *between* — in the indirect and discontinuous routes between self and other, without trying to possess, arrive at, or Know self and other — that response-ability can be performed.

The woman in Cameron's story, for example, as she addresses the "abyssal space of reading" by the lynching mob, has no way of knowing to whom her words may or may not speak.

Like testimony, performance art, and the ethical weight of being hailed into a listening before that listening can be "justified," (Readings, 1996, p. 162) the woman's address to the mob comes too soon. It inscribes "(artistically bears witness to) *what we do not yet know of our lived historical relation to events of our times*" (Felman & Laub, 1992, p. xx).

Performative pedagogy, as Readings (1996) implies, tries "to hear that which cannot be said but which tries to make itself heard. And this is a process incompatible with the production of (even relatively) stable and exchangeable knowledge" (p. 165). He continues: "My turn to the pedagogical scene of address, with all its ethical weight, is thus a way of developing an accountability that is at odds with accounting" (p. 154).

Butler (1992) paradoxically locates accountability on that rackety bridge between self and other:

Performativity describes [the] relation of being implicated in that which one opposes, [the] turning of power against itself . . . to establish a kind of political contestation that is not a "pure" opposition, a "transcendence" of contemporary relations of power, but a difficult labor of forging a future from resources inevitably impure. (p. 241)

The teacher's performance is never in full possession of itself. And yet, we perform the pedagogical relation every day, and in doing so, we give material and creative validation of the absolute necessity of speaking and responding.

Perhaps one possibility of performing a pedagogical relationship lies in the active acceptance of the inevitability of a suspended performance, a performance that leaves no visible trace of its happening, a performance that paradoxically manipulates teachers/students into taking on responsibility for producing partial texts that reconfigure what counts as the world, and by doing so, what counts as valued and valuable bodies and lives in that world.

10

A Fourth Paradox: Teaching as Performance Suspended in Time— Interactive Pedagogy in New Media

I THINK that my current preoccupation with mode of address in pedagogy, aside from nostalgic longing for my grad school days of film studies, has something to do with the fact that nearly every newspaper and magazine I pick up contains something about what journalists have dubbed "edutainment." Some of the filmmakers whom I studied in grad school are now becoming educators. And many educators are now designing and producing multimedia CD-ROMs.

You might say that what's happening in this crossing of genres is the desire and search for a hybrid mode of address. Historically, the who that Hollywood films thought you were was not the who that your classroom textbook thought you were. Can interaction designers succeed in getting the distinctive modes of address that have differentiated entertainment from education to coexist or be recombined into something new? What would be the value (commercial, political, educational, cultural) of such a project?

Fueled by the sense that designers and educators have barely tapped the pedagogical potential and power of interactivity, a billion-dollar race is on to find the holy grail of multimedia and engagement in education: a truly interactive medium. A medium that, like life, returns a difference.

Yet, even as interaction designers seek "true interactivity," there's a nagging suspicion that is sometimes more, sometimes less, explicit in the ways producers of edutainment speak of interactivity. It's the suspicion that just as you can't *make* someone learn, no matter what pedagogy you've designed, you can't design interactivity. Designed interactivity is an oxymoron. Planned interactions can't return a difference. They might be able to add more and more into their systems, opening out to more and more information, but this only expands the illusion of openness—as when CD-ROMs connect directly to the Internet.

The mode of address of interactive media is a paradoxical one, inviting the user to make something happen—to create a trauma—yet to do so within a contained universe of choices. Such an address can be both frustrating and fascinating.

What I want to explore here is this: Instead of trying to break through from "partial" interactivity to "true" interactivity, what if interaction designers and teachers approached interactivity as an unstable equilibrium? What if we approached interactivity as a constitutive structure of in-between in which "there is *constantly something to be settled*" (Chang, 1996, p. 102)?

What if we approached educational interactivity as if it were something like, for example, the unstable equilibria of tickling and being bored?

This thought occurred to me as I was reading Adam Phillips's *On Kissing, Tickling, and Being Bored: Psychoanalytic Essays on the Unexamined Life* (1993). I hadn't been reading that book through my interest in pedagogical modes of address. But when Phillips started discussing paradoxical and perverse structures of address, and when he began to link them to the pedagogical functions of psychoanalysis and the teaching of psychoanalysis as a craft—I shifted gears.

Both being tickled and being bored, according to Phillips (1993), are paradoxical, precarious states of desire that are easily upset or overthrown. What becomes crucial to the scenarios of each of these states are the structures of relations—the scenes of address—that surround them and make up their contexts. Both tickling and being bored require, as Phillips puts it, particular kinds of "holding environments" (p. 69). If the holding environment isn't just right, tickling can become humiliation. And in the scenario of being bored, the "wrong" holding environment can sabotage the important work that being bored performs for the psyche.

I'm interested in these questions: Drawing on Phillips's discussions of tickling and being bored, what use might it be to teachers and new media designers to conceptualize interaction design as the design of paradoxical environments of desire? And what might teachers learn from Phillips's provocative definition of what constitutes a perverse pedagogical mode of address?

TICKLING AND BEING BORED AS STRUCTURES OF ADDRESS

Phillips (1993) speaks of tickling as an interaction predicated on the paradoxical desire for *both* trauma (the trauma of chaotic, unpredictable openness and loss of control) *and* containment (the containment of order, predictability, limits, boundaries). Tickling is an "unstable equilibrium, easily upset or overthrown, insecure, tottering" (p. 10). Its often "frenetic contact

. . . quickly reinstates a distance, only equally quickly to create another invitation" (p. 11).

While tickling has no climax, it's not an open-ended scenario either. It can end too soon. It can end too late. As a repertoire of intrusions, it requires an environment of mutual accommodation, in which the tickler stops "at the blurred point" (Phillips, 1993, p. 10) which is poised precariously between pleasure and pain; understanding and confusion; play and real humiliation; affection and violation.

Much about new media interactivity is similar to tickling. The participant in an interactive web site, for example, is invited to make something happen—to, in other words, create a difference, a disturbance, a trauma— but to do so within a contained universe of choices. In this way, and like tickling, multimedia interactivity blurs boundaries between choice and closure, responsibility and manipulation, self and other.

While surfing the web, the poise between staying on a text and moving through it to something else is a precarious one. Web pages, in their bids to become *the* page to arrest my attention, often address me in a frantic manner, trying to make "frenetic contact"—through hot colors, bold graphics, in-my-face addresses. But just as quickly, they "reinstate a distance" by impelling me to move on, to check out other related sites, to click here for this, click here for that, click there to go off to distantly related or even randomly selected sites. And this distance is solicited "only equally quickly to create another invitation" to reestablish contact: *return to home, visit us again, check back to see what's new, don't miss what's coming next.*

Boredom, like tickling, is a precarious state of paradoxical desire. Phillips (1993) describes boredom as "a mood of diffuse restlessness which contains that most absurd and paradoxical wish, the wish for a desire" (p. 69).

Boredom is a "transitional state"—from one position within structures of relations to another—but its destination is unclear (Phillips, 1993, p. 72). Its destination *must* be unclear for boredom to perform important and necessary work for the child—the work of becoming conscious of one's "preconditions for desire," and for letting one's desire develop (p. 74).

According to Phillips (1993), one of the most oppressive demands of adults—and, I would add, of most pedagogies and learning environments— is that the child should be interested, rather than take time to find what interests her. There is always the risk that free-floating attention will be assaulted by invitations proffered by "impinging auxiliary egos," soliciting "premature flight from uncertainty," and proffering orgies "of promiscuous and disappointing engagements" (p. 70).

But the environment most helpful to the work that boredom performs is one that presents an invitation, suggests without imposing, "not exactly asserting itself, [it] is at least tentatively promising; hinting, as it were" (Phillips, 1993, p. 74).

Interaction designs that hold my activity as a surfer on the web must perform a double labor: They must arrest or engage my free-floating attention or boredom, in order to send me on to another site, and they must send me on to another site in order to arrest my boredom. It would be a "failure" of the "webness" of a web site, or the "hyperness" of a CD-ROM, if I stayed on one page or screen or section or site, without maximizing the potential of linking and interaction with others. Likewise, it would be a failure of the interactivity of webness if all I did was stay bored, clicking one "here" after another without making any contact.

This is where the interaction designer shares a recurrent dilemma with the psychoanalyst and the teacher. Each must try to provide an environment in which the client/student/user can be bored, can take the time to find what interests her. But a student/client/user who is unable to be anything else but bored is a failure of psychotherapy, teaching, and interaction design. And this brings us back to teaching and psychoanalysis as impossible professions:

> [J]ust as, for example, we cannot know beforehand which of the day's events from what Freud calls the "dream-day" will be used as day-residues in the dream-work, we cannot necessarily know what will serve as a transformational object. . . . An analysis can . . . be arranged. But it cannot, alas, organize epiphanies, or guarantee those processes of transformation—those articulations—that return the future to us through the past. (Phillips, 1993, p. 77)

Tickling, being bored, learning, psychotherapy, and interactivity are all precarious, transitional states, in which the holding environment makes all the difference. The holding environment—the mode of address, if you will—of the tickler, the teacher, the therapist, makes all the difference between amusement and humiliation, a hint and an imposition, an epiphany and a deadening lesson. But no mode of address can guarantee an epiphany.

PERVERSE PEDAGOGICAL MODES OF ADDRESS

Significantly enough for the interests I have both as a feminist and as a teacher, in his series of essays, the one and only place where Phillips (1993) explicitly refers to gender is in his discussion of pedagogy—of the instructions given to psychoanalysts on how to behave as a psychoanalyst. Some instructions, especially those from British object-relations theory, looked to mothers for answers to the question, "From whom, by what process can a person learn—or later, become—an analyst" (p. 102)? As part of their turn toward social engineering after World War II, psychoanalysts in Great Britain began to write as though they could be taught what to do by mothers. They used a version of "the pre-oedipal mother as psychoanalytic mentor. As such, [looking to the mother for answers about how to teach psychoanalysis] were bids to determining the analyst's function through a gender-specific identification" (p. 105).

Phillips's (1993) fear about this approach is that the psychoanalytic context or holding environment would become gendered through the assumption that at the "deepest" levels of the patient's personality, the analyst will be experienced as the patient's mother. His problem with this is not a problem with being gendered per se—as a woman or as a man. Rather,

> it is integral to the psychoanalytic process that the analyst cannot know beforehand which sex he is going to be. The analyst is always waiting for the patient to tell him—and then to discover what the assumed, the unconscious consequences are of such an invitation. The psychoanalytic setting is a frame for unanticipated invitations. (p. 101)

It's a problem then, when the holding environment, the frame, is preemptively structured through *any* gender. And the problem consists in this:

> [A]ttributions of apparent sexual identity bring with them a largely unconscious repertoire of permissions and prohibitions to act, of wished-up assumptions of sexual entitlement. Each sex is categorized according to unconscious fantasies of function, which are always fantasies of possible drama. (p. 101)

For example, on the web, when interpretations of what surfing "really means" or "should mean" or where it "should go" are made in terms of gender, the conscious and unconscious work that requires boredom and free-floating attention is interrupted—it is replaced by repertoires of permissions and prohibitions to act, by unconscious fantasies of possible drama.

After visiting a number of educational web sites addressed to women and girls, I'm left with this question: Are states of tickling and being bored invited at these sites? How is gender figuring into the design of web sites as environments of desire for women and girls?

This has become an issue for me because several such sites not only construct a who that they think I am through their modes of address as my attention arrests on a particular page; they also construct a who for who I will be as I move on—as I continue surfing through and away from their sites. Often, that who is a woman for whom making contact, arresting her attention, has to do with survival in a hostile environment. Stopping at a site, visiting it, making contact, is tied to empowerment, networking, organizing, locating resources, taking up space for women on the Internet, taking control of women's self-representation on the Internet. Reinstating a distance, moving on, surfing, means going to another site like this one, giving my support to another site that needs it, needs my help.

As such, moving on isn't really reinstating a distance, it's a substitution — substituting one gendered environment for another just like it. Surfing turns into a form of work — political, social, cultural labor. Unlike the state of boredom, here, things have to be done; and I'm helping or can help by patronizing women-owned businesses and other women's sites, by making my presence as a woman felt on the Net. Not an environment for holding or sustaining boredom or tickling, this labor turns surfing into the other way to use the web, namely, knowing exactly what I want and finding it.

In other words, at these sites, there is no way to surf "as a woman." There is no way to be bored as a woman, or to tickle or be tickled as a woman. As a woman turns surfing, tickling, and being bored into a perversion. Perversion, as Phillips (1993) puts it,

> in the only meaningful sense of the term [is] knowing too exactly what one wants, the disavowal of contingency, omniscience as the cheating of time; the mother who, because she knows what's best for us, has nothing to offer. (p. 108)

For Phillips then, perversion entails thinking that there is nothing new to know. To give surfing a gender is to arrest gender-in-the-making and turn it into taking on and performing an already constructed gender. Perversions, according to Phillips, are always prefigurings:

> We could say that we are being perverse whenever we think we know beforehand exactly what we desire. To know beforehand is to assume that otherness — whether it be a person, a medium, an environment, is redundant — that it has nothing to offer us, that it brings nothing — or just rage and disappointment — to the occasion. . . . I think, the so-called pervert, in his apparent knowingness, [is] an implicit parody of a certain kind of analyst. (1993, p. 63)

Namely, the analyst, the teacher, the feminist activist web designer — who thinks she can give the correct, knowledgeable interpretation of who I am when I surf as a woman.

Judith Butler (1990) begins her essay "Gender Trouble, Feminist Theory, and Psychoanalytic Discourse" with this: "Within the terms of feminist theory, it has been quite important to refer to the category of 'women' and to know what it is we mean" (p. 324). Then she goes on to question, "But does feminist theory need to rely on a notion of what it is fundamentally or distinctively to be a 'woman'" (p. 324)? Her answer, given in an essay on feminism and postmodernism, is no:

> [O]n the contrary, if feminism presupposes that "woman" designates an unde-signatable field of differences, one that cannot be totalized or summarized by a descriptive identity category, then the very term becomes a site of permanent openness and resignifiability. (1992, p. 16)

Paradoxically, Butler argues, it may be that only through releasing the category of women from a fixed referent that something like politicized feminist "'agency' becomes possible" (p. 16).

So, Butler argues that a feminist politics which requires a stable, known, knowable, teachable subject will always be normative, and there-fore exclusionary. And here, I want to suggest that the gendering of an environment of desire, a web site that genders its address to me, that thinks it knows who I am as gendered, constitutes a perverse mode of address: It knows too exactly what I want, who I am; it disavows contingency; its omniscience cheats time.

Might this perversion of address account for some of the resistance of many women to feminist modes of address in teaching?

A perverse pedagogical address thinks it knows who I am, and implic-itly or explicitly, then, tells me what to do. Phillips (1995) asks whether the aim of a psychoanalysis should be "to know who you are, or to tolerate and enjoy the impossibility of such knowing" (p. 101). But how could a teacher advocate tolerating and enjoying the impossibility of knowing? Because, Phillips tells us, psychoanalysis teaches us that "knowing is not the only thing we can do" (p. 104). It teaches us that there are valuable and useful states of mind other than that of knowing. These result from teaching people "how to get lost again (in thought)" (p. 102), teaching people "the capacity to be absorbed," inviting students into states of mind that are "either inarticulate or on the verges of representation, that defy or confound the already known" (p. 103).

What Phillips says of psychoanalysis can be said of pedagogy: If teach-ing doesn't also facilitate students' capacities not to know themselves and others, "it becomes merely another way of setting limits to the self; and the [teacher] becomes an expert on human possibility, something no one could ever be, despite the posturing of our own favorite authorities" (1995, p. 104).

THE PERVERSITY OF TEACHING "THE POSSIBLE"

Too often, the unknown is allowed into pedagogy and celebrated in teaching only as a tease (not a tickling) before finally reaching and ultimately achieving the known. Too often in discourses of critical or humanist pedagogies, the as yet unknown of human and social "possibility" are thought to be decidable. Possibility becomes a thing that can and will eventually be named and pursued. Such pedagogies address me, as teacher, as someone who is to teach "for possibility," or to name, through assisting students in discovering their authentic voices, what is possible for them so they can pursue it.

But teaching as interminable, meaning as undecidable, and self as an interminable process inextricable from world and others, makes not only meaning and knowledge undecidable—they also make possibility undecidable. Paraphrasing Chang on the undecidability of meaning then, the undecidability of possibility does not point simply to a future that is ambiguous or interpretable in different ways. Nor does it suggest merely that social futures and future selves will be differently accented in terms of ideology, class, geography, or history. More than ambiguity or multiplicity, Derrida's radical notion of undecidability suggests that possibility is *"essentially indeterminable,"* no matter what. And this is because actions taken in the world to give it meaning—such as writing or teaching—are "inaugural, in the primal sense of the word." Writing—and teaching—"does not know where it is going, no knowledge can keep it from the essential precipitation toward the meaning it constitutes, and this is, primarily, its future" (Chang, 1996, p. 204).

This may be what many people, including teachers, are sensing about the web—and why they're excited about it. The web is inaugural, in the primal sense of the word. It does not know where it is going, and when we surf it, neither do we. The web precipitates toward its future. When we surf it, we too can sometimes seem to precipitate toward an indeterminable future.

And maybe this is how these new interactive media can appear to us to be closer to reality, can appear as virtual reality—because like the futures of our lives and selves, the future of the web as text is unknowable. What we do with the web is more like writing than it is like spectating. Surfing the web is more like writing the web than watching the web. And writing the web, like all writing, makes a final reading of the web, like reading all texts, impossible. A final interpretation can never be arrived at; we never arrive at the web's future, or at the future of what our surfing has written through the web.

This may be an interesting place for pedagogy design to meet interaction design: at the undecidability of both meaning and possibility.

All of this is to say that teaching, like other forms of performativity, then, could be seen as inaugural. When, precisely, is a learning produced? Is it stated or produced when the teacher declares; "Now you've got it!" or when the student declares, "I get it!" The question of when learning happens can't be decided, because "all thoughts are afterthoughts" (Phillips, 1995, p. 102):

> *The mind always comes in afterwards* [after insight or learning] (to repair, to reflect, to reconstruct, to formulate, to consider, to fetishize, etc.) . . . because the mind always comes in afterwards . . . it always runs the risk of being a pre-emptive presence. (Phillips, 1995, p. 102)

That which "is learned" does not exist until the self-who-learned performs an afterthought. And paradoxically, the self-who-learned did not exist until after the learning. The "primal scene" of learning, in other words, did not exist when the learning took place, for it "came into existence only when one (re)visited the [staging of learning] *afterward for the first time*" (Chang, 1996, p. 213). The commonsense notion that teaching is a cause-effect relation, that there is a temporal precedence in teaching (the teacher teaches, the teacher causes learning, first comes teaching and then comes learning) is in deep trouble here. Teaching is a performance suspended in time.

There is an undecidability to teaching. The good teacher is the one who gives what s/he doesn't have: the future as undecidable, possibility as indeterminable.

11

A Fifth Paradox: Pedagogy as a Performance Suspended in Thought— The Power of a Magical Realist Address in Academic Writing

> And that...is what reading magical realism requires: a faculty for boundary-skipping between worlds.
>   –Rawdon Wilson, "The Metamorphoses of Fictional Space"

WHEN I READ Patricia Williams's book *The Alchemy of Race and Rights: Diary of a Law Professor* (1991), I feel as though I'm "being taught" by a "good teacher," one who gives what she doesn't have: the future as undecidable, possibility as indeterminable.

Teaching about and across difference without driving toward or prizing assimilation or the sameness of understanding requires an ability to allow plural worlds to exist side by side. As Williams (1995) writes, the riot in Crown Heights between blacks and Jews posed the question of "how— or if—we human creatures can live together while observing very different cultural practices" (p. 191).

And in her analysis of women writing in the literary style of magical realism, Sturgis (1991) writes:

> How do worlds held apart by custom come together? As women of different classes, cultures, ages, places, the question is posed for us, as we encounter each other, our own pasts, the histories of our people, the life of the land we live on. What we glimpse of the answers may disorient, terrify, horrify us— and exhilarate and empower us at the very same time. It doesn't yield to idealistic prescriptions or rational explanations. To what, then? (p. 5)

What Williams suggests through her practice as a teacher, a scholar, and a political activist, is that this question may not yield to linear and logical argument or analysis. The question of how worlds can "live together" when they are held apart by very different cultural practices and by the conflicted and power-inflected histories that engendered those practices "cannot be answered by an individual moral stance" or the understandings or knowledges of an emancipated autonomous subject (Readings, 1996, p. 162). Such a question exceeds "individual consciousness of justice" (p. 154). It may, however, yield to some other economy.

As a teacher and scholar, Williams dares to explore the uses—the efficacy—of paradox in academic writing and in pedagogy. Exploring the simultaneities of terror and exhilaration, disorientation and empowerment, in both scholarship and teaching, Williams leaves normal school. Paraphrasing and quoting Phillips (1995), "like the so-called neurotic, whose project is to be extremely normal," teaching has always struggled to distance itself from supposedly discredited things like psychotherapy, mysticism, the aesthetic, theater, eroticism, passion, "and all of the scapegoated 'alternative'" educations (p. 18).

Williams explores the uses and power of parable, parody, poetry, dreams, and the unconscious—in a particular relation to analysis and argument—in the task of working against racism as a teacher and a scholar. She writes simultaneously to and from multiple social positionings, histories, logics, and languages. Working on an intimate basis with such discredited things, she troubles the normalizing project that has required so many other teachers to be neurotic—as in "extremely normal."

In *Alchemy*, Williams offers a series of analytical essays on critical legal theory, race, culture, and teaching. She writes in a style that, for an academic book, is remarkable. Its mode of address requires me to be able to boundary-skip between multiple conceptual and experiential worlds.

Williams (1991) needs, as she puts it, a reader with the faculty for an "ambivalent, multivalent way of seeing." This way of seeing has to do, she says, with

> a fluid positioning that sees back and forth across boundary, which acknowledges that I can be black and good and black and bad, and that I can also be black and white, male and female, yin and yang, love and hate. (p. 130)

She needs a reader like that because, as a commercial lawyer and teacher of contract and property law, she writes from "the center of a snarl of social tensions and crossed boundaries" (Williams, 1991, p. 6). Those tensions are caused by her status as an "oxymoron" (p. 8). She is a commercial lawyer, Harvard educated, black, woman, tenured university professor, great-great-granddaughter of a slave and a southern white slaveholder lawyer. She is something that the history of power relations in the United States never intended to allow. And she's something that the politics of representation entwined with that history never intended to be intelligible.

She writes that there is "a paradigm at work, in the persistent perceptions of me as inherent contradiction: a paradigm of larger social perceptions that divide public from private, black from white, dispossessed from legitimate" (Williams, 1991, p. 7). Williams's struggle as an oxymoron in the academy is to construct a mode of address to her readers and students that makes it difficult for us to read her through this paradigm. She does not want to be read as either black *or* professor, woman *or* lawyer, Harvard educated *or* great-great-granddaughter of a slave, black *or* white, dispossessed *or* legitimate. Nor does she want me to read her as either an inherent contradiction *or* as coherent, univocal, and one who has finally arrived at the academy's center—to speak from its center. Instead, she addresses me, as her reader, in a way that attempts to put me in motion, offering me fluid positionings across these either/ors.

Williams (1991) writes from what she describes as the "gaps between those ends that the sensation of oxymoron marks" (p. 8). She writes from the conceptual, historical, geographical, legal and pedagogical spaces between black and white, male and female, public and private, social and individual, historical and current, large social perceptions and small unique incidents.

This is where Williams's academic writing shares something with the literary form known as "magical realism." Writing from the space-between, Williams "strikes the mind's eye" with the "doubleness of conceptual codes, the irreducibly hybrid nature of experience." Like magical realism, her academic prose inscribes "boundaries that fold and refold like quicksilver, can superimpose themselves upon one another" (Wilson, 1995, p. 210).

For several semesters, I've been assigning Williams's *Alchemy of Race and Rights* to students in my seminar on postmodernism and education. That seminar is, in part, about the challenges that the postmodern poses to academic practices—including the kinds of teaching we practice when we write academic books and articles. How do we teach, write, and do research once we encounter the epistemological crisis provoked by postmodernism—the crisis of having no privileged center from which to speak to or about culture, race, politics, history?

In *Alchemy*, Williams (1991) says that one of her goals is to pose this very challenge to her own field of commercial law and to the students whom she teachers there. She says that she wants to "challenge the usual limits of commercial [law] discourse by using an intentionally double-voiced and relational, rather than a traditionally legal black-letter, vocabulary" (p. 6).

Something has happened to many of my seminar students' relationships to their own academic writing since they have read Williams's (1991) attempt to "create a genre of legal writing to fill the gaps of traditional legal scholarship" (p. 7). Something has happened to their academic imaginations since they have witnessed Williams's efforts to write in a way that reveals the intersubjectivity of legal constructions, that forces the reader both to participate in the construction of meaning and to be conscious of that process. Thus, in attempting to fill the gaps in the discourse of commercial exchange, I hope that the gaps in my own writing will be self-consciously filled by the reader, as an act of forced mirroring of meaning-invention. To this end, I exploit all sorts of literary devices, including parody, parable, and poetry. (pp. 7–8)

Williams refuses to fill the gaps in her own writing; in fact, she embellishes them, elaborates them, flags them so that they won't go unremarked. Since reading *Alchemy* through these gaps, something has also happened to students' and my relations and responses to race and to the politics of social and cultural difference. Something has happened since we have been paradoxically manipulated—through textual strategies of discontinuity, intertextuality, multiplicity, and destabilized positions that Williams offers us as readers—into participating with her in meaning-invention. Namely, we have not found ourselves placed on opposing ends of a racial divide—in a face-off. Nor have we found ourselves addressed as committed to finding the enemy in an unjust world.

Instead, we have found ourselves addressed through a different ethic. It's an ethic committed to conflict without, paradoxically, needing the idea of an enemy. It is an ethic that operates not within the logic of oppositions and mutual exclusions, but within the logic of paradoxes and spectrums. "And a world of paradox is a world without revenge: retaliation is a false cure for contradiction" (Phillips, 1996, p. 84). The pedagogy of Williams's mode of address paradoxically manipulates us into a fluid positioning that sees back and forth across boundaries, and as a result, requires us to take on responsibility for the meanings we will construct out of this fluidity by bringing it to a (temporary) stop (Marshall, 1992, p. 154).

There's been an eventness that has surrounded the readings of *Alchemy* in these seminars—a breaking off of the status quo of academic reading and writing. And I'd like to get better at responding to it as a teacher. Not to define or name it, but to extend and enfold it into problems and practices of pedagogy. I'm wondering what becomes possible for me as a "teacher of Williams's book," and as a "student of Williams's book," when I read her "through" magical realism.

And so I've been reading about magical realism as a literary form and as a cultural practice. And I like what that's been doing to my academic and pedagogical imaginations.

What I'd like to explore here is this: What questions can magical realism be used to pose to the practice and reading of academic writing as—dare I say it—a "literary form"? And I want to explore what challenges magic realism as a cultural practice offers to pedagogy as a cultural practice. What might be the value, for teachers, of getting curious about magical realism and its significance for our research, writing, and teaching?

MAGICAL REALISM

As a literary form, magical realism is often associated with Latin American writers. But recently, literary critics have begun to explore magical realism as an influential worldwide phenomenon with a long history. Writers often identified with magical realism include Toni Morrison, Günter Grass, Salman Rushdie, Derek Walcott, Abe Kobo, Gabriel García Márquez and many others (Zamora & Faris, 1995).

Critics are discussing magical realism, as a textual strategy, in relation to postcolonial literatures and contexts, and as a major component of postmodern fiction. Recently, film reviewers have labeled as magical realist several popular films that have done well at box offices and awards ceremonies, including *Like Water for Chocolate* and *Antonia's Line*.

Here are some of the characteristics that various critics have used to distinguish magical realism as a literary form.

In their introduction to a recent collection of essays on magical realism, Zamora and Faris (1995) speak of magical realism's literary strategies in terms of its political implications:

> Magical realism is a mode suited to exploring—and transgressing—boundaries, whether the boundaries are ontological, political, geographical, or generic. Magical realism often facilitates the fusion, or coexistence, of possible worlds, spaces, systems that would be irreconcilable in other modes of fiction. . . . So magical realism may be considered an extension of realism in its concern with the nature of reality and its representation . . . at the same time it resists the basic assumptions of post-enlightenment rationalism and literary realism. Mind and body, spirit and matter, life and death, real and imaginary, self and other, male and female: these are boundaries to be erased, transgressed, blurred, brought together, or otherwise fundamentally refashioned in magical realist texts.
>
> Magical realism's assault on the basic structures of rationalism and realism has inevitable ideological impact. . . . Magical realist texts are subversive; their in-betweenness, their all-at-onceness encourages resistance to monologic political and cultural structures, a feature that has made the mode particularly useful to writers in postcolonial cultures and, increasingly, to women. . . . John Erickson [calls magical realism] "a corrosion within the engine of system," an admission of the exceptional that subverts existing structures of power. (pp. 5–6)

Many literary critics have read Toni Morrison's *Beloved* as a magical realist text. Marshall (1992), for example, who uses *Beloved* to teach postmodernism, describes the novel this way:

> This is a novel in which a family accepts the daily presence of a poltergeist who later takes human form as the grown-up version of the child, Beloved, slain by the mother, Sethe, 18 years earlier. The physical presence of the once-dead daughter causes a certain commotion in the lives of the women of 124 Bluestone Road, but no surprise. For Sethe and her daughter, Denver, the addition to their lives of a poltergeist is just one more thing to accept as "natural." Listen to Baby Sugg's response to Sethe's suggestion that they could move to another house to get relief from a dead "baby's fury at having its throat cut": "What'd be the point? . . . Not a house in the country ain't packed to its rafters with some dead Negro's grief." (p. 180)

Marshall goes on to argue that while the magic of magical realism "may appear to add to, to be superfluous to, an accepted reality," it also works to "replace what is missing: the assumption is that it is . . . realism . . . that is lacking, and thus needs supplementing" (pp. 180–181). All rhetorics, including the rhetoric of realism, must "leave some things unsaid in order to be able to say others" (Chang, 1996, p. 208). These become structuring absences—exclusions that configure the text, "some dead Negro's grief" that props up the rafters of every house in this country.

> Within the context of *Beloved* we could refer to the material world of a people so devastated by the institutionalized brutality of slavery that the supplement of magic to the realism of slavery and its effects was a strategy for survival. As author Morrison stated in an interview, "One of the things that's important to me is the powerful imaginative way in which we deconstructed and reconstructed reality in order to get through." (Marshall, 1992, p. 181)

Magical realism constantly poses the question, then, What's counting as "real" here? What's counting as unreal, excessive, distorted? Who's counting it as real and why?

> In magical realist texts, ontological disruption serves the purpose of political and cultural disruption: magic is often given as a cultural corrective, requiring readers to scrutinize accepted realistic conventions of causality, materiality, motivation. (Zamora & Faris, 1995, p. 3)

"Accepted" reality, in other words, is always someone's reality, constructed in and through particular intentions and interests, and from particular locations on multiple networks of power relations. That which is rejected by accepted reality has no place within that reality. It can't be represented there — it makes no sense there — it is excessive.

The insight of magical realism, and its challenge to many current ways of thinking about power and of teaching against racism or sexism, for example, is the way it insists that structuring absences do not simply exist alongside or parallel to the inclusions that they structure. The are not simply alternatives standing as choices to be made outside of the authorized and legitimized realities or stories.

Rather, magical realism takes inclusions and exclusions to be equiprimordial — each inhabits the other as its own essential constitutive element. Butler (1994) points this out when she writes about how the social construction of gender, race, and sexuality are "constitutive constraints." They

> not only produce the domain of intelligible bodies, but produce as well a domain of unthinkable, abject, unlivable bodies. This latter domain is not the opposite of the former, for oppositions are, after all, part of intelligibility; the latter is the excluded and illegible domain that haunts the former domain as the specter of its own impossibility, the very limit to intelligibility, its constitutive outside. How, then, might one alter the very terms that constitute the "necessary" domain of bodies through rendering unthinkable and unlivable another domain of bodies, those that do not matter in the same way. (p. xi)

And in her work of literary criticism, *Playing in the Dark: Whiteness and the Literary Imagination* (1992), Morrison locates the equiprimordial doubleness of the world of American literature. The Africanist presence, she argues, is the ghost in the machine of American literature. It is the repressed that returns as twisted and distorted narrative structures, corroding the realism of American fiction. Whereas American literature acts as if there is a "single axiom" "from which everything descended, or from which the world hung," in fact there have been "instead two codes that were interwound, twisted in a grip closer than blood and mind, in a tight choreography" (Wilson, 1995, p. 212). The doubleness of the world of American literature exceeds logics of opposition and mutual exclusion.

And yet, no matter how tightly the choreography between the domain of intelligible white bodies and the domain of abject, unlivable black bodies, they never merge, connect, or resolve. There is no match, no perfect fit, between the lived realities of slavery, on the one hand, and the conceptual maps, the reasoning, the legal discourses, the stories told to justify or explain slavery, on the other. Magical realism, like the grotesque, operates in the space of difference between perception and consciousness, sensation and language.

ACADEMIC WRITING AND MAGICAL REALISM

The particular in-between that Patricia Williams (1991) writes from and writes to is the in-between of "lived experience and social perception" (p. 8). She writes from within the gap between lived experience and codified (mis)understandings that take the form of legal discourses and practices. But her goal is not to close, fill, or transcend that gap once and for all. Rather, she wants to highlight the intersubjectivity of legal discourse—by using a mode of address that "forces" the reader to participate in meaning-making and in the intersubjective construction of social perception.

And so Williams (1991) sets out as an academic writer to resist mono-logical political and cultural structures. This is because the logics of her academic field, "the hypostatization of exclusive categories and definitional polarities"; "transcendent, acontextual, universal legal truths or pure proce-dures" (p. 8); and the construction of "objective, 'unmediated' voices by which those transcendent, universal truths find their expression" (p. 9) all serve to brand some social actors with the legal status of "isolation of oxymoron, of oddity, of outsider" (p. 7).

Williams isn't the only academic writer who has resisted monological writing strategies, definitional polarities, universal truths, and the objective voice. Judith Butler, among others, resists these, but not through magical realism. Instead, she uses language ironically—as when she employs the conventions of academic writing to have them critique themselves. Her address to readers is also a multiple address, using language that enfolds within itself the possibilities of different readings. Often, she does this through the ironic or self-reflexive syntax of a single sentence or conceptual-ization. This can lead to some pretty convoluted syntax. Butler uses linear, logical, rationalist rhetorical and syntactical structures in her attempts to enfold at least two ways of seeing, and in attempts to see ambivalently, multivalently, and fluidly across boundaries. Consider the following prose:

> If gender is a construction, must there be an "I" or a "we" who enacts or performs that construction? How can there be an activity, a constructing, without presupposing an agent who precedes and performs that activity? How would we account for the motivation and direction of construction without such a subject? As a rejoinder, I would suggest that it takes a certain suspicion toward grammar to reconceive the matter in a different light. For if gender is constructed, it is not necessarily constructed by an "I" or a "we" who stands before that construction in any spatial or temporal sense of "before." Indeed, it is unclear that there can be an "I" or a "we" who has not been submitted, subjected to gender, where gendering is, among other things, the differentiating relations by which speaking subjects come into being. Subjects to gender, but

subjected by gender, the "I" neither precedes nor follows the process of this gendering, but emerges only within and as the matrix of gender relations themselves. (1993, p. 7)

By trying to say several things at once, and no single thing once and for all, writing styles like Butler's have given postmodernism its reputation as elitist, obstructionist, impenetrable. But there can be some pleasure in reading or writing linearly in ways that fold back on themselves. One of my favorite passages of academic writing is Trinh's (1986–1987) poetic academic prose:

After all, she is this Inappropriate/d Other who moves about with always at least two/four gestures: that of affirming "I am like you" while pointing insistently to the difference; and that of reminding "I am different" while unsettling every definition of otherness arrived at. (p. 9)

As an academic writer, Patricia Williams, however, takes another route. Her refusals, interruptions, and supplements most often take the form of stories predicated on the exceptional that subverts existing structures of power. She interwinds multiple worlds, histories, and geographies of power in and through the telling of excessive stories. She narrativises conceptual space (such as the conceptual space of rights discourse in the law) by showing that there's a history to this concept, to the construction of this conceptual space.

I've often commented to students in seminars that it's almost impossible to "quote" Williams. You have to quote an entire story—or two stories as they collide—to remake her point(s). Unlike most other academic writers who eventually supply the point or conclusion or implications of their argument or analysis, Williams supplies instead the doubleness, the absent ghost that structures what's present. Her summaries or conclusions most often take the form of a metaphor or a poetic condensation of the tension marked by the ends of an oxymoron. But the metaphors or poems make sense only in the context of the story or juxtapositions that surround them, and so they, too, cannot be easily extracted for quotation.

There are two moments in Williams's text that I'd like to look at closely here, to explore the power of magical realism as a pedagogical mode of address—especially when teaching about and across social and cultural difference. One is a story/analysis that Williams tells about how she was positioned (and positioned herself) as party to an anti-Semitic incident. The other moment is the repeated eruptions of polar bears into the last two chapters of Williams's book.

SHOPPING THROUGH ANTI-SEMITISM

Williams goes shopping for a sweatshirt. Her shopping trip came not long after she had interrupted an anti-Semitic remark made by a friend. This interruption resulted in Williams feeling "our friendship being broken apart" (1991, p. 125).

While shopping, she overhears several young saleswomen joking about Jews. "'Speak of the devil,' said one of them as four other young people came into the store" (Williams, 1991, p. 126). Williams watches and listens as the salespeople decide that the newcomers are Jews, murmur anti-Semitic remarks, imitate "Jewish" accents, and make scornful gestures behind the backs of these "designated Jews." Williams says nothing. "I wanted to say something and, since I'm usually outspoken about these things, I was surprised when no words came out" (p. 127).

Williams writes:

> I was surprised when no words came out. It is embarrassing but worthwhile nonetheless . . . to run through all the mundane, even quite petty, components of the self-consciousness that resulted in my silence. Such silence is too common, too institutionalized, and too destructive not to examine it in the most nuanced way possible. (1991, p. 127)

Minnie Bruce Pratt (1991) has written about similar moments of self-surprise. She writes, for example, about the moment when she heard the news that 50 miles from where she lived, in Greensboro, North Carolina, five people were killed in broad daylight when Klansmen and Nazis drove into an anti-Klan demonstration and opened fire. Her response to this news was to ask, "Am I not surprised and shocked that this could happen? Yet it did, and there must be a history to it" (p. 51).

Williams is surprised by her silence, Pratt by her ignorance. The surprise and the ignorance, as well as the violent incidents themselves, have erupted—from somewhere—unexpectedly into their seemingly normal, everyday worlds. Suddenly, several things become remarkable—require their response. Where have the surprise and ignorance come from? What other "worlds"—in whose other stories about "normal, everyday life"— would being let in on an anti-Semitic "joke" or hearing about Klan activity in the neighborhood not be surprising at all?

And, how are what Williams and Pratt have taken to be the normal, everyday stories of shopping as a professional black woman and living as a white woman in Greensboro not "real" at all—but "linguistic codification[s] of a particular privileged center's worldview" (D'haen, 1995, p. 197).

Williams fills four pages "running through" the history of the "self-consciousness" that underlay her few moments of silence in the store (p. 127). She writes about her surprising and "embarrassing" (p. 127) silence *in terms* of the history that there must be to the construction of that self-consciousness. Her narrative politicizes and problematizes the self-consciousness that results in her "paralysis" (p. 127). She does this by making the history of the social construction of this particular kind of "self-consciousness" copresent with the story of how it silenced her that day. Doing this, she avoids any purely psychological or privatized explanation for the crisis she experienced in the store. And so she refuses to offer guilt, pain, understanding, or a changed attitude as possible resolutions of her story. Her story is not one of linear self development or consciousness-raising.

For example, and paradoxically, she writes that her self-consciousness is both about being older than the salespeople telling the anti-Semitic jokes, *and* feeling "very young again" as she shopped in a store with posters that said "as advertised in *Seventeen Magazine*." She was afraid of being dismissed by the young saleswomen as "maternal" if she questioned their joking. Yet, this consciousness of feeling both young and old has a history to it:

> In some odd way that is extremely hard to admit in print, I wanted their approval. I was on the edge of their group, the odd person out (as I always was as a teenager, that time in one's life when attitudes about everything social — including race — are most powerfully reinforced). (Williams, 1991, p. 127)

An admission of seeking approval by not interrupting the anti-Semitic remarks "is extremely hard" to make in print, yet she performs this speech act of "admission." The difficulty of making this admission has a history to it which she tells: Williams grew up an "outsider," in a neighborhood "where blacks were the designated Jews" (1991, p. 127). In this store, she was "caught short" because of the smiling *openness* of the salespeople's anti-Semitism, which positioned her simultaneously, and paradoxically, as insider and outsider. Two histories, two worlds were made copresent in this moment:

> [I]t was irresistible, forbidden, almost thrilling to be on the inside. I was "privileged" to hear what these people thought, earmarked as someone who would not reveal them; I was designated safe. I was also designated as someone who didn't matter. (p. 128)

She felt included by their trust that she would not break the bond of their shared silence, and "at the same time, I realized that their faith in me was oppressively insulting . . . if I was 'safe,' I was also 'easy' in my desire for the illusion of inclusion" (p. 128):

> I remember the Woolworth sit-ins; I remember my father walking trepida-
> tiously into stores in Savannah, Georgia, shortly after desegregation, cau-
> tiously disbelieving of his right to be there, disproportionately grateful for the
> allowance just to be. Very much my father's daughter, I am always grateful
> when storekeepers are polite to me; I don't expect courtesy, I value it in a way
> that resembles love and trust and shelter. I value it in a way that is frequently
> misleading, for it is neither love nor trust nor shelter. (pp. 128–129)

Valuing courtesy in this context is, she concludes, a form of fear. She is both "relieved" when she is not thrown out of stores like this one, and "enraged by the possibility of this subsurface drama-waiting-to-happen." Despite her rage, she "can't kill" everyone, but neither can she "teach every-one" (p. 129).

Insider and outsider, safe and easy, trusted and insulted, privileged and of no consequence, the mature lawyer-professor and the teenager learning her place within race, grateful and fearful, relieved and enraged, neither avenger (I "can't kill everyone") nor savior (I can't "teach everyone")— Williams writes and reads herself in ways that blur the boundaries of each of these social and cultural positionings. She does this by showing how, in the store that day, these paradoxical identities, categories, and experiences were at the same time mutually constitutive and mutually deconstructive— both necessary to, and unsettling of, each other.

Williams writes the paradoxical "components of her self-conscious-ness" in a way that enacts their simultaneous dependance upon and under-cutting of each other. In this way, Williams breaks the conscious and un-conscious silences that are enforced when identities, positionings, and experiences are understood and lived out as monolithic, exclusive, and stable.

But breaking silence is not something that is done once and for all— either at the personal or at the social level. In and through writing in a way that calls up the "subsurface drama-waiting-to-happen," Williams con-structs a changed consciousness of self-in-relation-to-others. Yet, at the same time, she continues to encounter her own, and the surrounding cul-ture's, unwillingness and inability to be "fully and sufficiently awake" to events marked by surprising and traumatic eruptions of subsurface memo-ries, power relations, circles of enemy-making through revenge:

> [T]he distance between the "I" on this side of the store and the me that is
> "them" on the other side of the store—is marked by an emptiness in myself.

> Frequently such emptiness is reiterated by a hole in language, a gap in the law, or a chasm of fear. (1991, p. 129)

Frequently, she finds herself unwilling to break her own surprising silences in the face of "a chasm of fear." Frequently, she finds herself unable to break such silences because of holes in language and gaps in the law—the discourses needed are just not available. They are not yet historical and cultural achievements. Nevertheless, Williams writes an interruption of the silence that paralyzed her that day. That interruptive act is a transgression of (a preexisting) self, of cultural frames of reference, and of prexisting categories of perception. The interruption is achieved precisely by enfolding multiple discursive formations, histories, memories, lives. Her interruption consists in violating the supposed boundaries between past and present, between multiple selves, and between the "I" in this side of the store and the "'me' that is 'them' on the other side."

Such interruption too is paradoxical. It is not once and for all. It is not definitive. It is, at the same time, sinful and a pleasure, terrifying and addictive, discovery and loss.

Like Kirkov, Williams can't know the difference her transgressive story and its mode of address might make. But also like Kirkov, there is pleasure and renewal in this not knowing. Because this kind of transgression is fecund, it is inaugural—it does not know where it will go, but it unleashes (previously bound or unimagined) meanings over which she has no control.

To walk through the world and engage with its stores or university classrooms as a black woman Harvard-educated professor-lawyer great-great-granddaughter of a slave is to walk through enfolded worlds—each "bearing its own distinct laws" and histories, each bearing subsurface dramas capable of erupting to the surface (Wilson, 1995, p. 225). It takes effort to suppress the plural histories and power relations that are contained within, occulted, by an anti-Semitic joke told in front of a black woman customer. It takes effort to suppress the "abiding presence" of the African persona in American literature. When Morrison re-reads several American novels that historically have been considered critical failures she finds that their logics and aesthetics have broken under the strain of ignore-ance. She finds that the deformations of narrative structure and the implausibilities of characterizations in these novels can be traced to the effort the author had to expend to suppress the presence of African Americans in the shaping of American literary sensibility.

Morrison's discovery enlivens Wilson's points about the historical, social, and aesthetic costs of realism as a literary style. And what Wilson (1995) says about realism can also be said of the "typical limpidity" of academic prose:

> Realism's typical limpidity arises from the muscular suppression of narrative
> potential. . . . The actual world's diversity is canceled, cropped, or brushed
> out in order to create fictional worlds of great intensity, but narrow semiotic
> potential. Not many different *kinds* of things occur in dirty realism. The possi-
> bilities of border-crossing or boundary-skipping between domains are blocked,
> methodically delimited. . . . Magical realism, in its maximalist pyrotechnics,
> follows the path that narrative minimalism closes. (p. 226)

It seems obvious why Williams, who describes herself as an oxymoron,
would forge a unique academic writing style that appears to have much in
common with magical realism. After all, there is an oxymoronic aspect to
magical realism itself:

> The term "magic realism" is an oxymoron, one that suggests a binary opposi-
> tion between the representational code of realism and that, roughly, of fantasy.
> . . . Since the ground rules of these two worlds are incompatible, neither can
> fully come into being and each remains suspended . . . a situation which cre-
> ates disjunction within each of the separate discursive systems, rending them
> with gaps, absences, and silences. (Slemon, 1995, p. 409)

There's a history to Williams's innovative uses of language and style
when she writes "as" an academic. There's a history to why it has become
necessary for her to find a way to use language for the purpose gesturing
toward that which—because of the workings of history and power—is incompatible with (academic) language, and so remains suspended and disjoined in (academic) language.

TEACHING THROUGH HOLES IN LANGUAGE

How does one teach in and through historically constructed and politically
interested holes in language? How does one teach when there's no way to
say it—and yet something must be said? How does one employ language
that knows, but does not tell what it knows—language that is *in-formed* by
its ghost, by its Other, yet cannot speak that Other.

In *Alchemy*, Williams uses structural and stylistic devices to create
what might be called a magical realist *conceptual* and *analytical* space in
her deconstruction of legal discourses and practices. She uses fragmented
narrative; cinematographic montages of scenes, episodes, and chapters; dis-
solution of different times and spaces and the creation of a time-space
continuum; oral tradition; multiple points of view and perspective; and
dreams, visions, and hallucinations.

Space in a realistic novel is like a map in which "the navigational

routes, the lines on a map, the rational cartographical space, unfold lucidly
and unmistakably" (Wilson, 1995, p. 210) allowing you to move about
within it.

But space in magical realism has a plasticity which "displaces normal
expectations and learned behavior." It's as if

> two distinct geometries had been inscribed onto the same space. Think of it as
> co-presence . . . as different geometries at work constructing a double space.
> Magical realism focuses the problem of fictional space. It does this by suggest-
> ing a model of how different geometries, inscribing boundaries that fold and
> refold like quicksilver, can superimpose themselves upon one another. (Wilson,
> 1995, p. 210)

Writing as a scholar rather than as a novelist, Williams focuses the
problem of conceptual space in academic writing. The geometry of prevailing academic analysis and argumentation is like rational cartographical
space. It attempts to unfold lucidly and unmistakably, and apparently
allows the reader to move freely about within it—with an illusion of mastery and access.

But a Cartesian grid misses the ways that history and power inscribe
multiple, moving, enfolded, and conflicting social positionings onto the
same conceptual space. In Williams's conceptual space, boundaries of her
own multiple selves, of self and other, of privilege and exploitation fold and
refold like quicksilver. Multiple histories and power relations are copresent
in her analysis of the law, and superimpose themselves, working to construct doubled and tripled conceptual spaces.

As a reader, I can't move freely about within Williams's arguments or
analyses. Heading in any "straight" or "rational" line of argument with the
hope to arrive at some transcendent moment of mastery and conclusion, I
fall instead into the holes between disjointed discursive systems. I stumble
into the chasms opened up by lived experiences that map onto no known or
authorized concepts, words, or arguments. I am spun in place by mirrorings
of positions that are "supposed" (logically, physically, politically, historically) to be distinct—as when I encounter the I who is the them on the other
side of the room. The conceptual space that Williams constructs addresses
her reader through reversals, folds, superimpositions, simultaneity, both-
ands, looking glasses, multiple beginnings and endings, and double vision.

This address is an effort, I would suggest, to position her reader as a
subject-in-motion. But not just any motion. She places her readers within a
moving ellipse. That moving ellipse breaches the point of my observation.
That is, a difference is returned to both the location within relations of
power from which I observe, and to my point or motive for being there.

The return of a difference makes it possible to change my initial point of observation into a question — a question that, in the very process of its construction and articulation, changes my theorizing and practice already.

ERUPTIONS OF POLAR BEARS

Here's an example that I think demonstrates the intention of Williams's address to invite a return of difference. In *Alchemy*, Williams offers an elliptically recurring motif. It has repeatedly grabbed the attention of students who read *Alchemy* in seminar. It's the polar bears.

The polar bears first appear in the very early pages of Williams's book. She is trying to explain to her sister what her book is about:

> "But what's the book about?" my sister asks, thumping her legs against the chair impatiently.
>
> "Howard Beach, polar bears, and food stamps," I snap back. "I am interested in the way in which legal language flattens and confines in absolutes the complexity of meaning inherent in any given problem." (1991, p. 6)

And soon after:

> "What's so new," asks my sister, losing interest rapidly, "about a schizophrenic black lady pouring her heart out about food stamps and polar bears?"
>
> I lean closer to her. "Floating signifers," I whisper. (p. 7)

And then, as Williams continues to explain to her sister that she wants her readers to self-consciously fill in the gaps of her own writing:

> To this end, I exploit all sorts of literary devices, including parody, parable, and poetry.
>
> " . . . as in polar bears?" my sister asks eagerly, alert now, ears pricked, nose quivering, hair bristling.
>
> "My, what big teeth you have!" I exclaim, just before the darkness closes over me. (p. 8)

And this is all we hear of the inexplicable bears until much later in her book. By then, we've read that while Williams was doing research on contract law, in an archive, she discovered the contract written to sell her great-great-grandmother into slavery.

The polar bears' elliptical returns are integral to the work of the last two chapters of *Alchemy*. Both of those chapters are highly metaphorical discussions of the states of being "imagined property" and of being "the object of property."

The epigraph to the chapter entitled "Arm's-Length Intimacies (a diary of imagined property)" reads:

> Two polar bears who have become psychotic from the boredom of a lifetime in captivity are to receive psychotherapy at their zoo in Bristol, England. Micha, 20, and Nina, 30, have taken to napping long hours and to walking the same three steps forward and backward over and over again. Dr. Roger Mugford, an animal psychologist, has designed a treatment to save the bears from madness: he plans to vary their menus and to give them unbreakable toys. (Williams, 1991, p. 202)

What follows are Williams's descriptions of preparing materials for a class, leaving her office to go to an African dance class, running into several students who ask a question left unanswered from last semester, going home for Christmas, going at New Year's to New Orleans for back-to-back conferences on literary criticism and the law, having a dream about a lawyer-shaman in bear mask, going dancing on New Year's Eve, having a discussion about social engineering with a fellow conference goer, watching an old black man tap dancing on the street at night and a woman "with bags full of what looks like trash" "raging to herself, to another self" the next day. This chapter ends with a postscript entitled "Through the Looking Glass." Williams explains that she submitted this chapter to a "prominent law review" and it was promptly rejected. She then offers a paraphrased composite of rejection letters she's received.

In the last chapter, "On Being the Object of Property (a gift of intelligent rage)," Williams begins with a story of her mother's words to her as Williams left for law school, and goes on to discuss the forced sterilization of Native American and Puerto Rican women, the "treatment of blacks by whites in their law" (p. 219), market theory and master-slave relations, the power relations of white people looking at black people and black people looking at white people: "If I deflect, if I move out of the way, they will never know I existed" (1991, p. 222), contract law and surrogate motherhood, the death of her godmother, circles of barter, a Phil Donahue program on AIDS, the death of her great-aunt Jag, the mauling of an eleven-year-old boy by two polar bears in the Brooklyn Zoo who were then shot to death by police, and finally, the experience of being invisible before one hundred white prepubescent males attending basketball camp as they "loped" across Dartmouth's campus, "jostling," "smacking," and "pushing" her from the sidewalk into the gutter (p. 235).

In the meantime and through all of this, Williams manages to design a brilliant subversion of legal discourses that in various ways make human beings objects of property.

Polar bears help to pull off this subversion. Their reappearances throughout these chapters are unexpected and fleeting. Each time they surface, they appear in a different guise. They arise and clamor and rage in the back of Williams's head — voices of one self interrupting another self. They ask questions about underlying motivations, subtexts, and dangers, as one of Williams's selves becomes impatient with another. They arise as "comforting specters" within "gaps between [the] disciplines" of literary criticism and the law.

And they arise, she writes, to dissolve the walls that separate her classroom from . . . what?

> I sleep fitfully in the New Orleans humidity. I dream that I'm teaching my Uniform Commercial Code class. My students are restless and inattentive, bored to death with the sales of chattels. Suddenly, from somewhere deep in my psyche, polar bears rise. Silent, unbidden, they come to the dissolved walls of the classroom, the polar bears come padding to hear what this law will mean for them. It is snowing in their world. Hunching, they settle at the edge of the classroom, the walls of the classroom melt in the heated power of their breath, their fierce dark eyes are fixed upon me. They hunch and settle and listen, from beyond-language. (Williams, 1991, p. 207)

They come from beyond language, and this can be terrifying:

> (Why am I so terrified? Some part of me knows that it is intelligent for me to be schizophrenic. It is wise, in a way, for me to be constantly watching myself, to feel simultaneously more than one thing, and to hear a lot of voices in my head: in fact, it is not just intelligent but fashionable, feminist, and even postmodern. It is also wise, I know, to maintain some consciousness of where I am when I am other than the voice itself. If the other voice in my head is really me too, then it means that I have shifted positions, ever so slightly, and become a new being, a different one from her, over there. It gets confusing sometimes, so I leave markers of where I've been, particularly if it's not just a voice but a place I want to come back to in time. This season, those spots are marked with polar bears.) . . .
>
> But since I know they are nothing more than, as I have said, markers of where I've been, I get up the courage to calm myself, and settle in for the vision that their presence will have brought. In their turn, the bears give me back my listening, they ring me with their listening, beyond language. (Williams, 1991, pp. 207–208)

Beyond language. Williams writes from and to subject positions never intended by "normal" or "realist" academic language to be inhabited or spoken from. And there's a history to what has been relegated to the "outside" academic language. Williams also calls attention to that which exceeds language per se.

But she doesn't summon polar bears from beyond language in order to fill the holes in language opened up by her oxymoronic positionings. She doesn't drag the polar bears into language. They are left unexplained, inexplicable, they are sliding signifiers. What are we readers to make of these polar bears?

This brings us to the authorial voice in magical realist texts. Many literary critics have spoken of how the magical realist author manages the ambiguity that constantly threatens to disorient the reader. They speak of the necessity for "authorial reserve." This is because any explanation of the supernatural, inexplicable, and mysterious events on the part of the narrator, author, or the characters would destroy the simultaneous presence of the two conflicting codes, resolving them into a hierarchy.

In magical realism, the narrator accepts the "magic" as if it were nothing strange or disturbing. "The narrative voice bridges the gap between ordinary and bizarre, smoothing the discrepancies, making everything seem normal" (Wilson, 1995, p. 220).

Williams never "explains" the polar bears. And for me to try to interpret what they "mean" would be to destroy what I believe to be the very work Williams intends for them in her text. For me, the question, What do they mean? stops the work that the polar bears perform in her text from continuing on in my reading and uses of her text. What if I ask, instead, When the conceptual space inhabited by polar bears breaks through into the conceptual space inhabited by legal discourses that make human beings the object of property, what becomes possible and thinkable that was otherwise foreclosed in each of the separate spaces?

Here is what the polar bears make possible and thinkable for me as a teacher when I grapple with the question of pedagogy: In the final chapters of her book, Williams uses polar bears to interrupt herself *as* teacher. They melt the walls of her classroom—making it impossible to teach-as-usual. The polar bears arrive unbidden to interrupt Williams's explanations and analyses. There's more to it—more to what Williams can or will speak as teacher—some of it is beyond language, some of it is the ghosts of the dead seeking justice, some of it is her own surprising silences that cause her embarrassment. Just when her accomplishments in the previous chapters might appear to be too masterful, too neatly tied up, she dreams in the last chapter of bored-to-death students. The polar bears arrive to shift registers. Like a shift in register from uppercase to lowercase letters, they perform a shift in register from (the uppercase of) realist language to the (lowercase of) subsurface dramas. Those subsurface dramas are not only waiting to happen—they are happening all along. It's just that they've been rendered just out of sight, just out of memory, just beyond language, in forgettings, enfolded histories, misspeakings, fears, systematic as well as surprising silences, denials, guilty desires. And there's a history to this rendering—to what has been relegated to the uppercase of academic realism and to what has been relegated to the lowercase of subsurface drama.

Teaching is not normalizable. It happens in disjointed and yet enfolded conceptual and social spaces not unlike those mapped by the literary genre of magical realism. Its in-betweenness and all-at-onceness corrodes the engine of system. Where, when, and how teaching happens is an undecidable. This is what saves it from being a skill or a technology.

At this moment, perhaps one of the most strategically useful things that "radical" teachers could do would be to unsettle the normalizing relationship that exists between educational theorists and their beloved topic. At this moment, one of the most radical assertions may be to insist that educational researchers and reformers engage with challenges and possibilities raised by teaching's proximity to the literature of magical realism and to the pedagogy of psychoanalysis.

Coda

There are times in life when the question of knowing if one can think differently than one thinks, and perceive differently than one sees, is absolutely necessary if one is to go on looking and reflecting at all. In what does [philosophical activity] consist, if not in the endeavor to know how and to what extent it might be possible to think differently, instead of legitimating what is already known?... [Philosophical activity] is entitled to explore what might be changed, in its own thought, through the practice of a knowledge that is foreign to it.
                                    –Michel Foucault, *The History of Sexuality*

I STARTED WRITING this book at a time in my life when the question of knowing if I could think differently from how I had been about teaching was absolutely necessary if I were to go on teaching at all. And so I began to practice foreign knowledges.

Knowledges about things such as mode of address, the unconscious, and the space-between of texts and readings are made foreign to those of us in education in many ways. Disciplinary boundaries that separate film scholars from literary critics from performance artists from psychoanalysts can make their respective knowledges about teaching foreign to one another and to those of us working in the field of education. And so part of the task of trying to inhabit the text of teaching differently is to read teaching through dance or literature. Or to read psychoanalysis and film studies through teaching.

There are other ways that certain knowledges are made foreign. They can be discredited and separated out from the legitimate study of teaching. Some questions and curiosities have been banished from the domains of legitimate educational research. But they are residing very nearby. And the borders are permeable. They are the stuff of the subsurface dramas that constantly erupt into the best-laid lesson plans and research projects.

There's something provocative about teaching's proximity to discredited things such as trauma, surprise, discontinuity, tickling, the unconscious, paradox, magic, silence, obsession, invisible and unrepeatable events, and the movies. Here, I've tried to show what teaching looks like to me when I view it from its own shadows. I'm convinced that such an imagined viewpoint is possible and thinkable only because there are discourses and practices already afoot in the world that support and even demand such a re-visioning of teaching. They're being spoken and enacted by teachers such as Felman, Donald, Williams, Phelan, Morrison, Phillips, and Bollas, as well as many others. Maybe this means we might just be coming upon one of those times in a field of study when the question of knowing if we, as educators, can think differently from how we've been thinking and perceive differently from how we've been seeing is absolutely necessary if we are to go on looking and thinking at all.

This means interdisciplinary and cross-cultural work. But it also means straying into the alien yet uncannily familiar shadows cast by our field's own domesticated knowledges about teaching. Momentous things are happening right behind the teacher's back, and have been all along. Turning and facing them and getting curious about their fecundity is not about throwing a light on the shadow and making the foreign continuous with the domesticated. It's not about discovering something in teaching's others that can then be added into or used to correct our understanding of teaching.

Rather, to practice knowledges foreign or discontinuous to teaching is to engage yet another paradox. How can any knowledge "foreign" to teaching be taught? How did I or anyone else "learn" it if it was foreign to teaching? How can I, why would I "as" a teacher and in the name of teaching, practice something discontinuous to teaching?

This is a good paradox to end with, because like all paradoxes produced by socially and historically constructed knowledge, it is inaugural, not final. It traces the limits of teaching and at the same time it breaches those limits from within. In order to turn and face what is going on behind the teacher's back, we have to stray afield of "education" as it's currently defined in academe, and practice knowledges foreign to us. Doing so, we breach the circle of education in the name of becoming educated about what the field of education itself prevents us from thinking and seeing.

Happily, by turning and facing the shadows of our own practices, we will not find ourselves and our practices "reflected" there. We will not find ourselves and our practices "as" teachers confirmed, enlightened, emancipated, or made continuous with our interests, understandings, or desires. Instead, we will find ourselves and our practices unsettled by the paradoxes of teaching. Turning and facing the third participant in the structure of relations between teacher and student, we are paradoxically and productively both empowered and condemned to the interminable cultural production that is teaching.

References

Bahovec, E. D. (1993, Winter). Turning the screw of *Sentimental Education* [Review of the book *Sentimental education: Schooling, popular culture and the regulation of liberty*]. *New Formations,* 165–172.

Baldwin, J. (1963; rpt. 1988). A talk to teachers. In R. Simonson & S. Walker (Eds.), *Multi-cultural literacy* (pp. 3–12). Saint Paul, MN: Graywolf Press.

Baldwin, J. (1976; rpt. 1990). *The Devil finds work.* New York: Dell.

Bollas, C. (1995). *Cracking up: The work of unconscious experience.* New York: Hill and Wang.

Burbules, N. C. (1993). *Dialogue in teaching: Theory and practice.* New York: Teachers College Press.

Butler, J. (1990). Gender trouble, feminist theory, and psychoanalytic discourse. In L. J. Nicholson (Ed.), *Feminism/postmodernism* (pp. 324–340). New York: Routledge.

Butler, J. (1992). Contingent foundations: Feminism and the question of "postmodernism." In J. Butler & J. W. Scott (Eds.), *Feminists theorize the political* (pp. 3–21). New York: Routledge.

Butler, J. (1993). *Bodies that matter: On the discursive limits of "sex."* New York: Routledge.

Butler, J. (1997). *Excitable speech: A politics of the performative.* New York: Routledge.

Carr, C. (1994, February 1). An American tale: A lynching and the legacies left behind. *The Village Voice,* pp. 31–35.

Chang, B. G. (1996). *Deconstructing communication: Representation, subject, and economies of exchange.* Minneapolis: University of Minnesota Press.

Cohen, R. (1995, March 12). A Balkan gyre of war, spinning onto film. *The New York Times,* Section 2, pp. 1, 24–25.

Cook, P. (Ed.). (1985). *The cinema book: A complete guide to understanding the movies.* New York: Pantheon Books.

Crimp, D. (Ed.). (1988). *AIDS: Cultural analysis, cultural activism.* Cambridge: MIT Press.

Davies, B. (1993). *Shards of glass: Children reading & writing beyond gendered identities.* Cresskill, NJ: Hampton Press.

Derrida, J. (1978). *Writing and difference* (A. Bass, Trans.). Chicago: University of Chicago Press.

D'haen, T. L. (1995). Magical realism and postmodernism: Decentering privileged centers. In L. P. Zamora & W. B. Faris (Eds.), *Magical realism: Theory, history, community* (pp. 191–208). Durham, NC: Duke University Press.

Donald, J. (Ed.). (1991). *Psychoanalysis and cultural theory: Thresholds*. London: Macmillan Education.

Donald, J. (1992). *Sentimental education: Schooling, popular culture and the regulation of liberty*. London: Verso.

Felman, S. (1983). *The literary speech act: Don Juan with J. L. Austin, or seduction in two languages* (C. Porter, Trans.). Ithaca: Cornell University Press.

Felman, S. (1987). *Jacques Lacan and the adventure of insight: Psychoanalysis in contemporary culture*. Cambridge: Harvard University Press.

Felman, S., & Laub, D., M.D. (1992). *Testimony: Crises of witnessing in literature, psychoanalysis, and history*. New York: Routledge.

Flax, J. (1993). *Disputed subjects: Essays on psychoanalysis, politics and philosophy*. New York: Routledge.

Foucault, M. (1977). *Language, counter-memory, practice: Selected essays and interviews*. (D. F. Bouchard & S. Simon, Trans.). Ithaca: Cornell University Press.

Foucault, M. (1979). *Discipline and punish: The birth of the prison*. New York: Vintage Books.

Foucault, M. (1985). *The history of sexuality: Vol. 2. The use of pleasure*. (Robert Hurley, Trans.). New York: Vintage Books.

Green, J. (1996, September 15). Flirting with suicide. *The New York Times Magazine*, pp. 38–45, 54–55, 84–85.

Griffin, J. H. (1961). *Black like me*. Boston: Houghton & Mifflin.

Kuhn, A. (1982). *Women's pictures: Feminism and cinema*. London: Routledge & Kegan Paul.

Lacy, S. (Ed.). (1995). *Mapping the terrain: New genre public art*. Seattle: Bay Press.

Mayne, J. (1993). *Cinema and spectatorship*. New York: Routledge.

McRobbie, A. (1984). Dance and social fantasy. In A. McRobbie & M. Nava (Eds.), *Gender and generation* (pp. 130–161). London: Macmillan.

Marshall, B. K. (1992). *Teaching the postmodern: Fiction and theory*. New York: Routledge.

Masterman, L. (1985). *Teaching the media*. London: Comedia.

Mizell, L., Benett, S., Bowman, B., & Morin, L. (1993). Different ways of seeing: Teaching in an anti-racist school. In T. Perry & J. W. Fraser (Eds.), *Freedom's plow: Teaching in the multicultural classroom* (pp. 27–46). New York: Routledge.

Morrison, T. (1992). *Playing in the dark: Whiteness and the literary imagination*. Cambridge, MA: Harvard University Press.

Neale, S. (1980). *Genre*. London: British Film Institute.

O'Shea, A. (1993). [Review of the book *Sentimental education: Schooling, popular culture and the regulation of liberty*]. *Media, Culture and Society, 15*, 503–510.

Patton, C. (1990). *Inventing AIDS*. New York: Routledge.

Phelan, P. (1993). *Unmarked: The politics of performance*. New York: Routledge.

Phillips, A. (1993). *On kissing, tickling, and being bored: Psychoanalytic essays on the unexamined life.* Cambridge, MA: Harvard University Press.

Phillips, A. (1995). *Terrors and experts.* Cambridge, MA: Harvard University Press.

Pratt, M. B. (1991). *Rebellion: Essays 1980–1991.* Ithaca, NY: Firebrand Books.

Readings, B. (1996). *The university in ruins.* Cambridge, MA: Harvard University Press.

Rooney, E. (1989). *Seductive reasoning: Pluralism as the problematic of contemporary literary theory.* Ithaca, NY: Cornell University Press.

Sedgwick, E. K. (1990). *Epistemology of the closet.* Berkeley: University of California Press.

Slemon, S. (1995). Magic realism as postcolonial discourse. In L. P. Zamora & W. B. Faris (Eds.), *Magical realism: Theory, history, community* (pp. 407–426). Durham, NC: Duke University Press.

Sturgis, S. (1991). *Tales of magic realism by women: Dreams in a minor key.* Freedom, CA: Crossing Press.

Tompkins, J. P. (1996). *A life in school: What the teacher learned.* New York: Addison-Wesley.

Trinh, T. M. (1986–1987, Fall–Winter). Introduction. *Discourse, 8,* 3–9.

Trinh, T. M. (1989). *Woman, native, other.* Bloomington: Indiana University Press.

Willard, N. (1993). *Telling time: Angels, ancestors, and stories.* New York: Harcourt Brace & Co.

Williams, P. (1991). *The alchemy of race and rights: Diary of a law professor.* Cambridge, MA: Harvard University Press.

Williams, P. (1995). *The rooster's egg: On the persistence of prejudice.* Cambridge, MA: Harvard University Press.

Wilson, R. (1995). The metamorphoses of fictional space: Magical realism. In L. P. Zamora & W. B. Faris (Eds.), *Magical realism: Theory, history, community* (pp. 209–233). Durham, NC: Duke University Press.

Zamora, L. P., & Faris, W. B. (Eds.). (1995). *Magical realism: Theory, history, community.* Durham, NC: Duke University Press.

Index

About the Author

ELIZABETH ELLSWORTH is Professor of Curriculum and Instruction at the University of Wisconsin-Madison. In the Educational Communications Technology Program, she teaches courses on the production and analysis of educational media. Her teaching and research focus on the politics of representation and the social construction of knowledge; theories and practices of pedagogy using media; and feminist and postmodern approaches to educational inquiry. As a Vilas Fellow at the university, she currently is researching the relation between interaction design and pedagogical modes of address in new media.